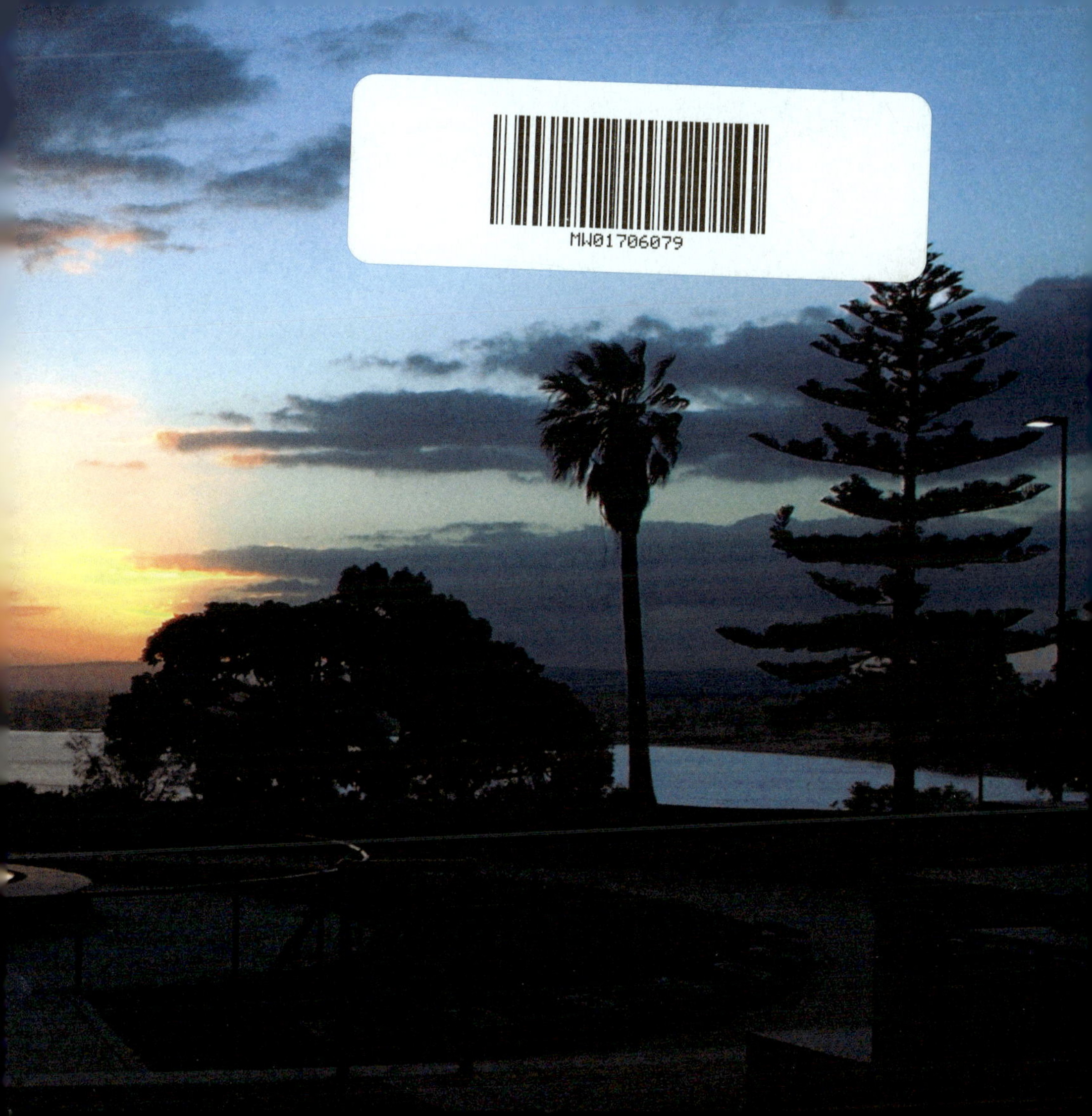

perth
fremantle
rottness island

western . australia

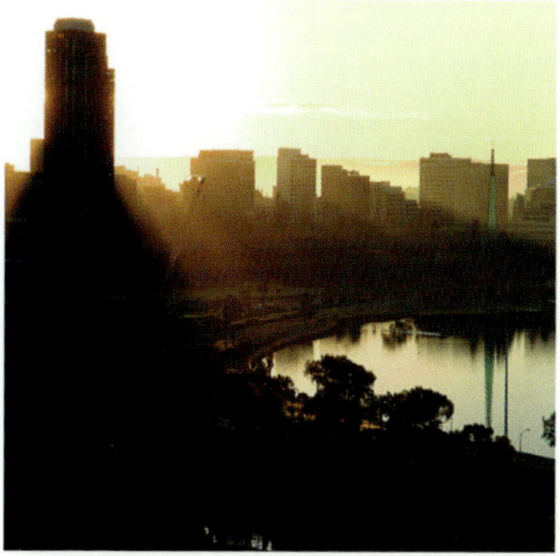

a photographic essay.
peter emanuel's
impressions of perth, fremantle and
rottnest island, western australia.
thankyou God for your creation.

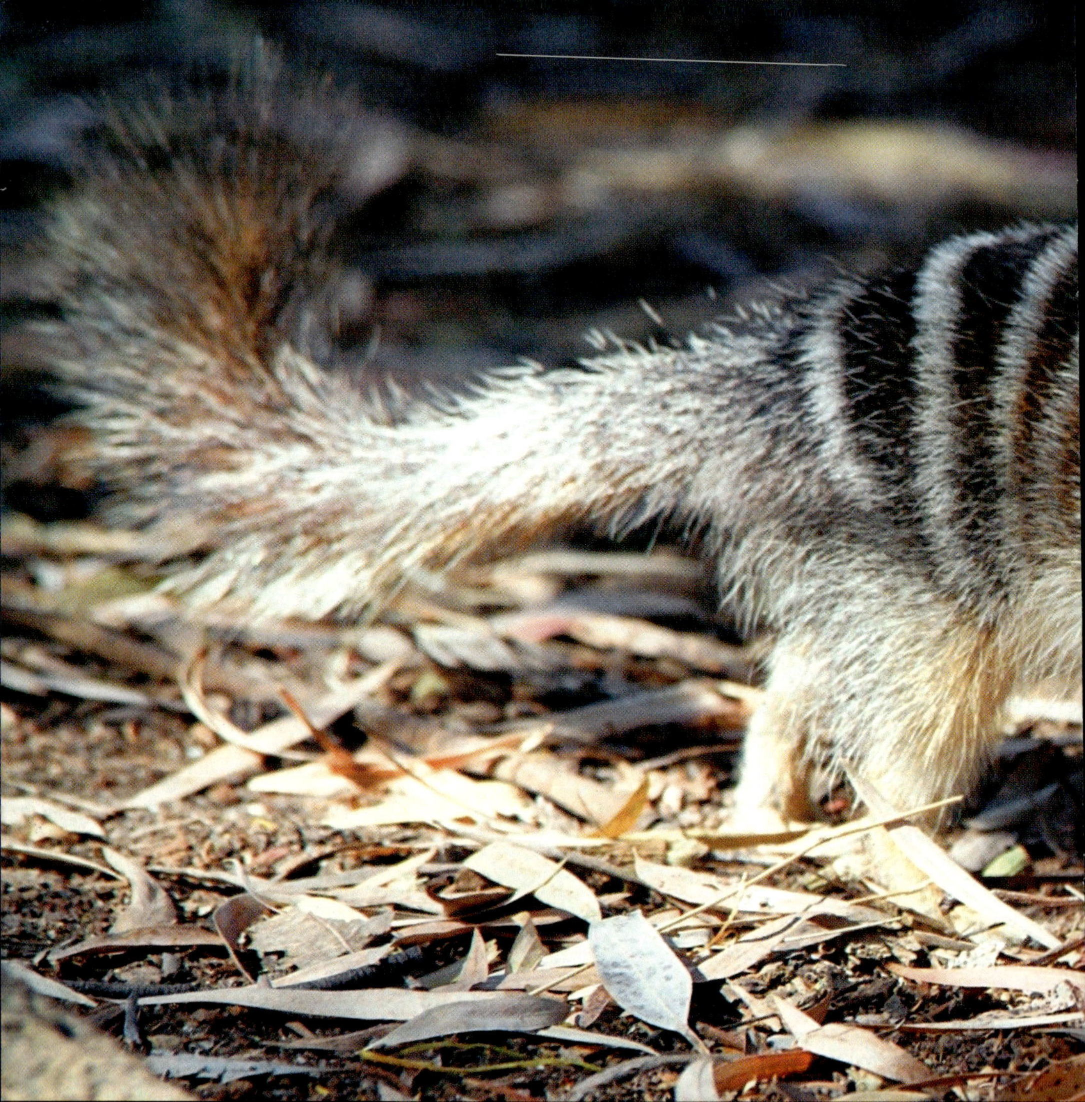

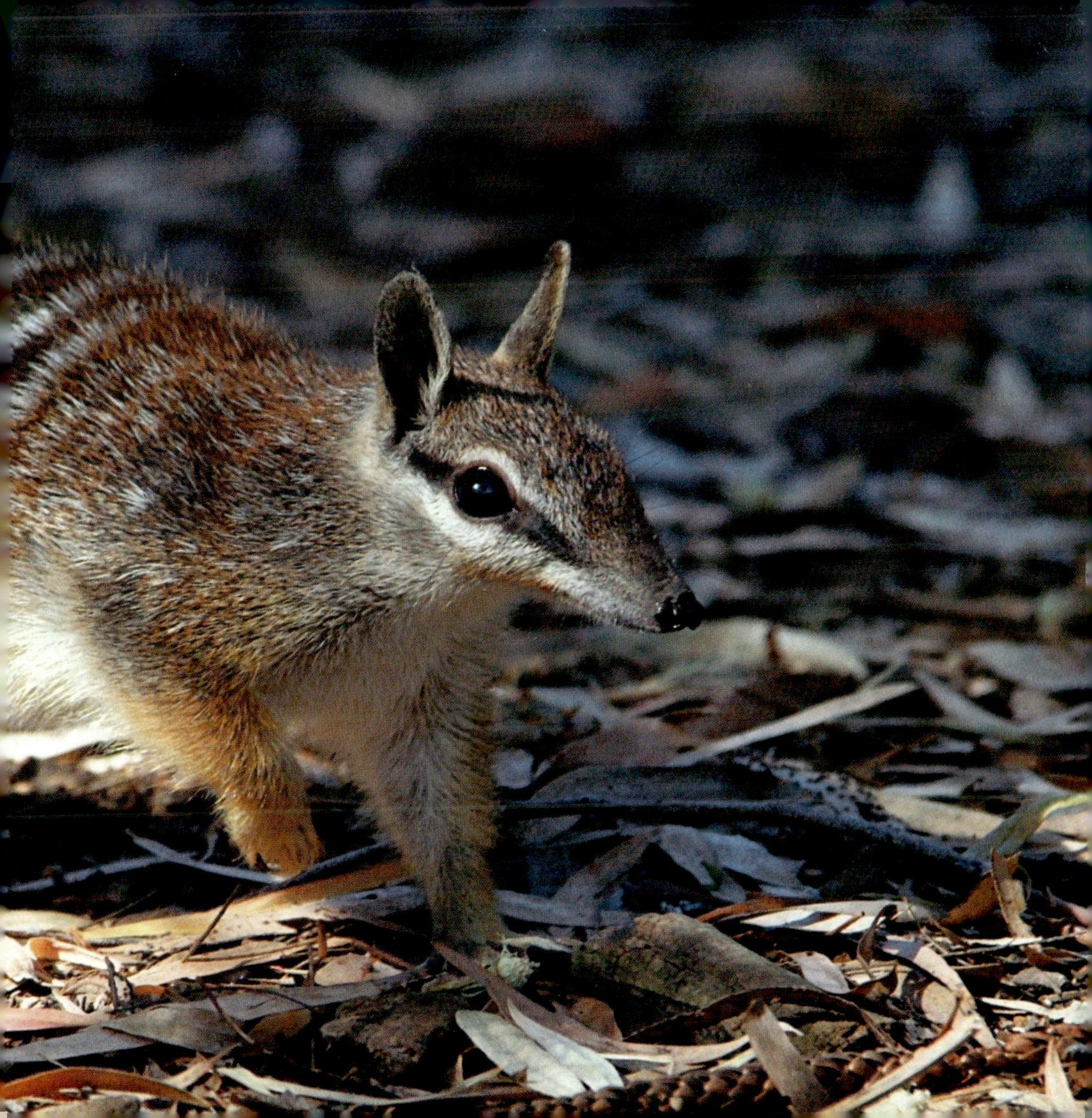

previous page. numbat

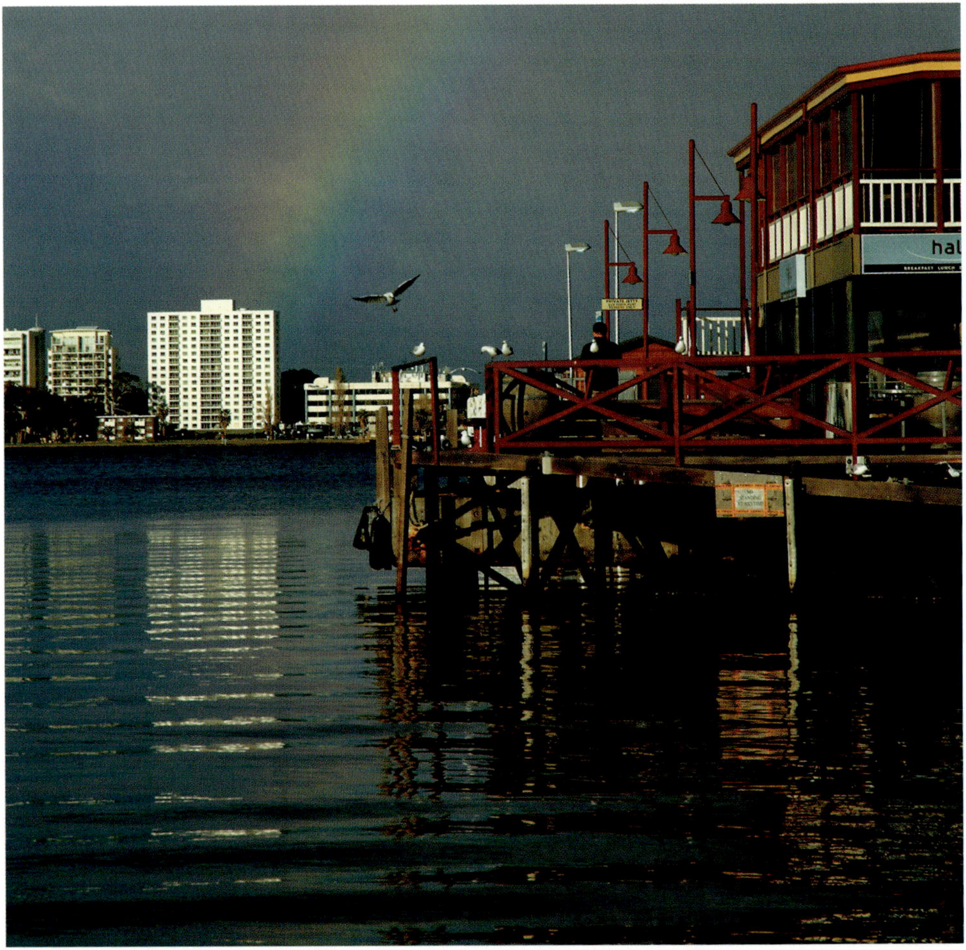

4. barrack square jetty

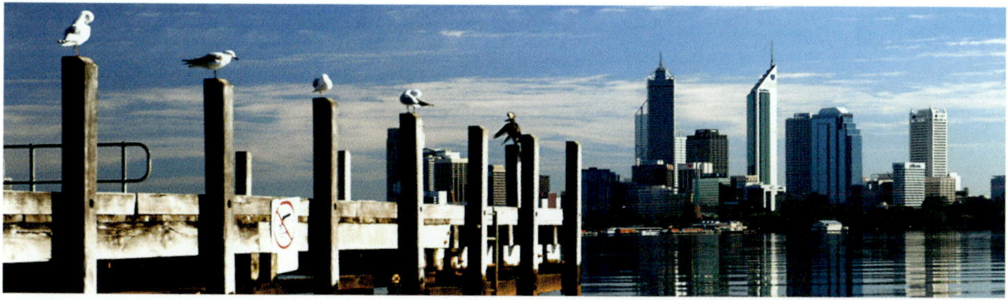

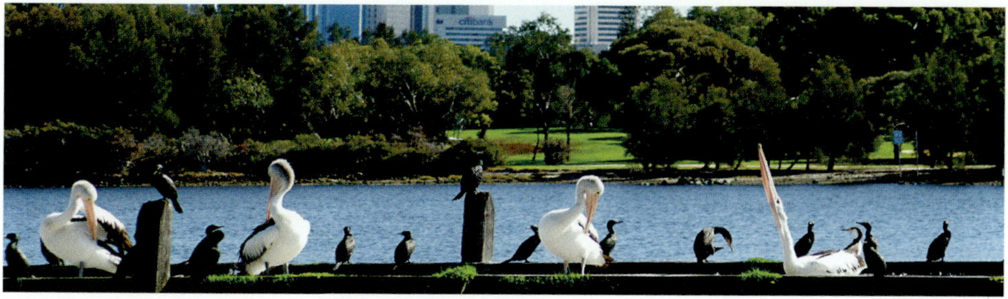

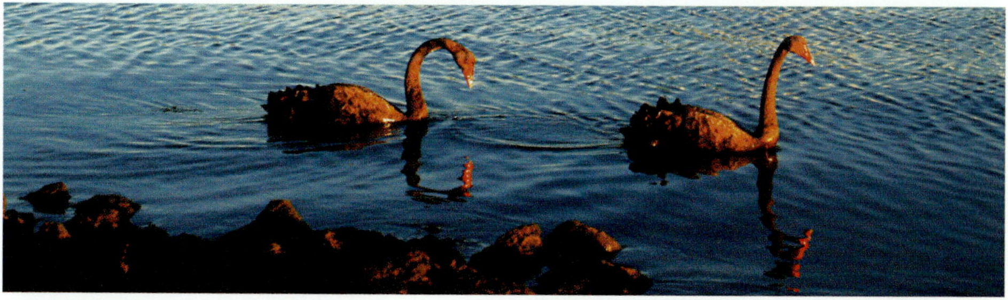

a. coode street jetty b.&c. birds by the swan

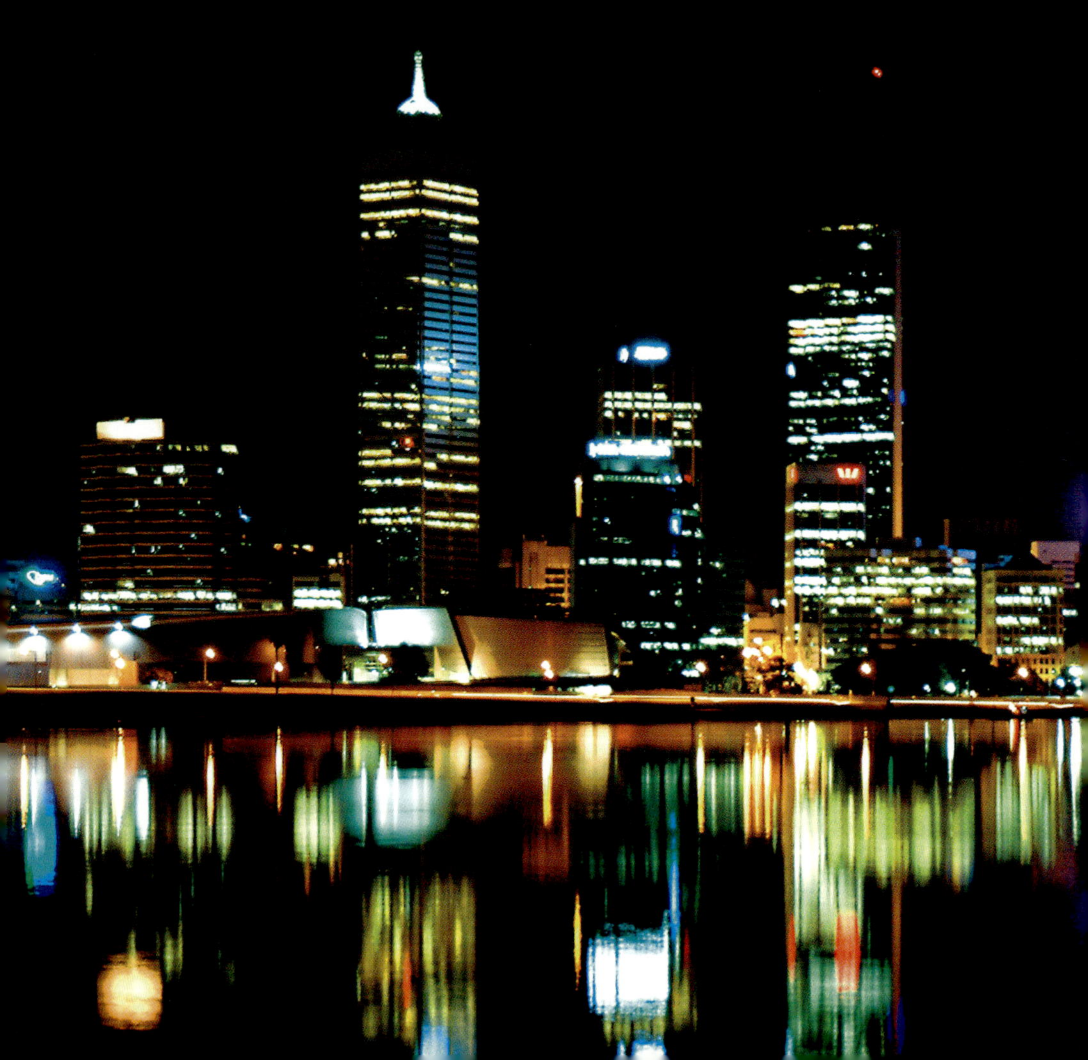

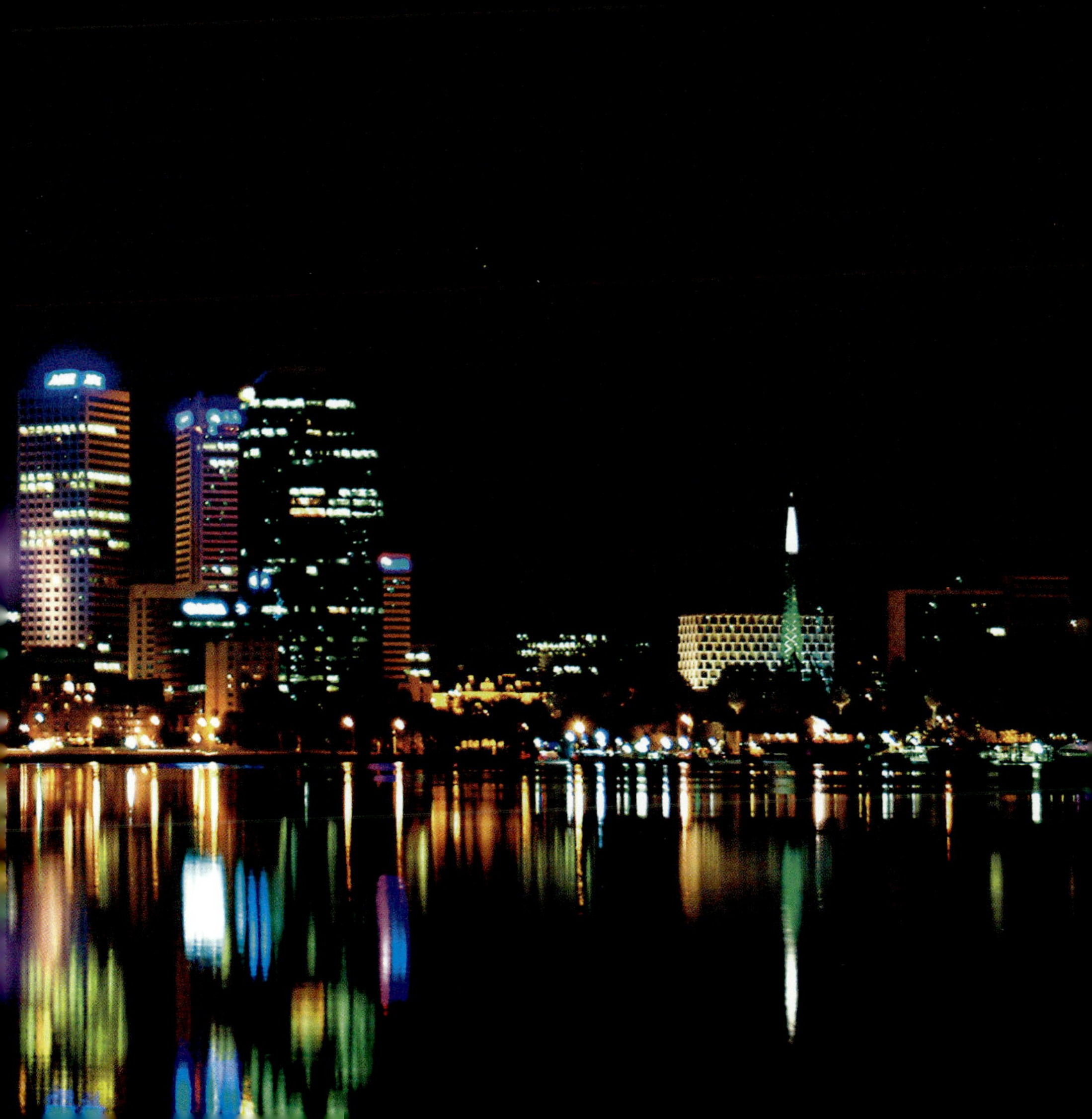

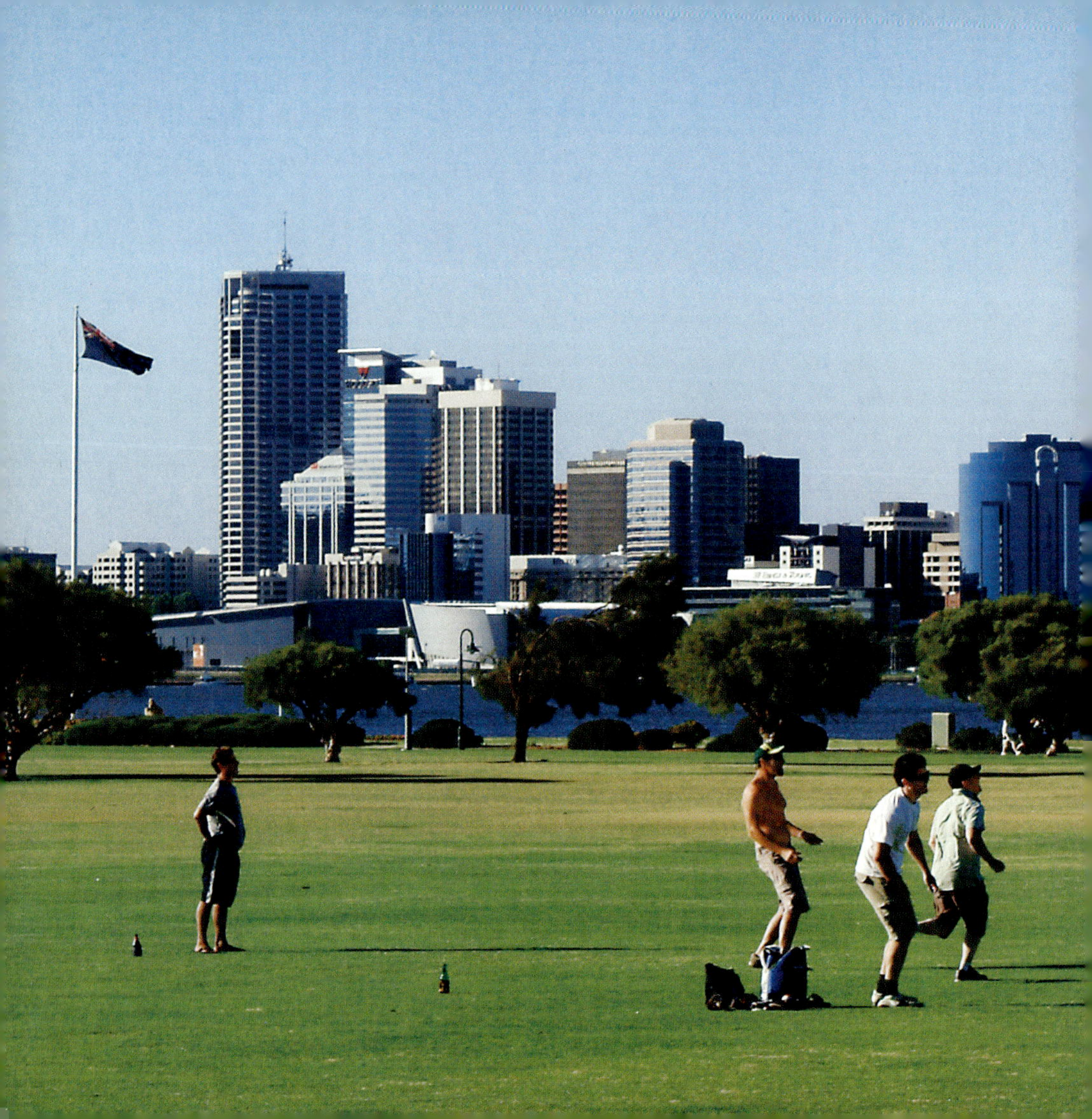

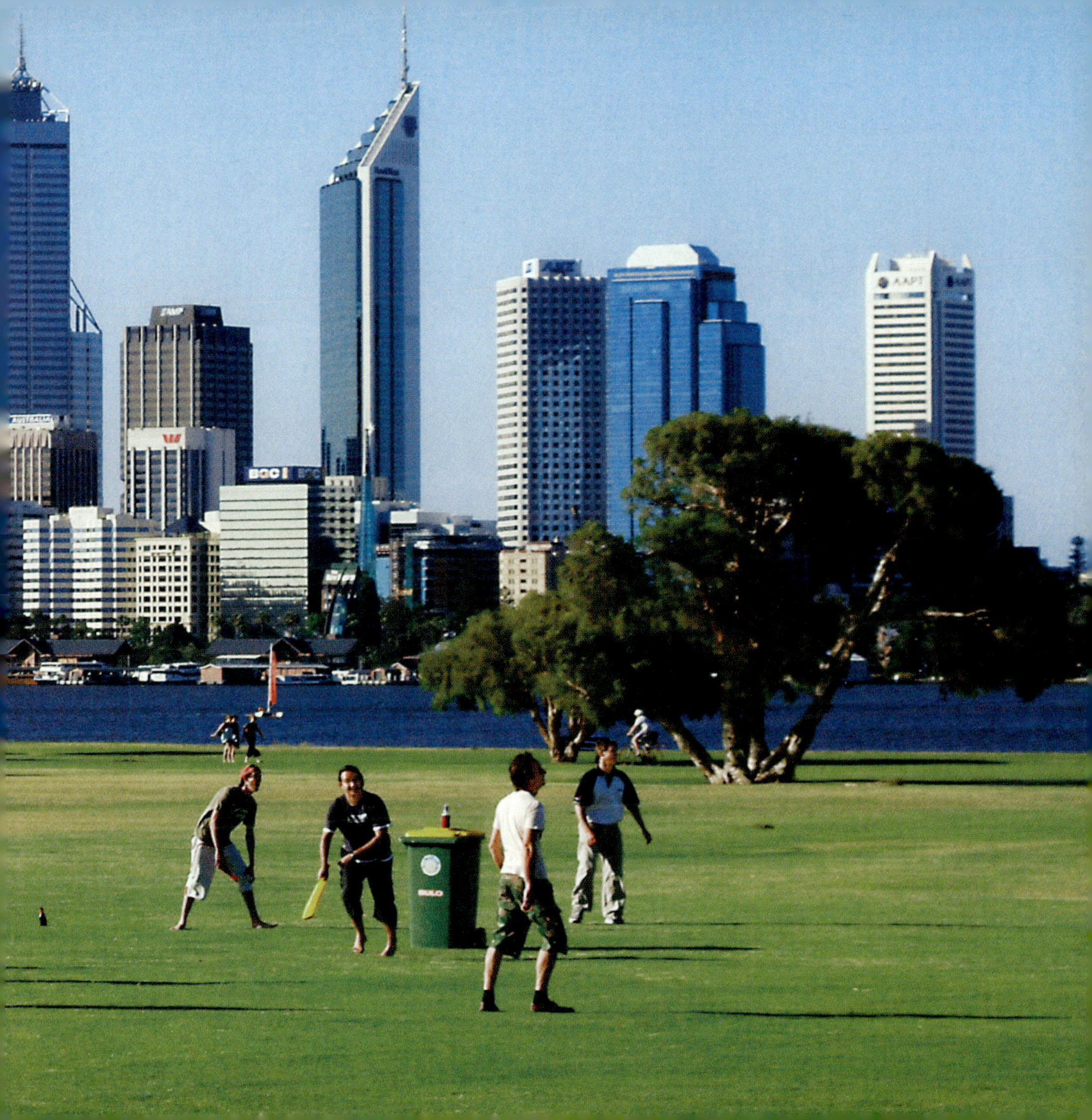
AAPT

previous page. sir james mitchell park

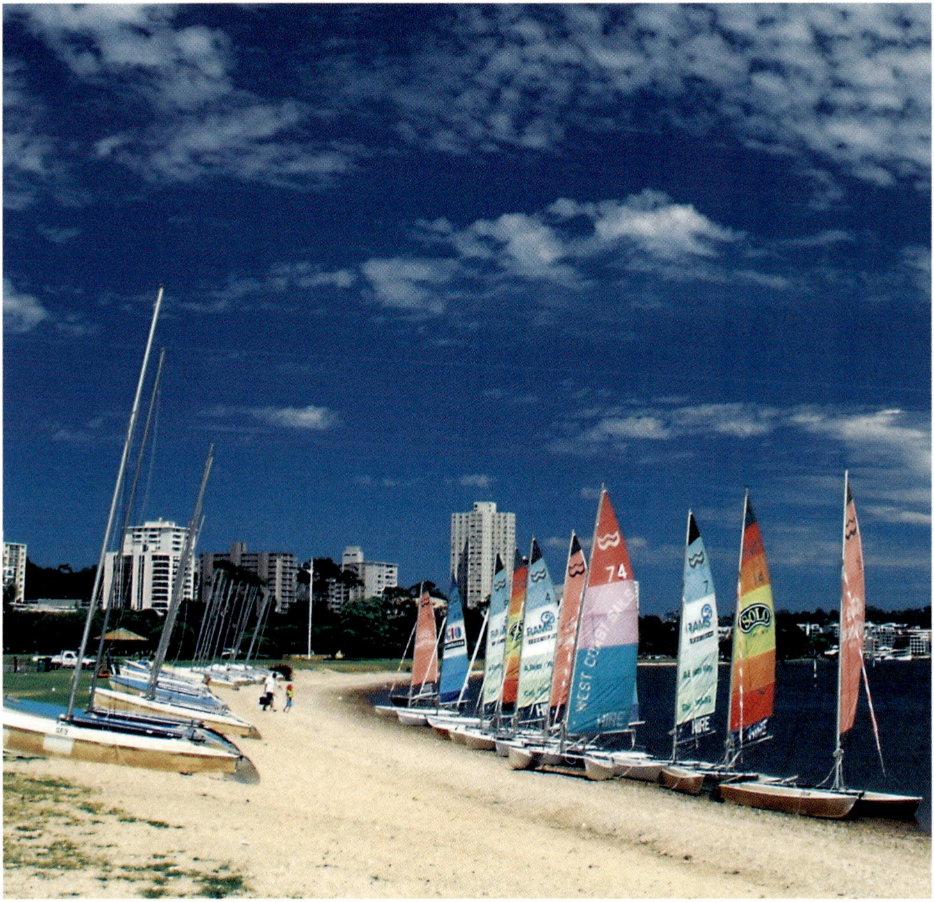

10. beach at edge of perth water

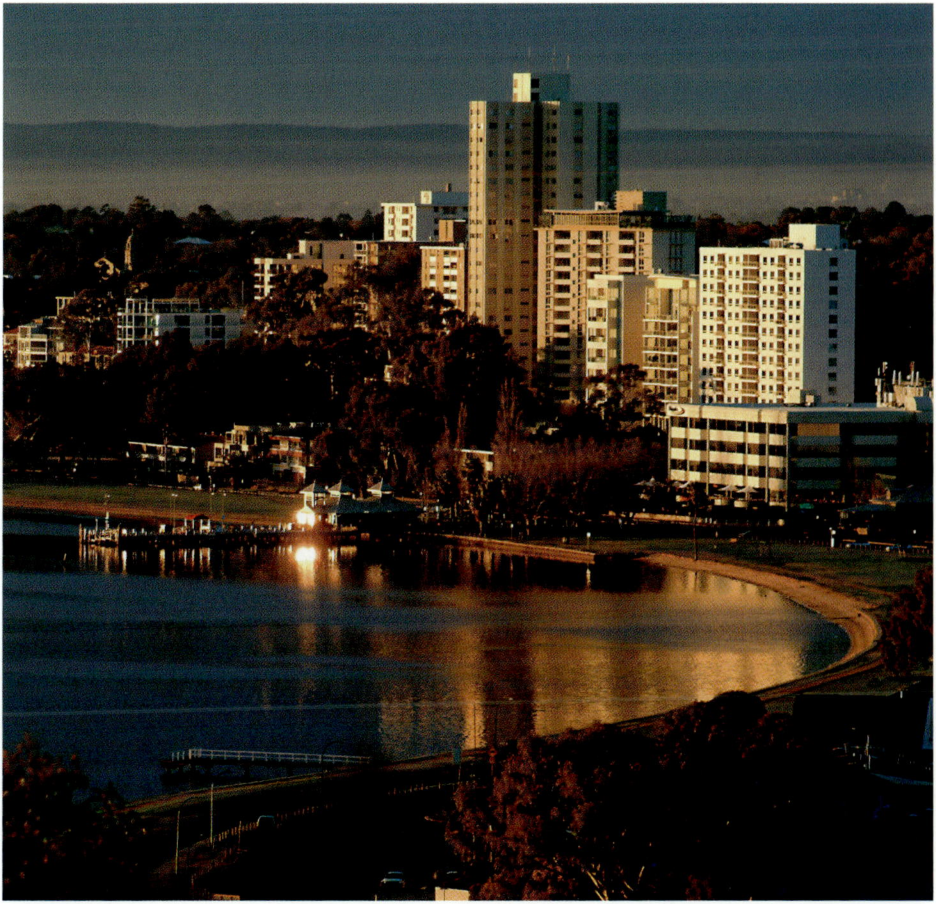

next page. northbridge

south perth

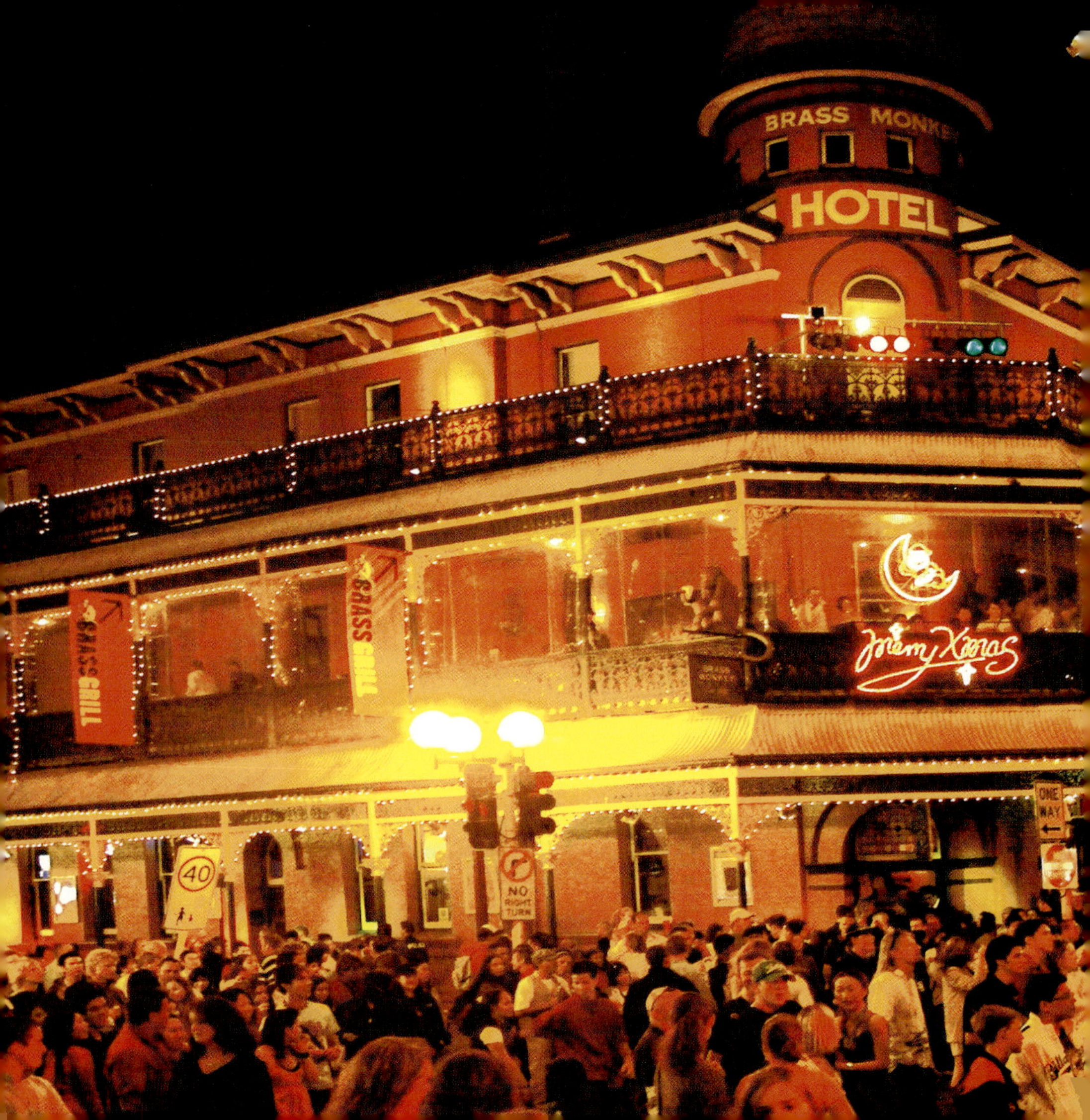
BRASS MONKE
HOTEL
BRASS GRILL
BRASS GRILL
Merry Xmas
40
NO RIGHT TURN
ONE WAY

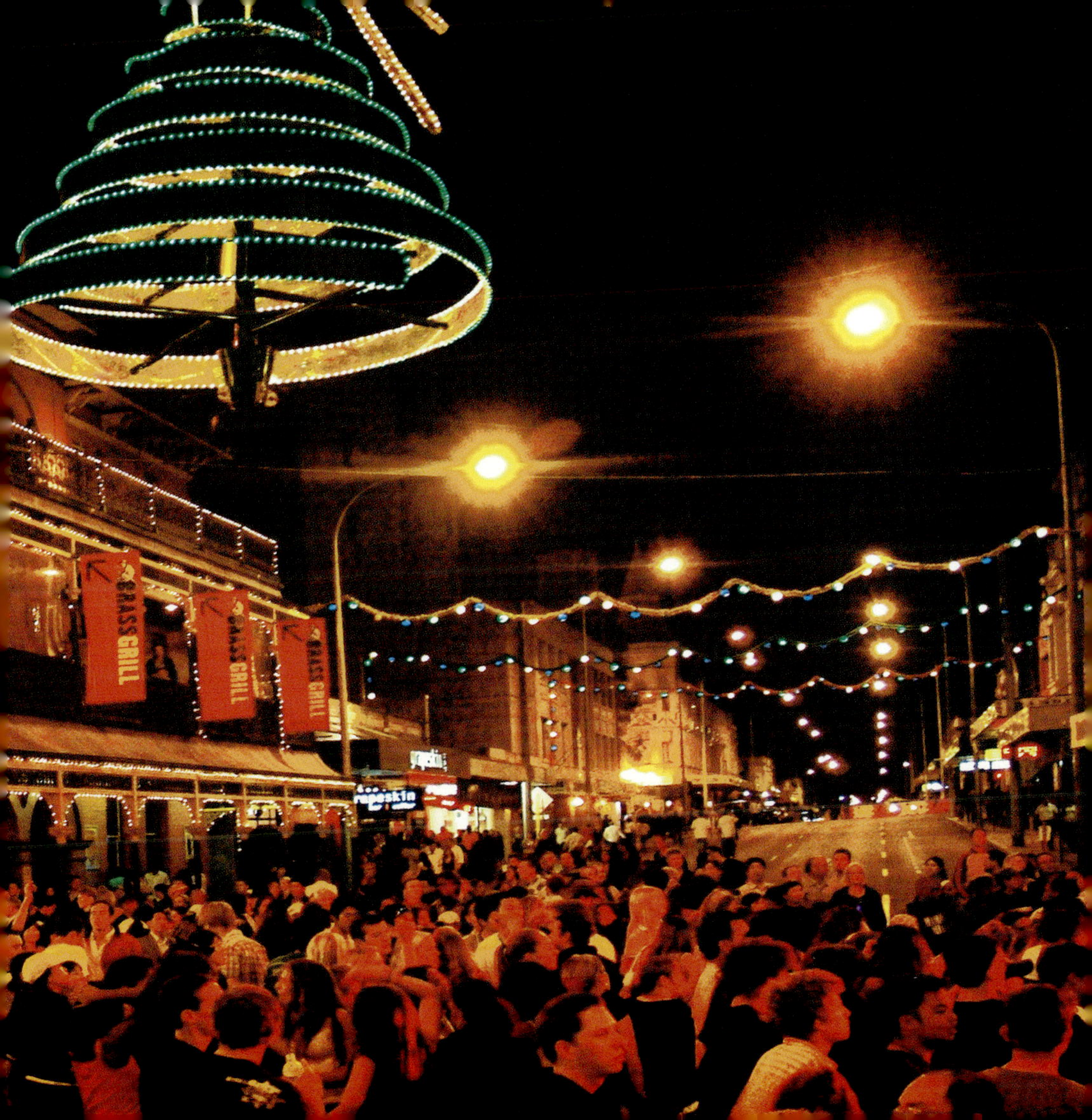
BRASS GRILL
BRASS GRILL
BRASS GRILL

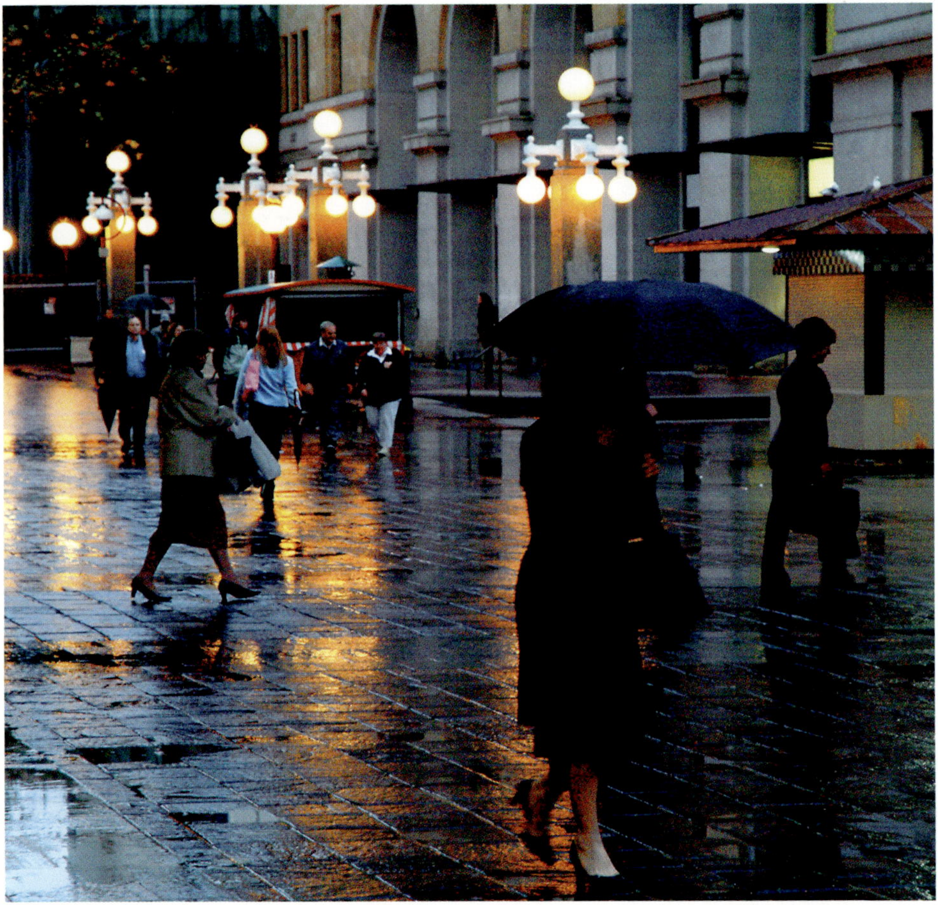

14. murray street mall

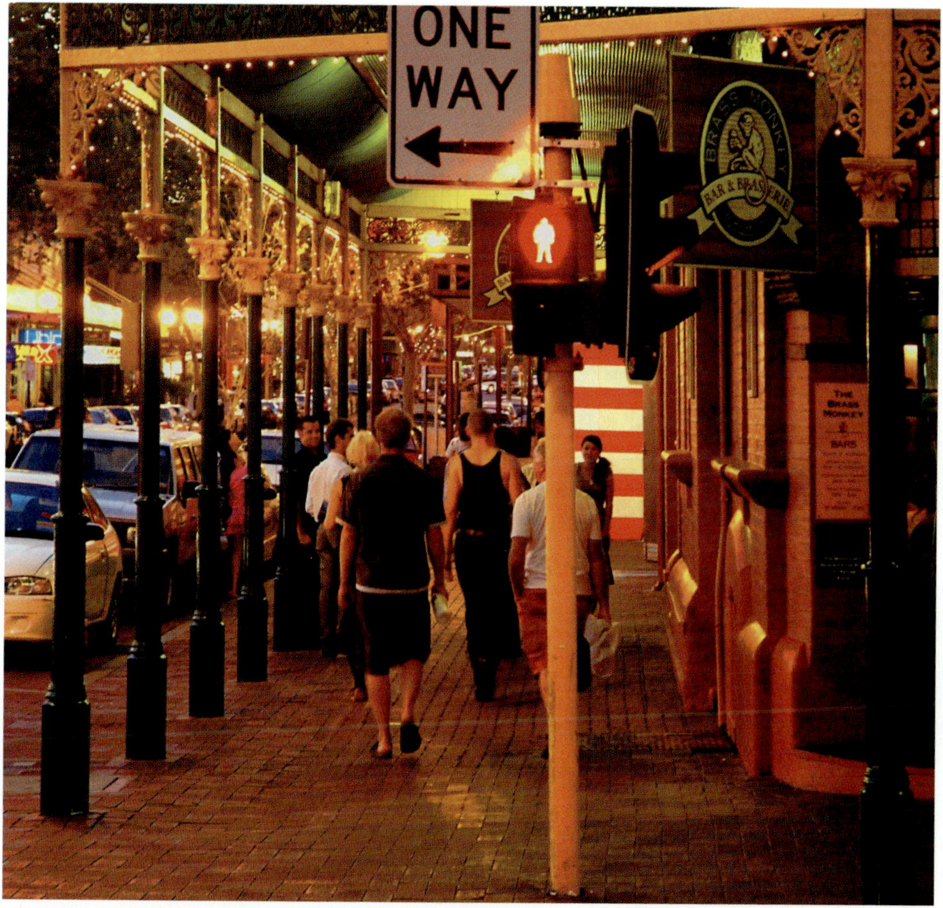

next page. murray street mall

brass monkey hotel, northbridge

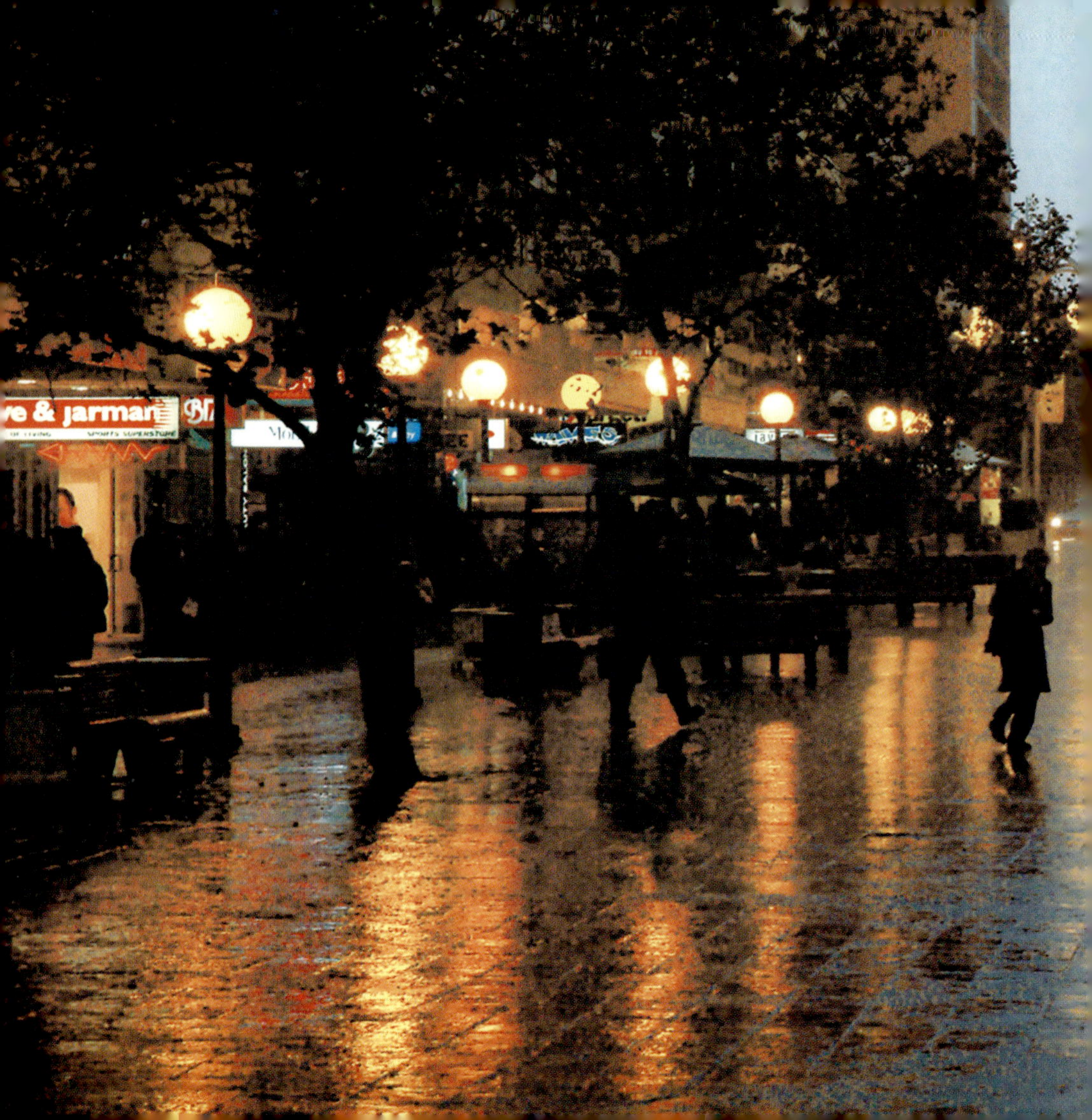
ve & jarman

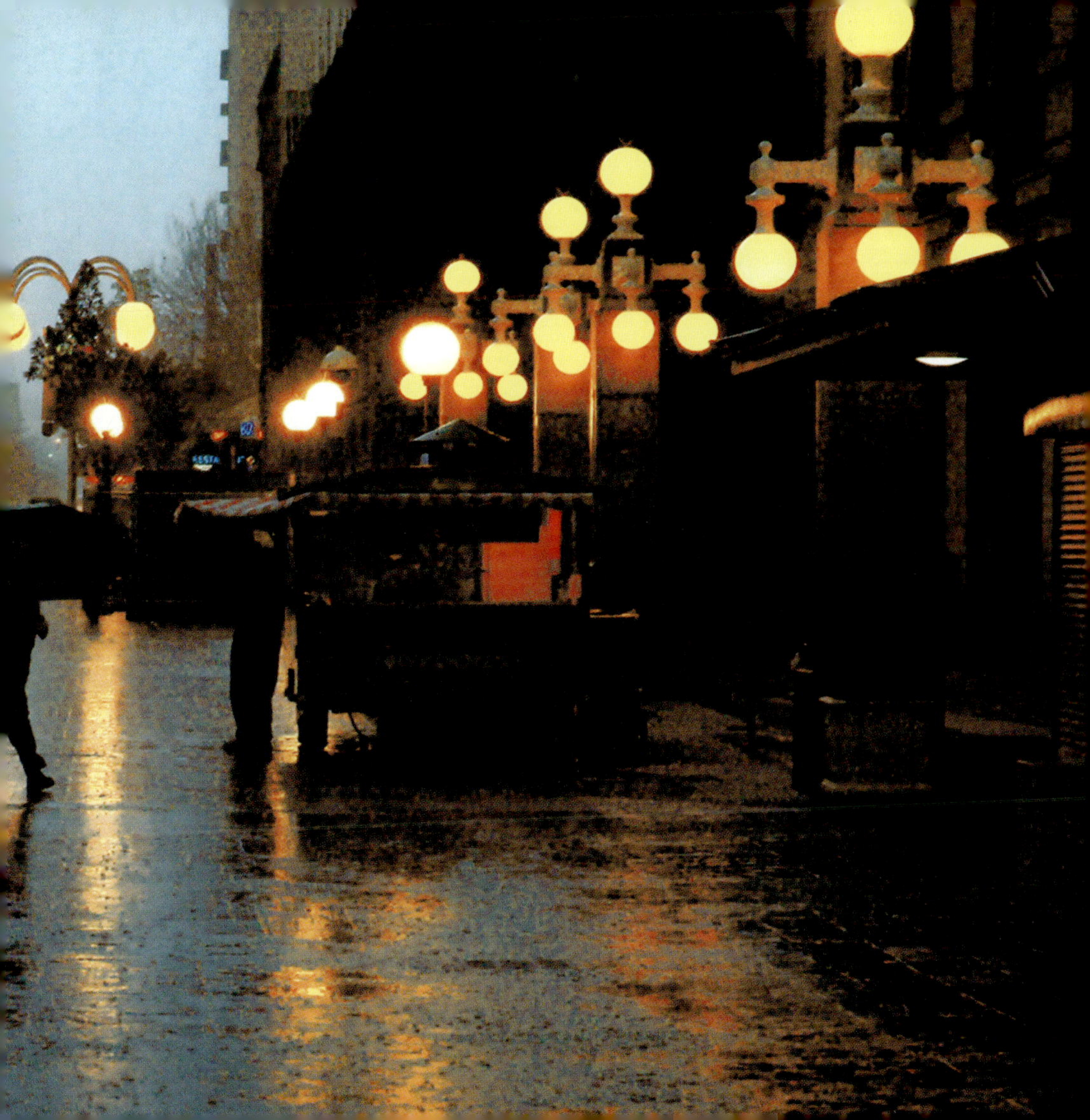

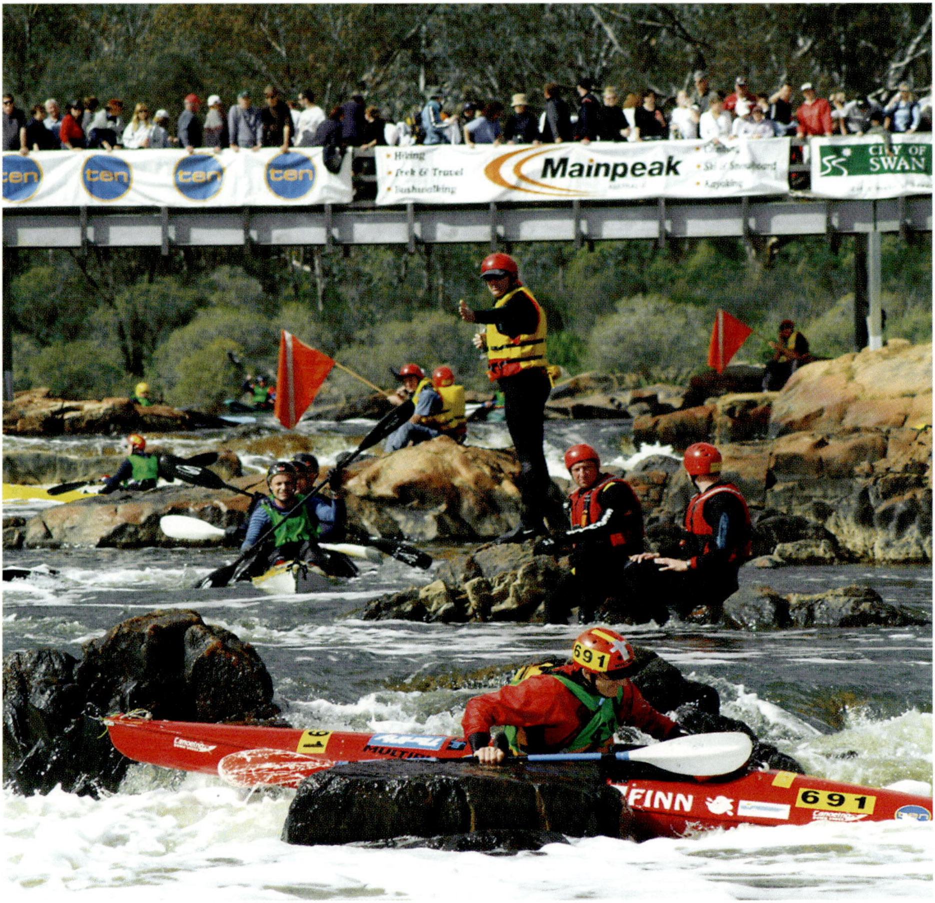

18. avon descent

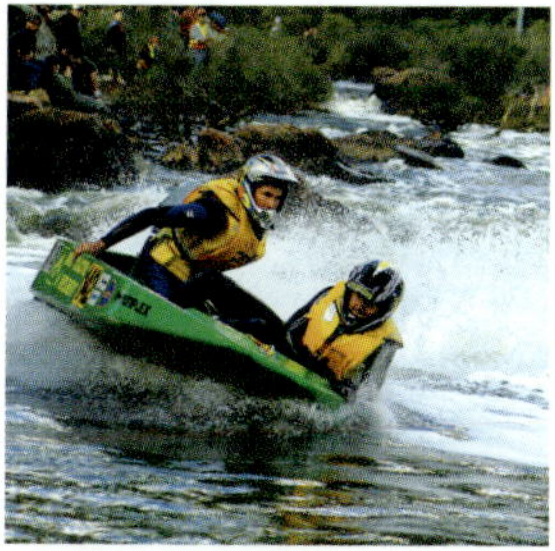

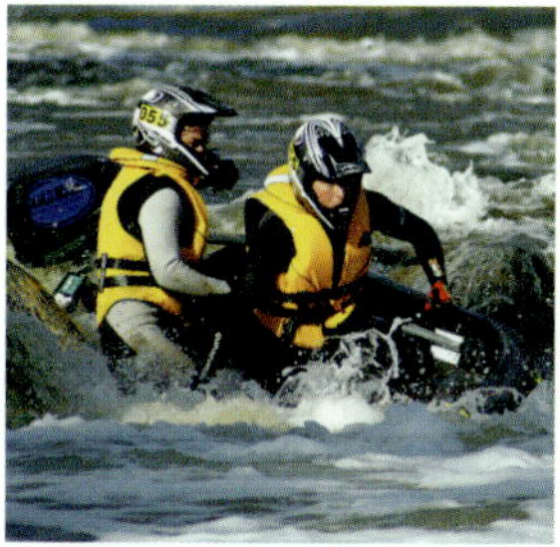

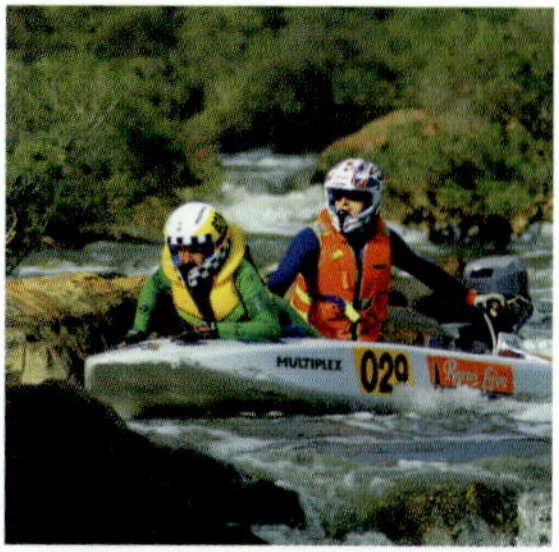

next page. windsurfing at cottesloe

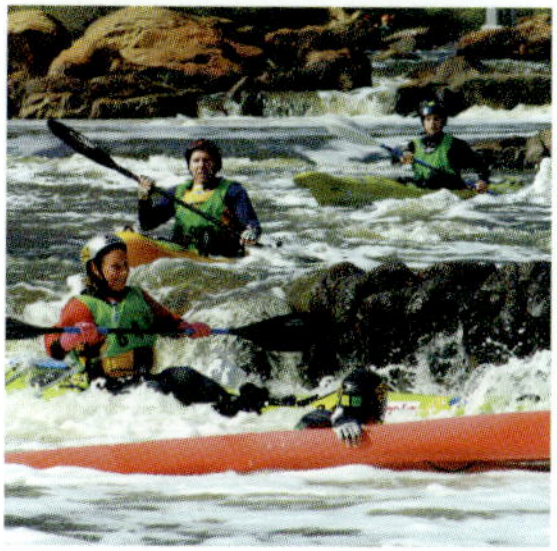

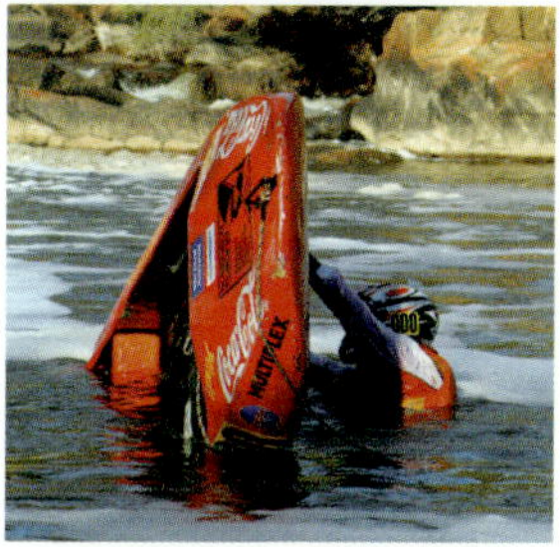

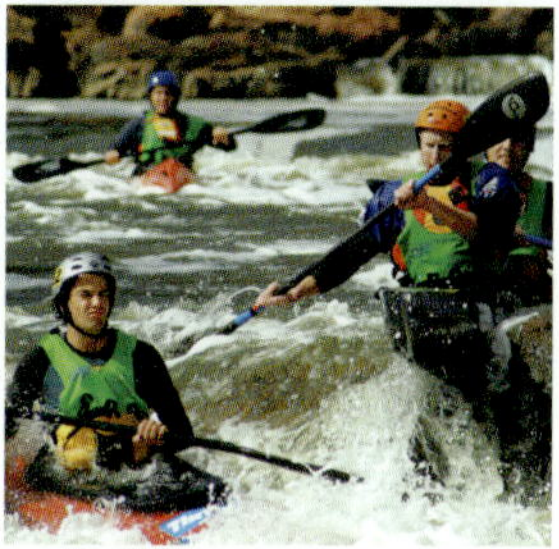

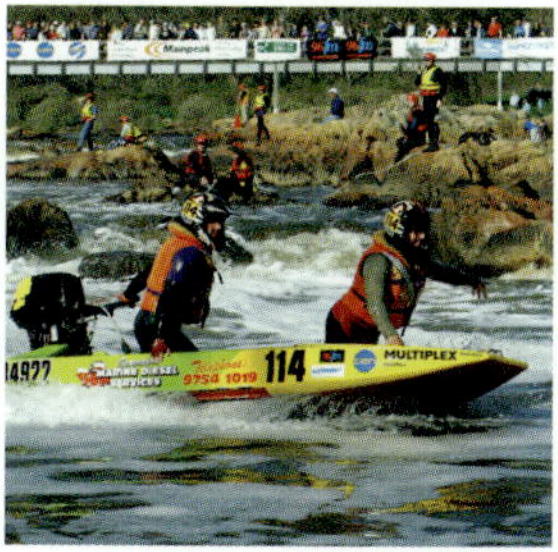

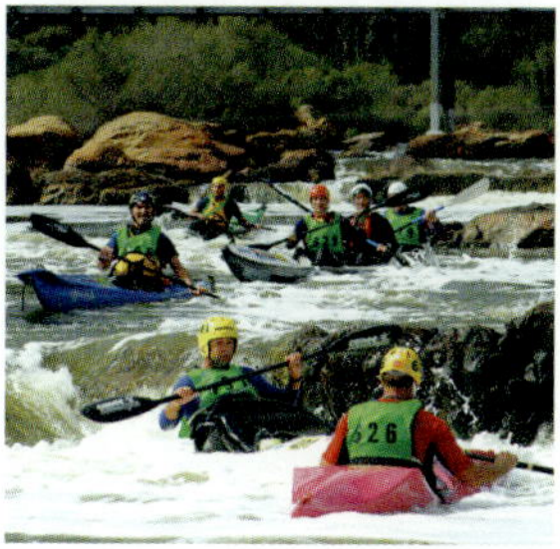

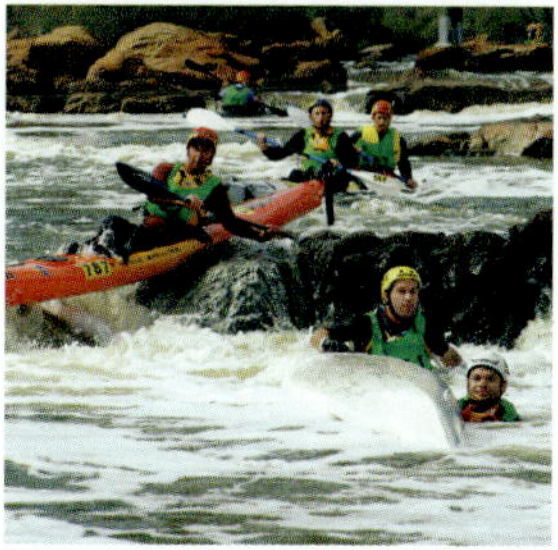

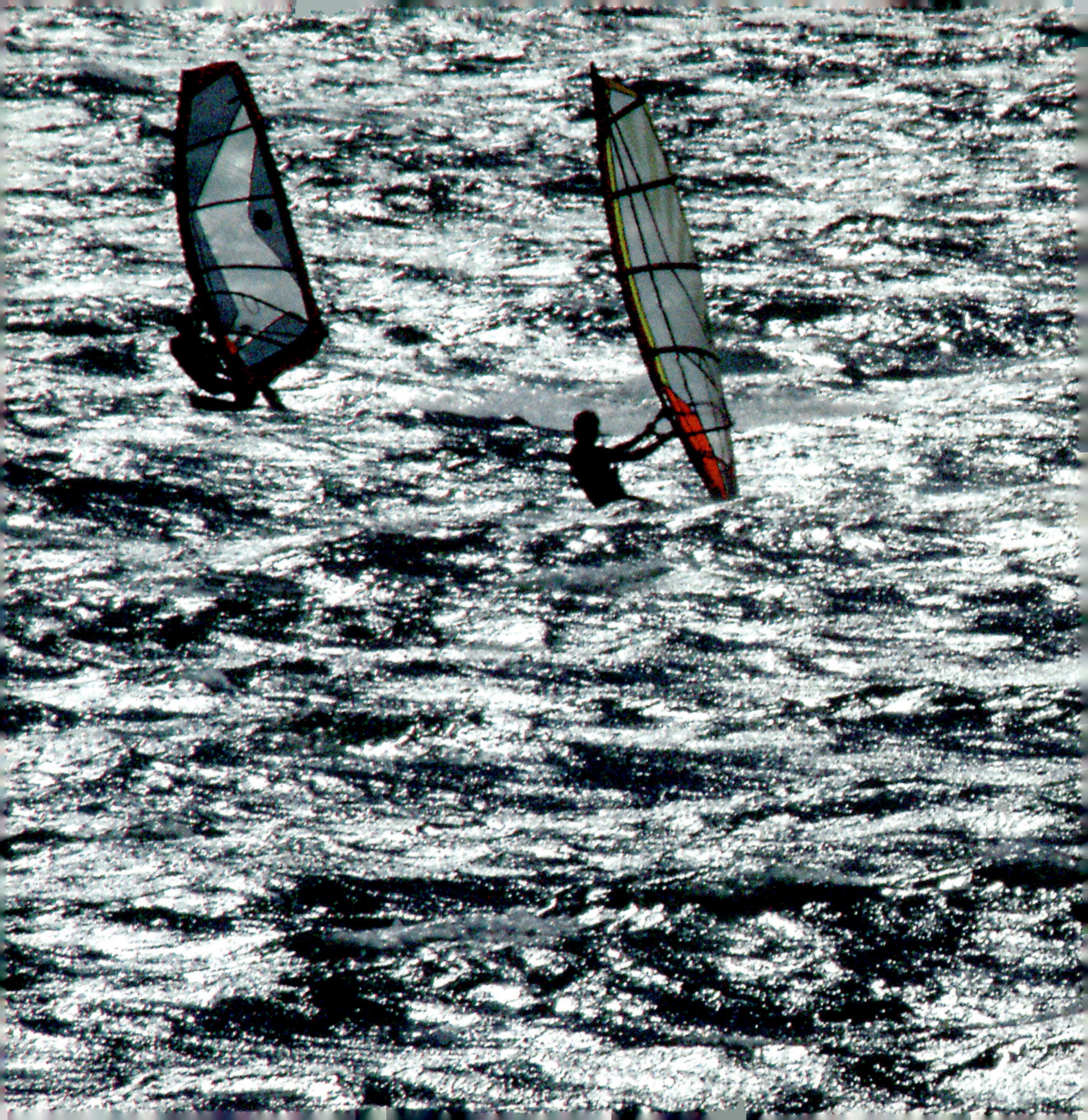

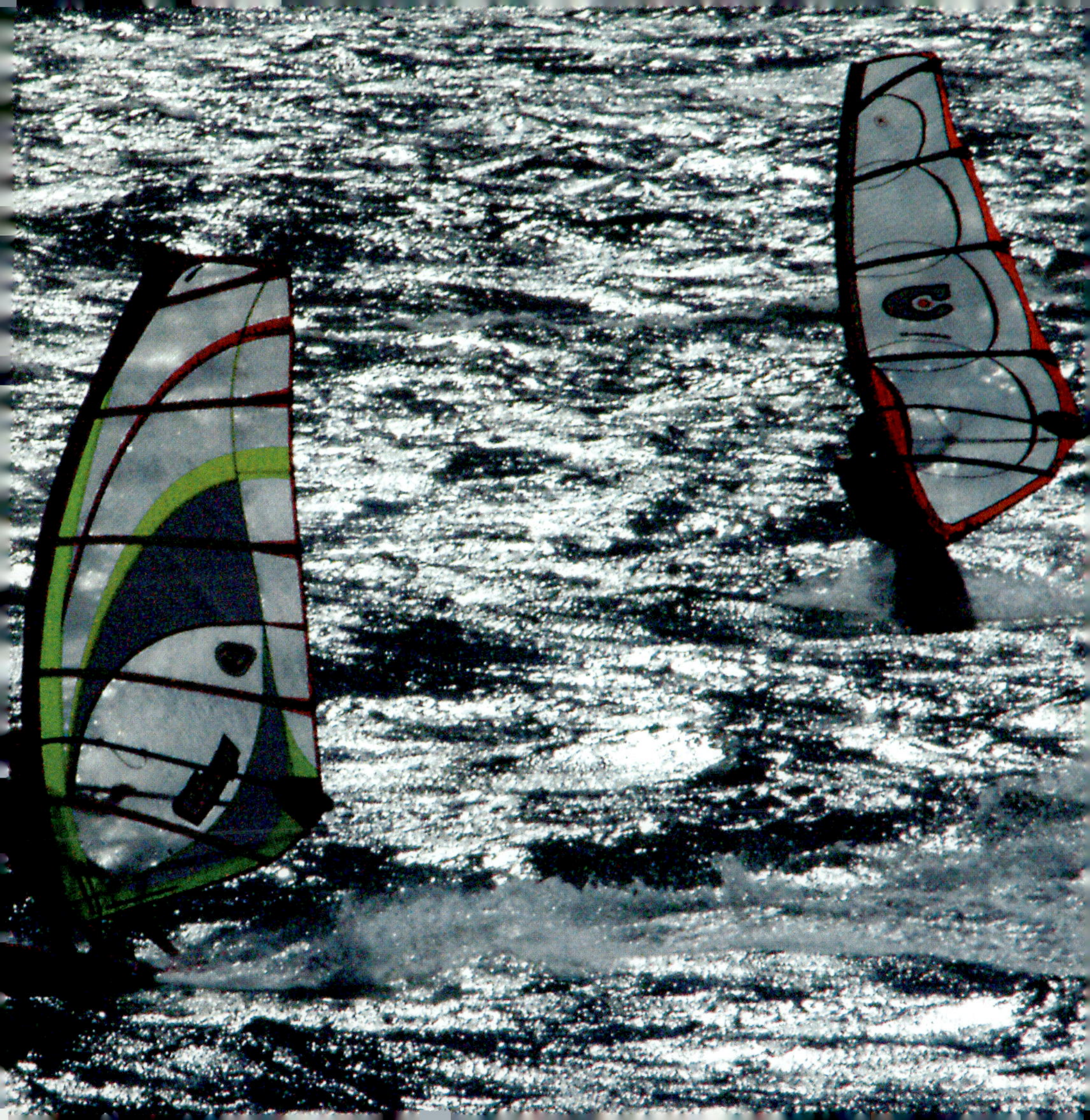

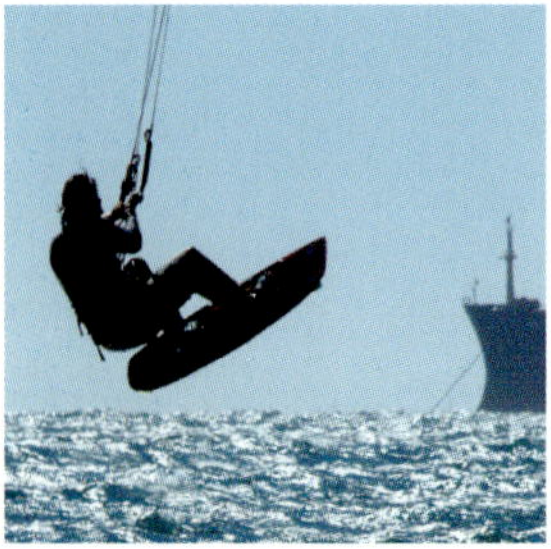
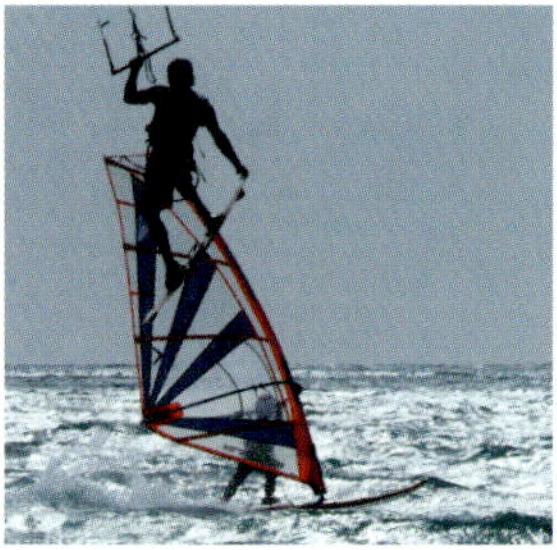
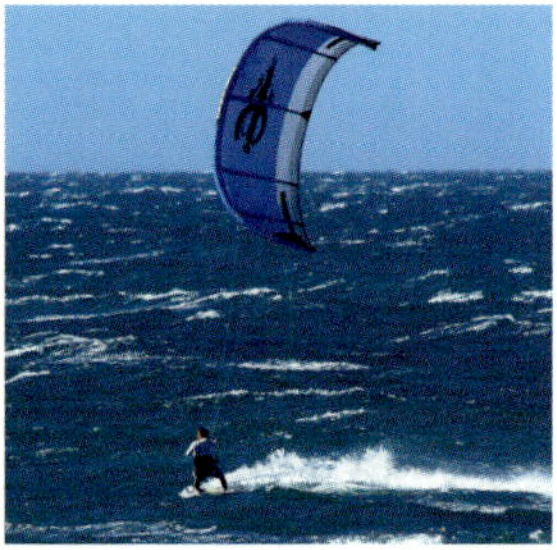
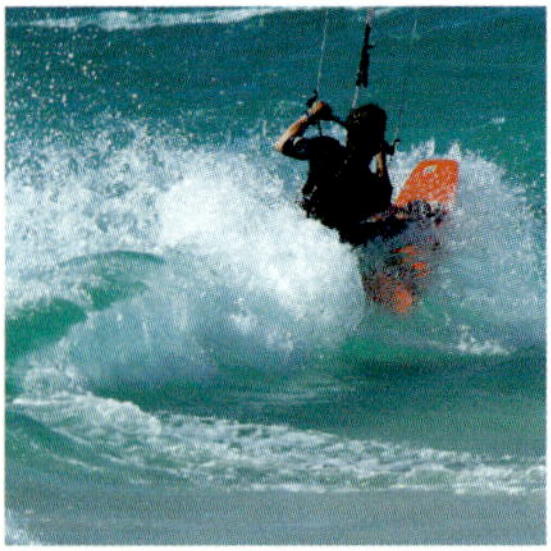
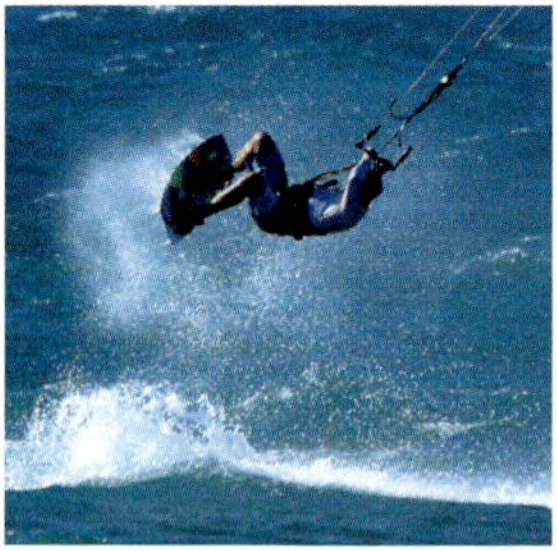
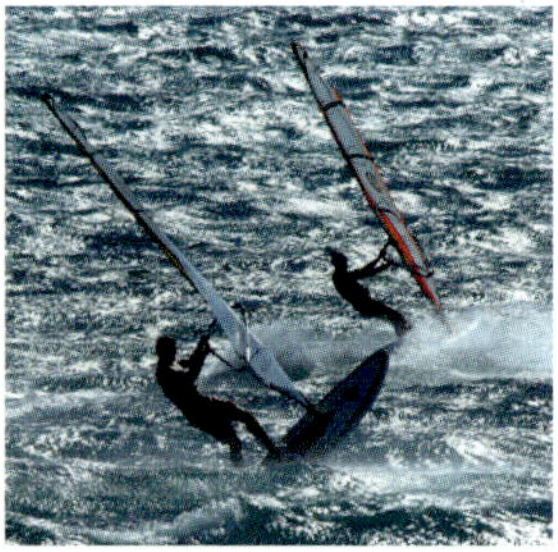
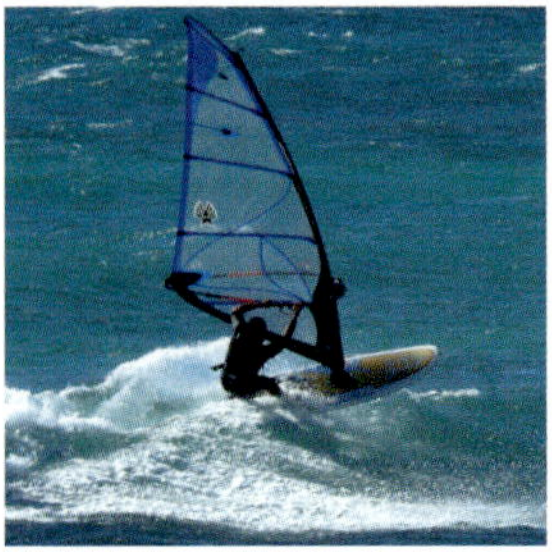
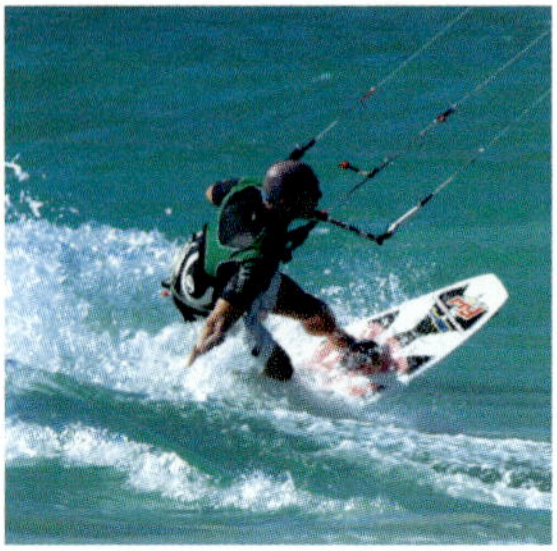
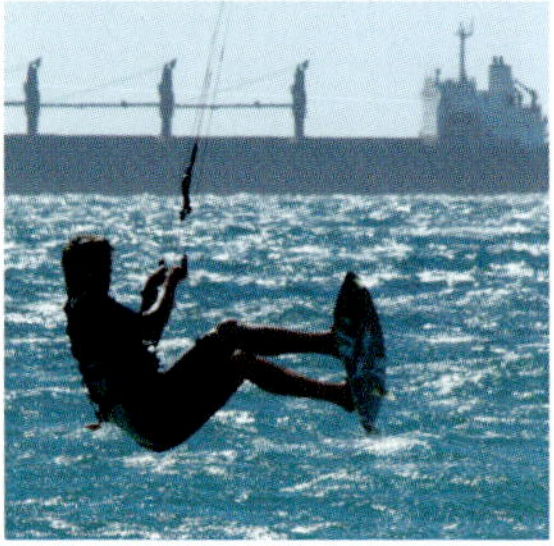

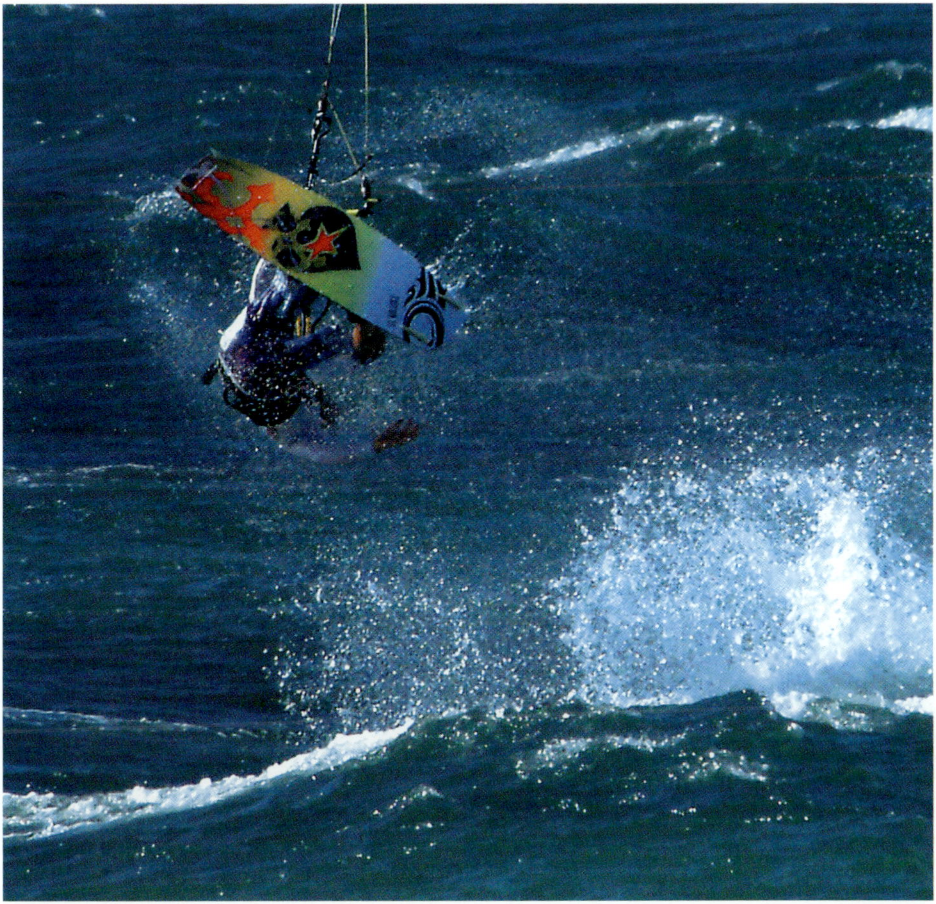

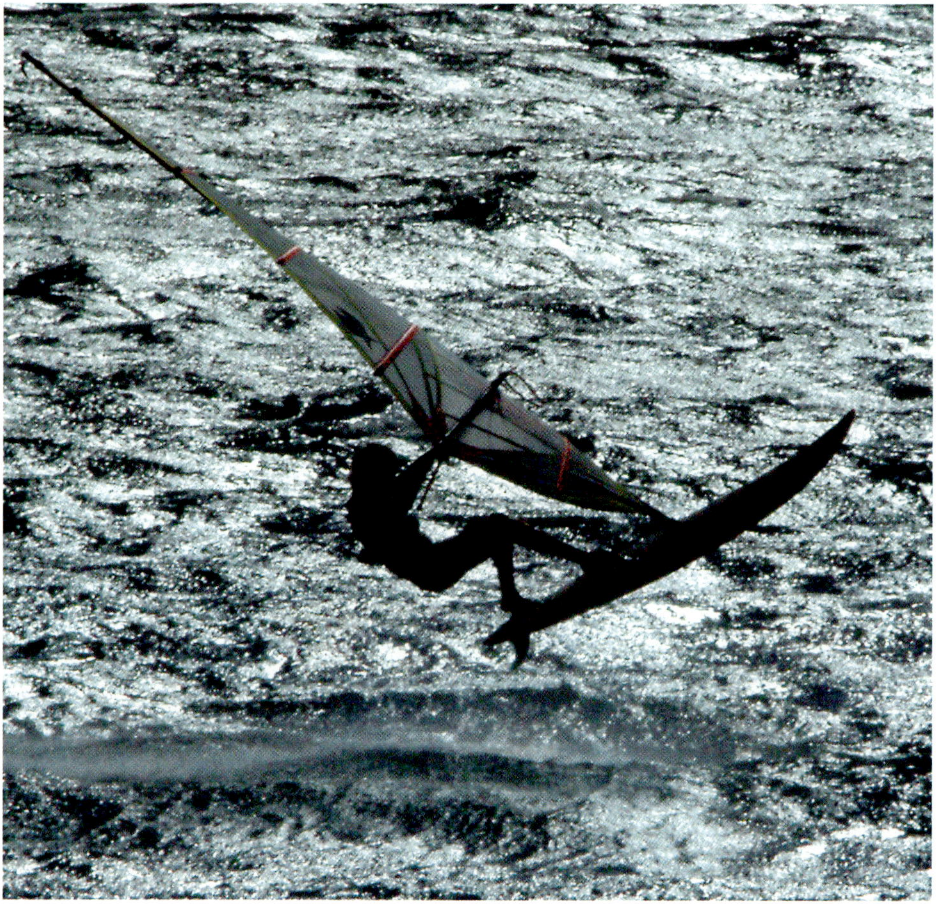

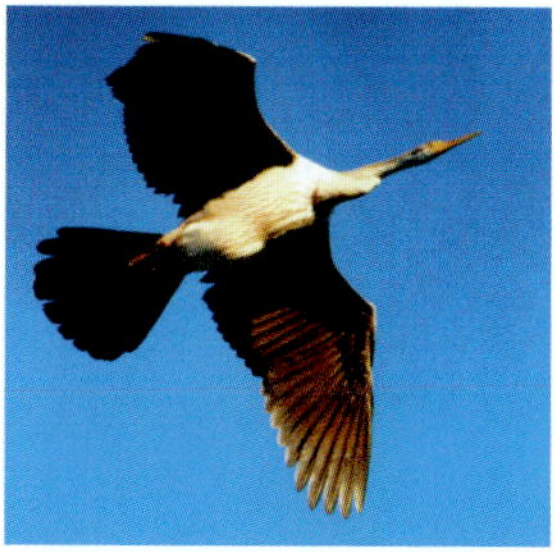
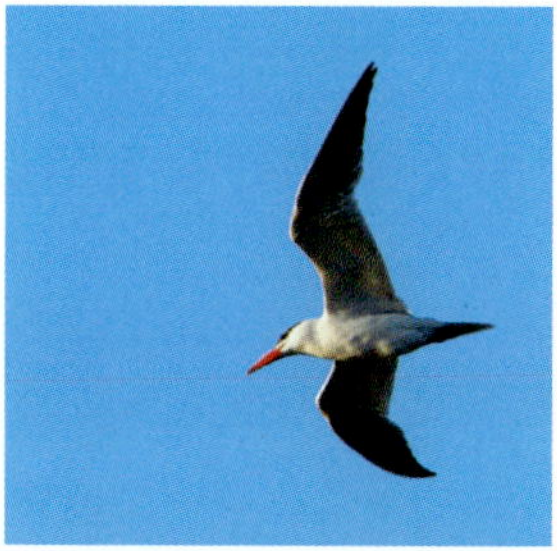
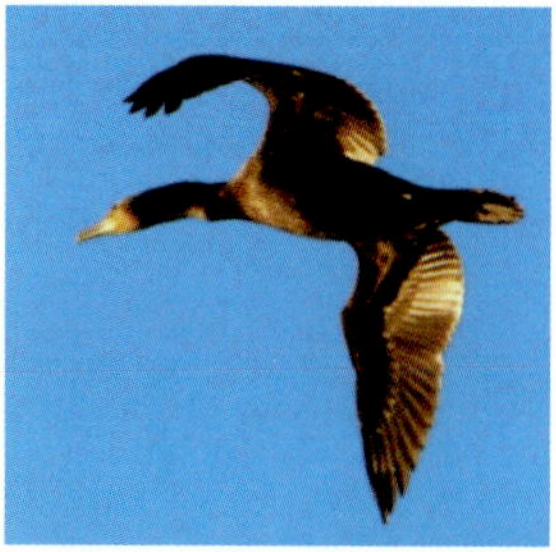

next page. the old swan brewery

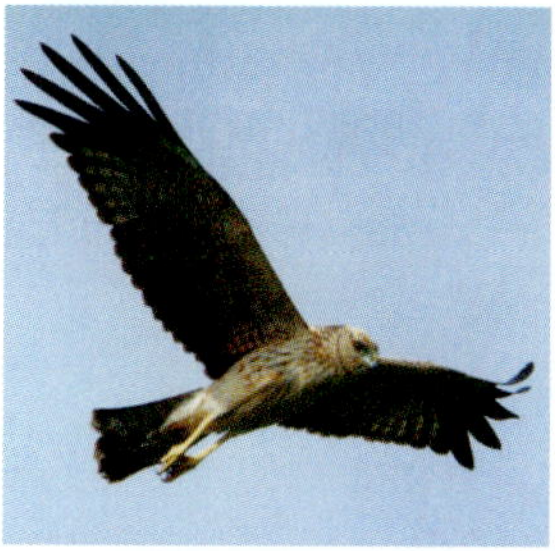
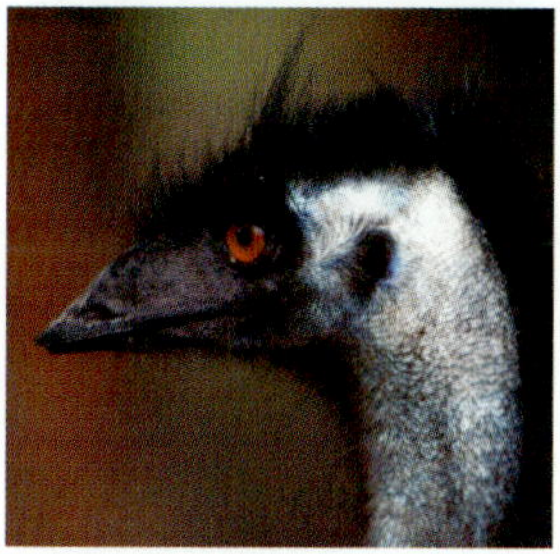
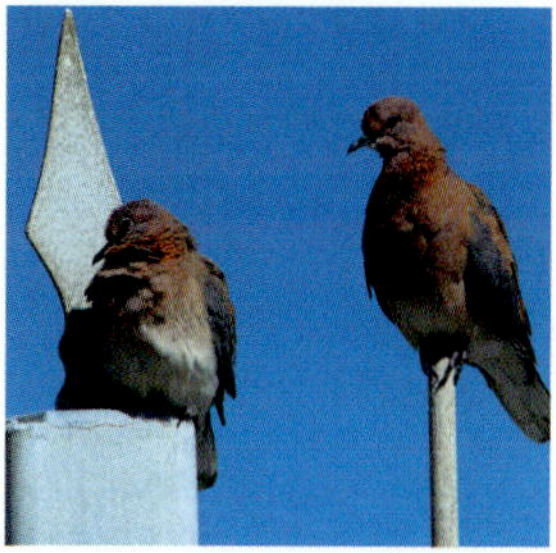
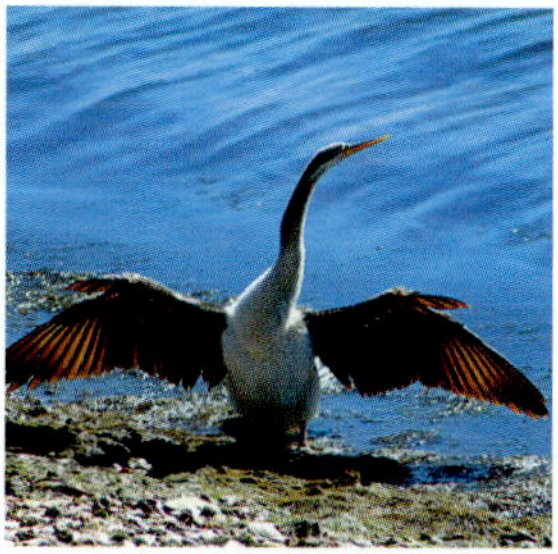
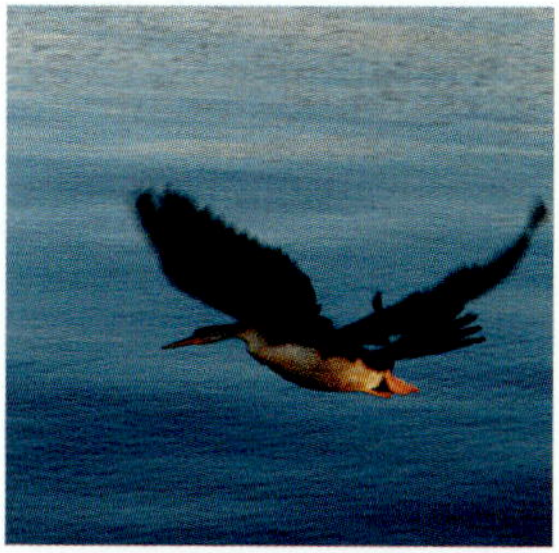
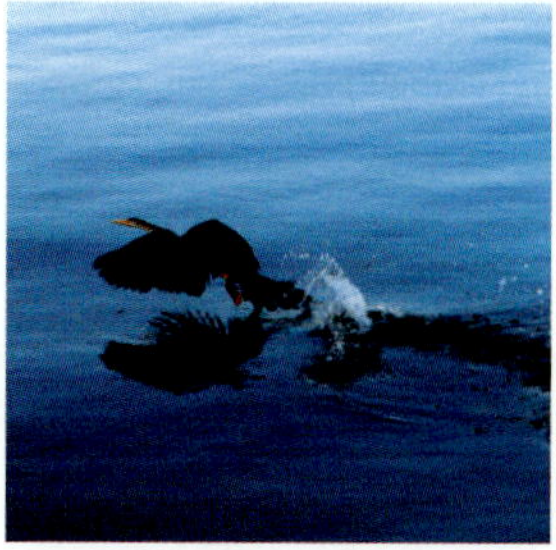

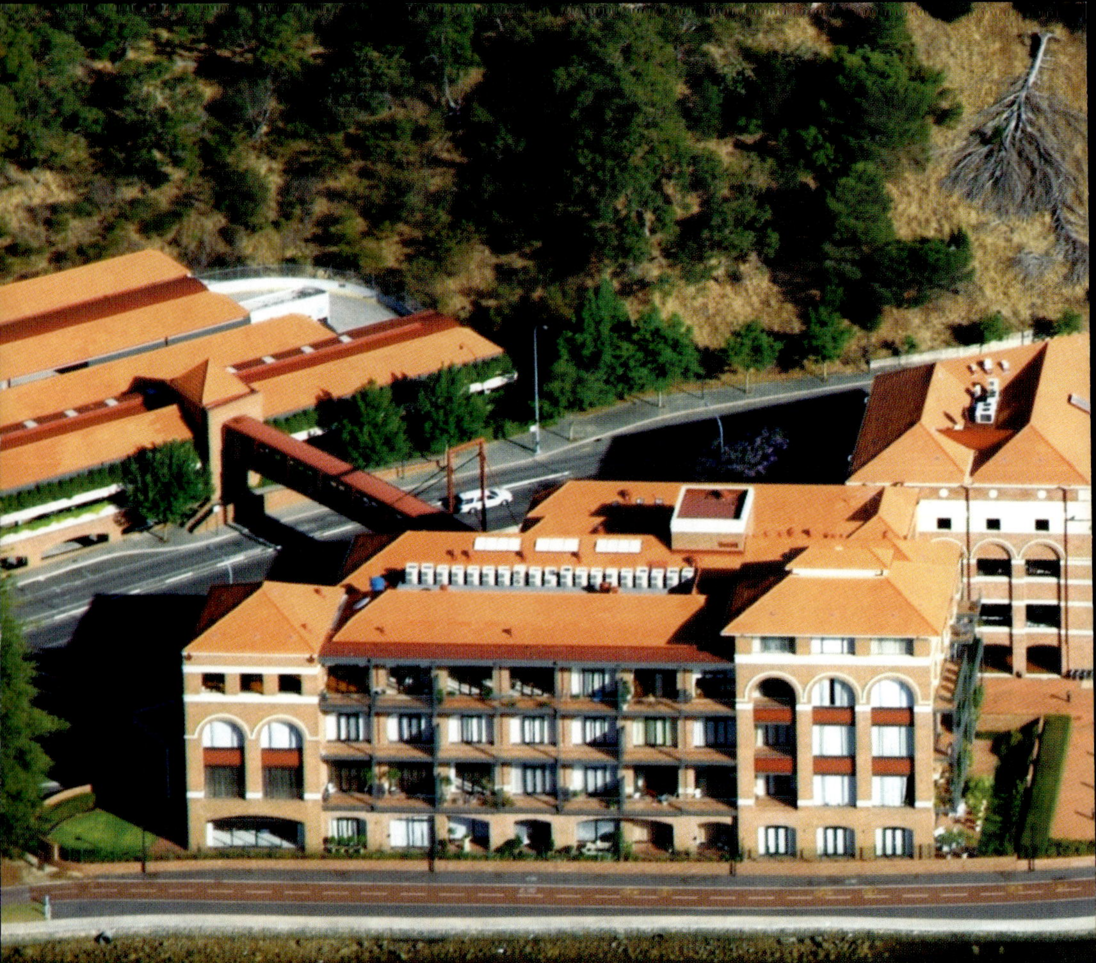

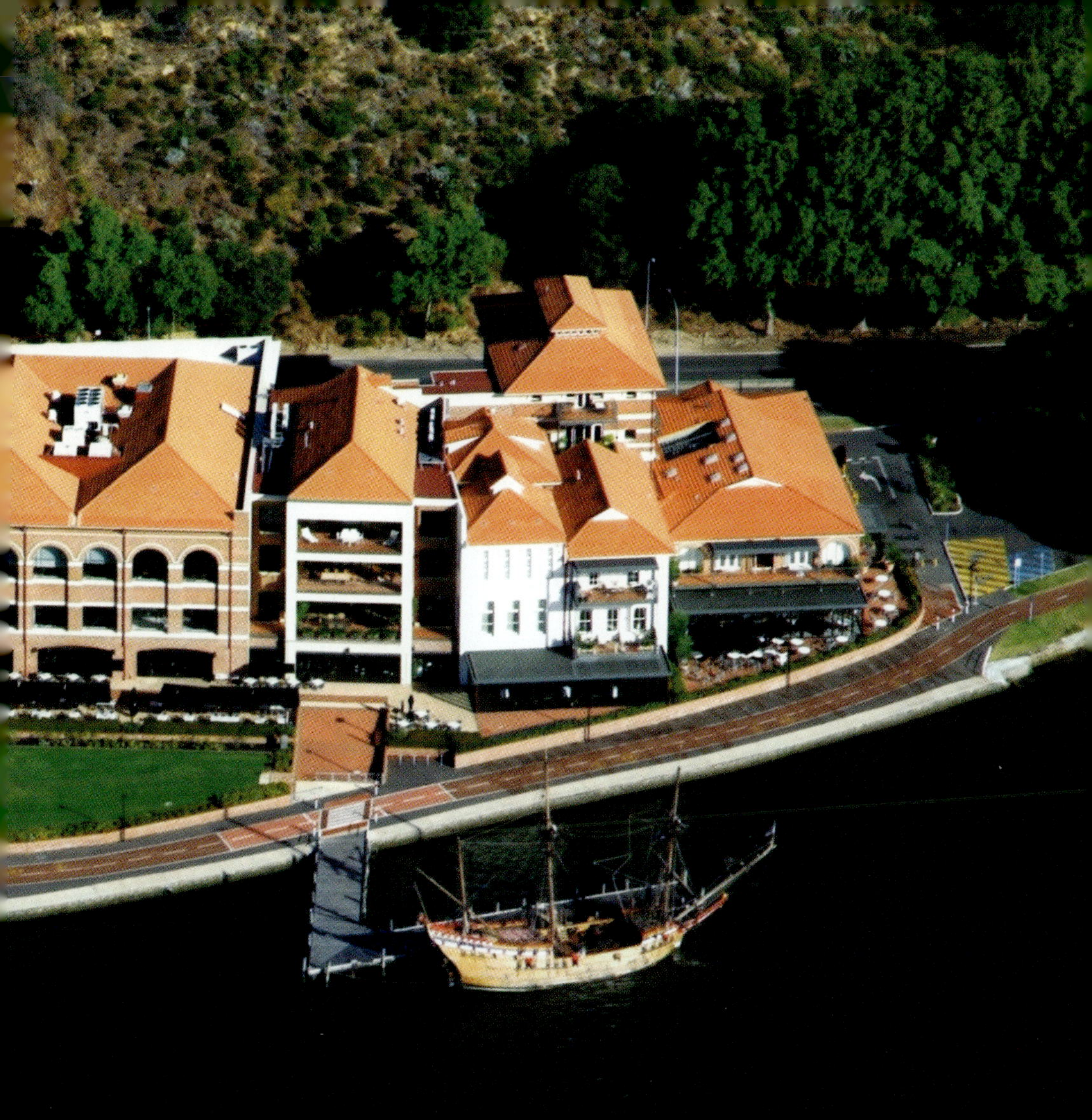

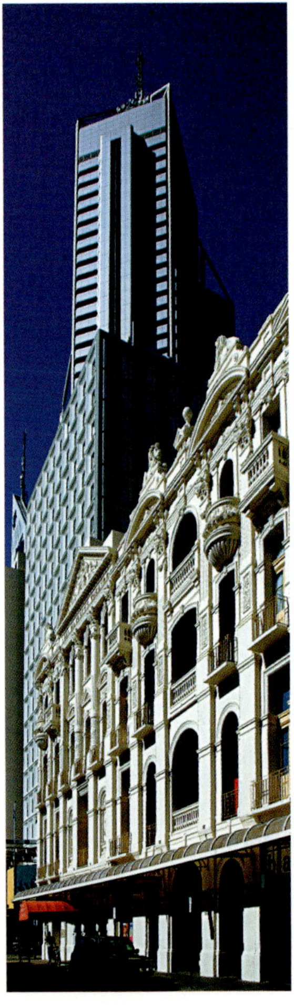

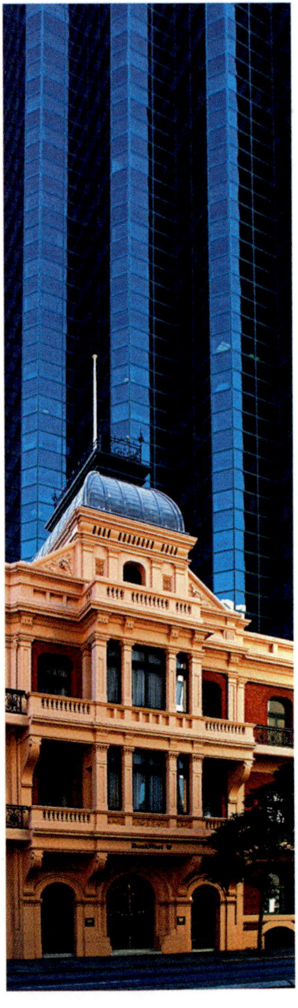

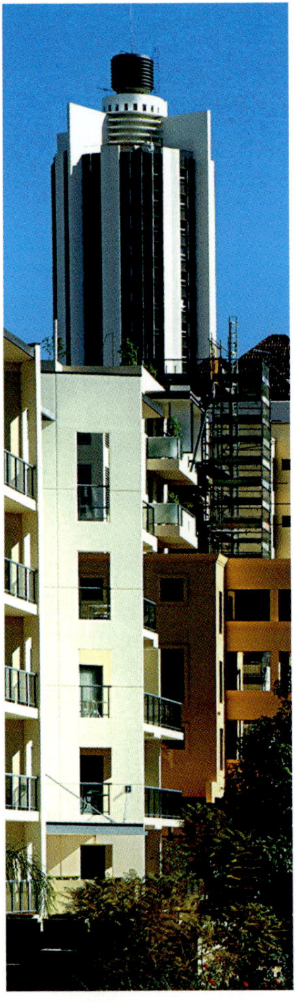

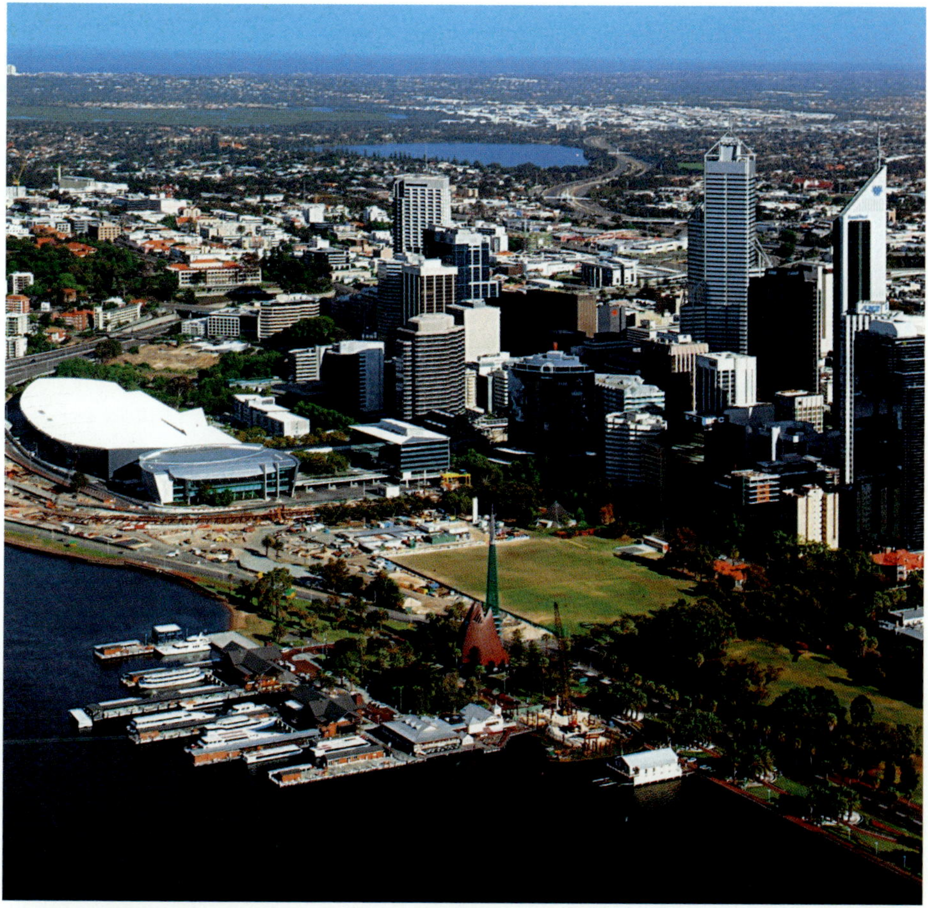

next page. kings park

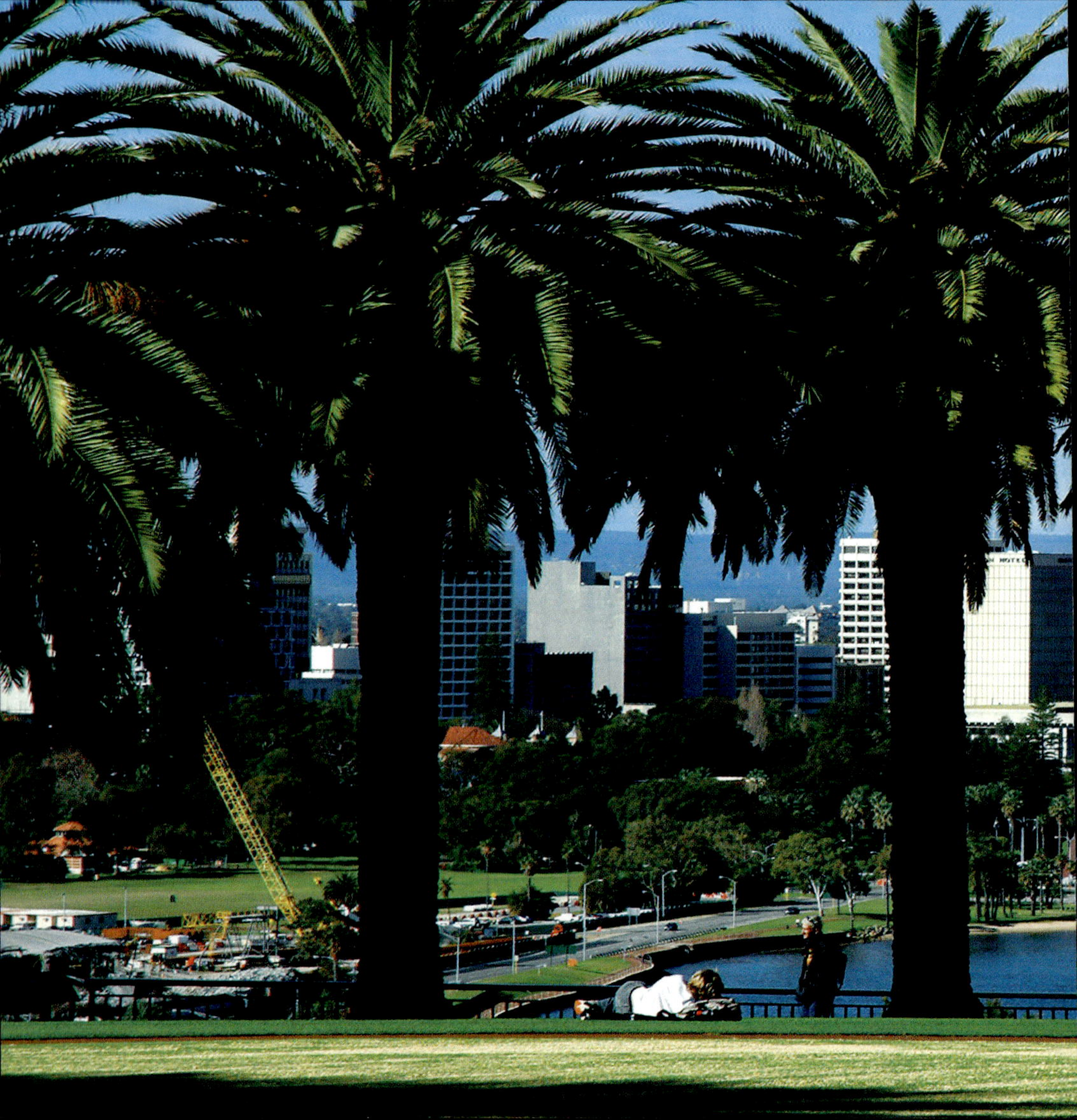

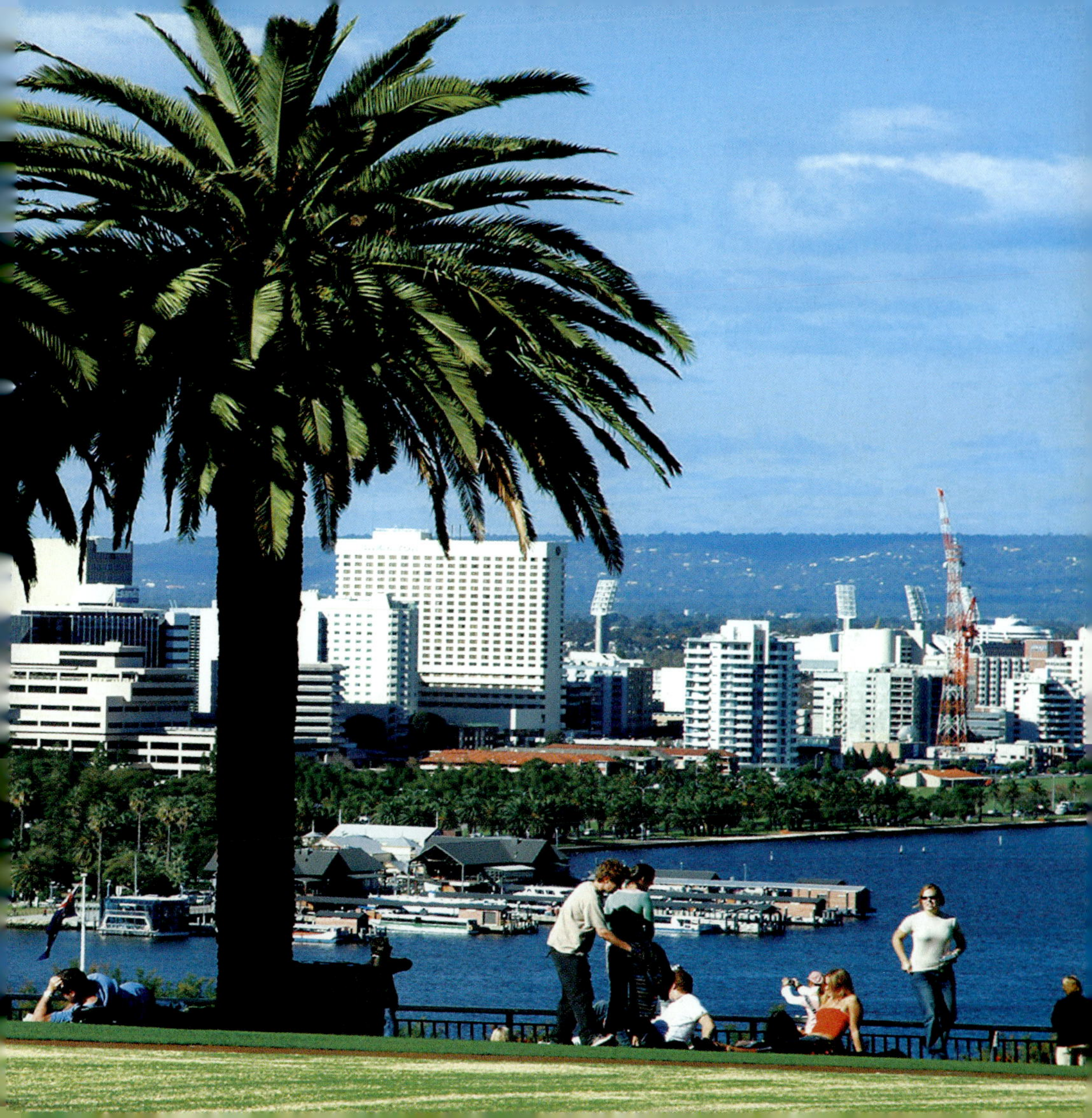

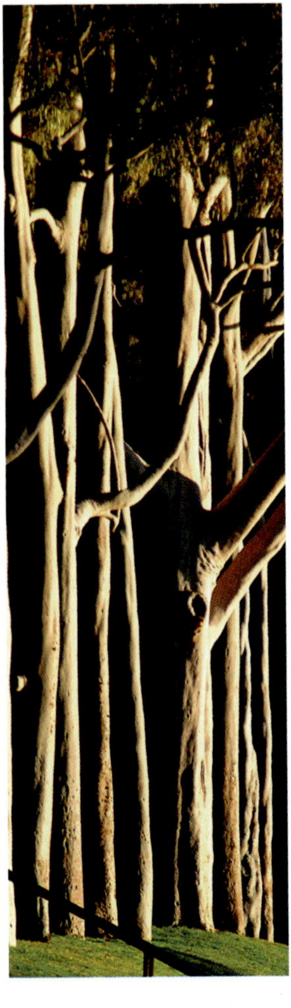
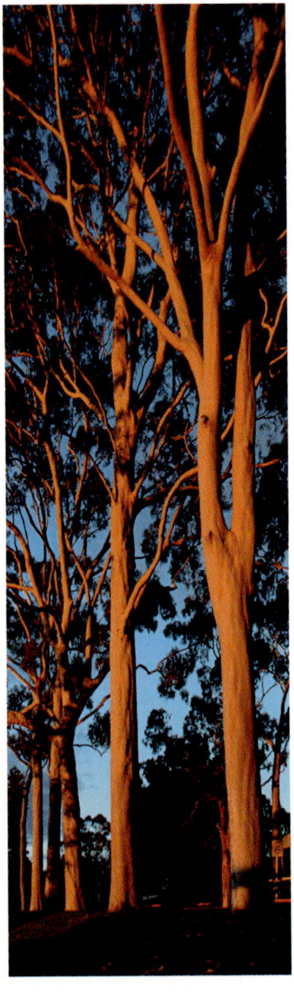
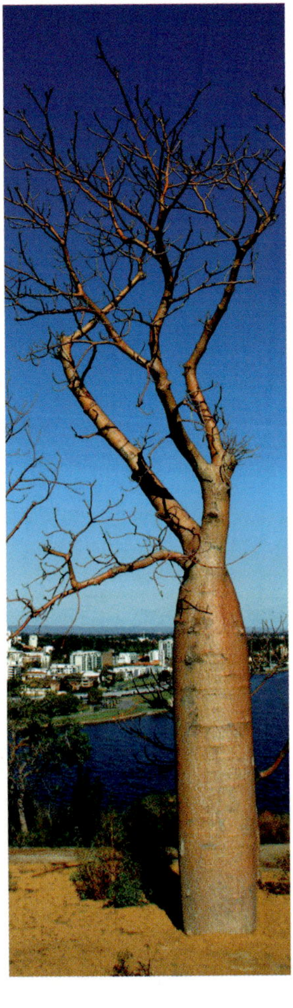

32. kings park

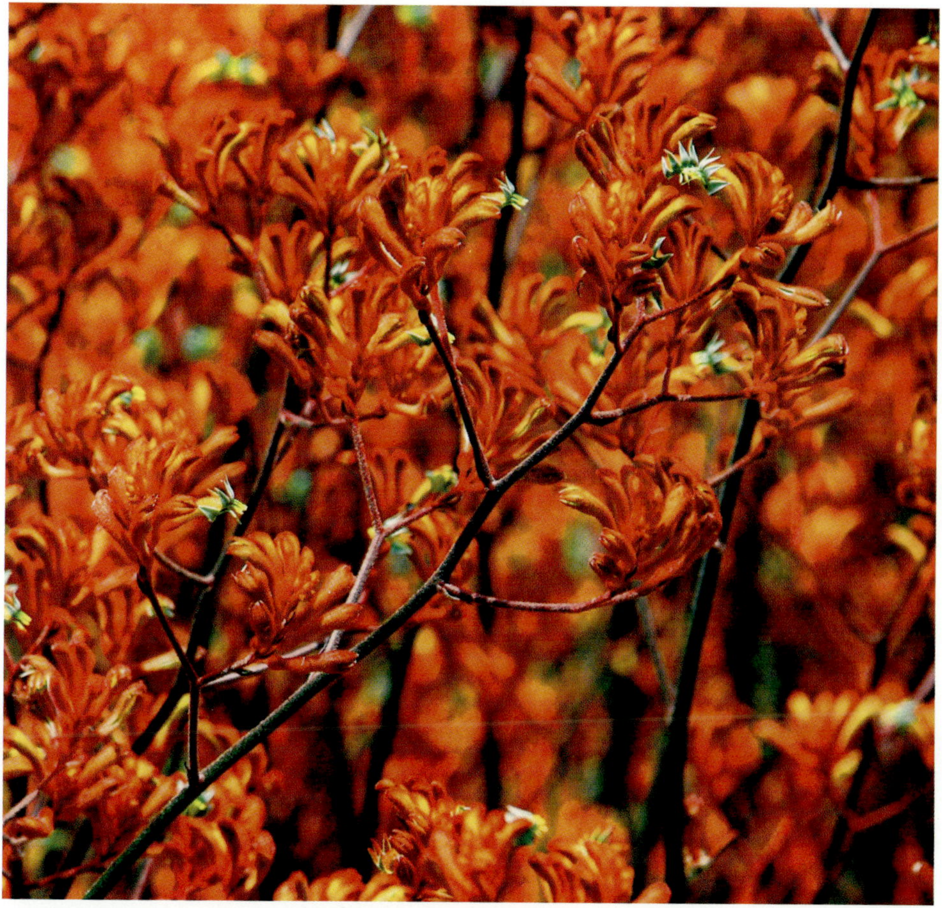

next page. barrack square

kangaroo paw

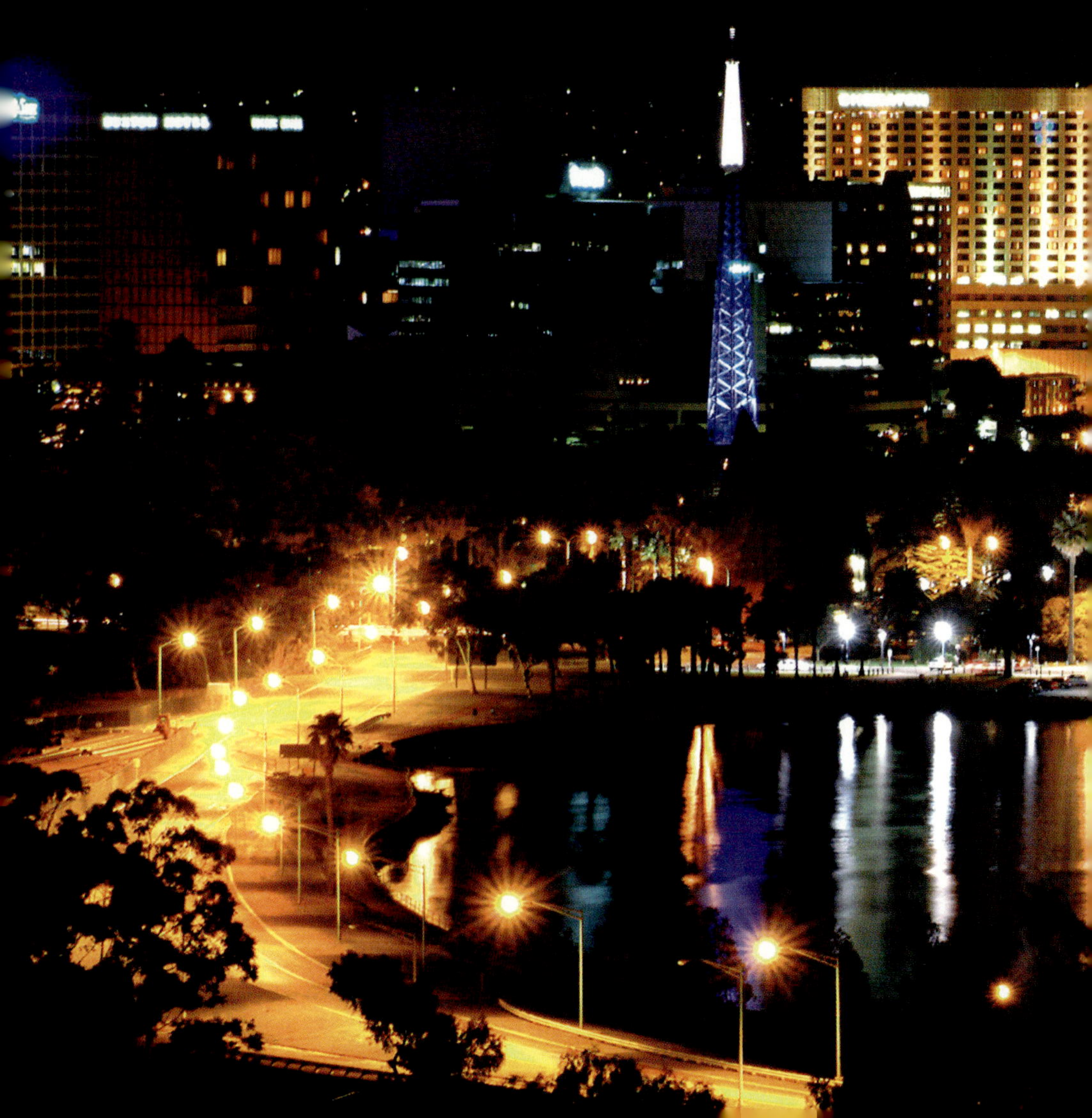

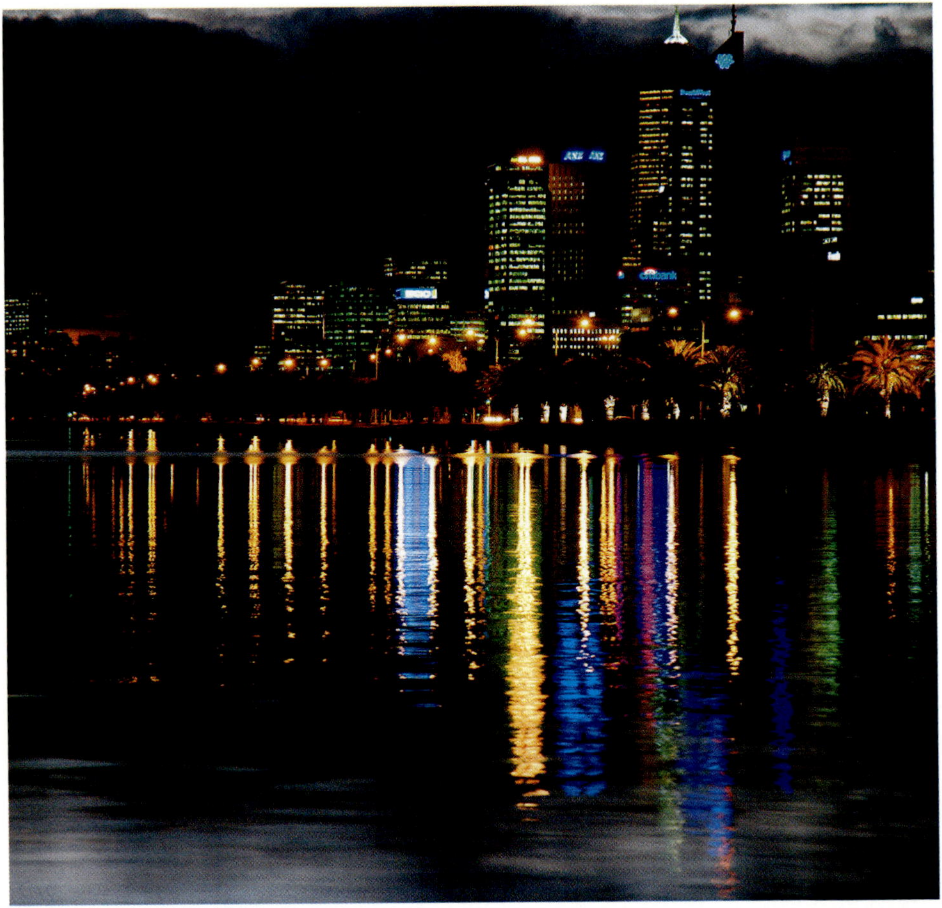

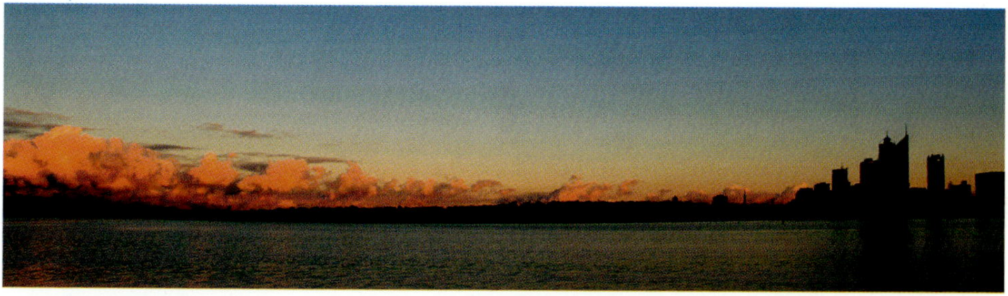

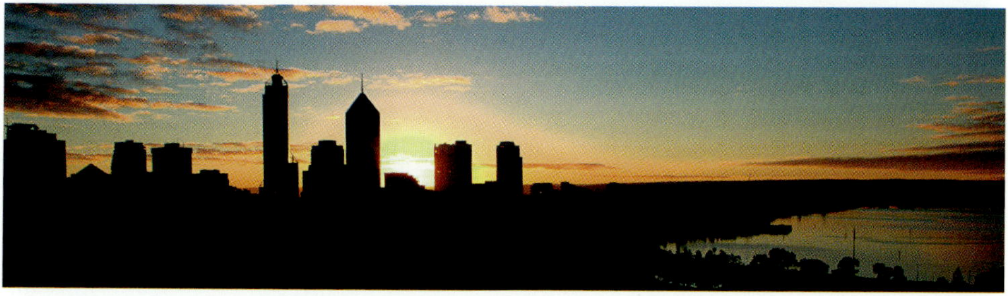

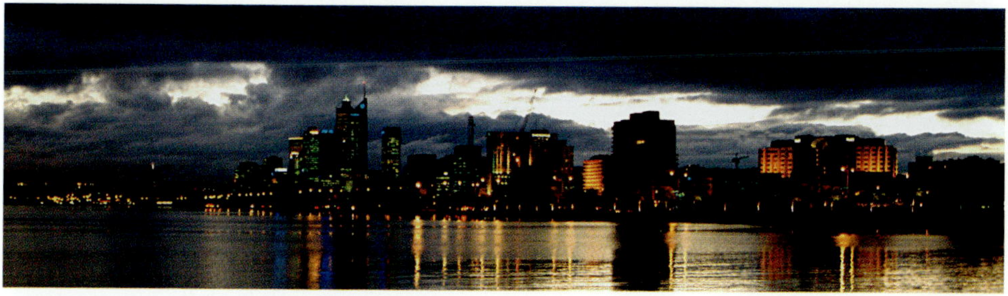

next page. southern cross fountain, convention centre & mitchell freeway

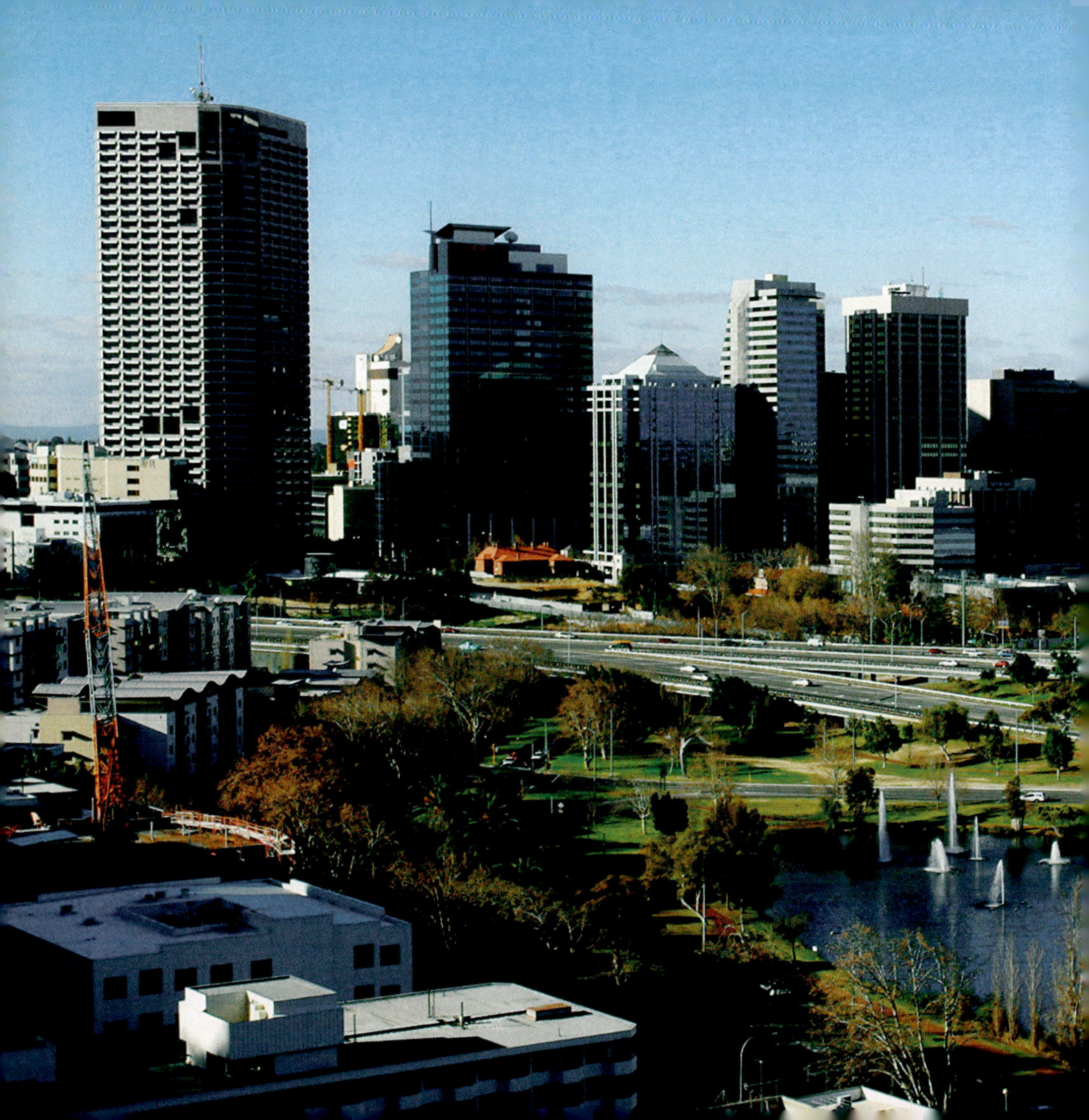

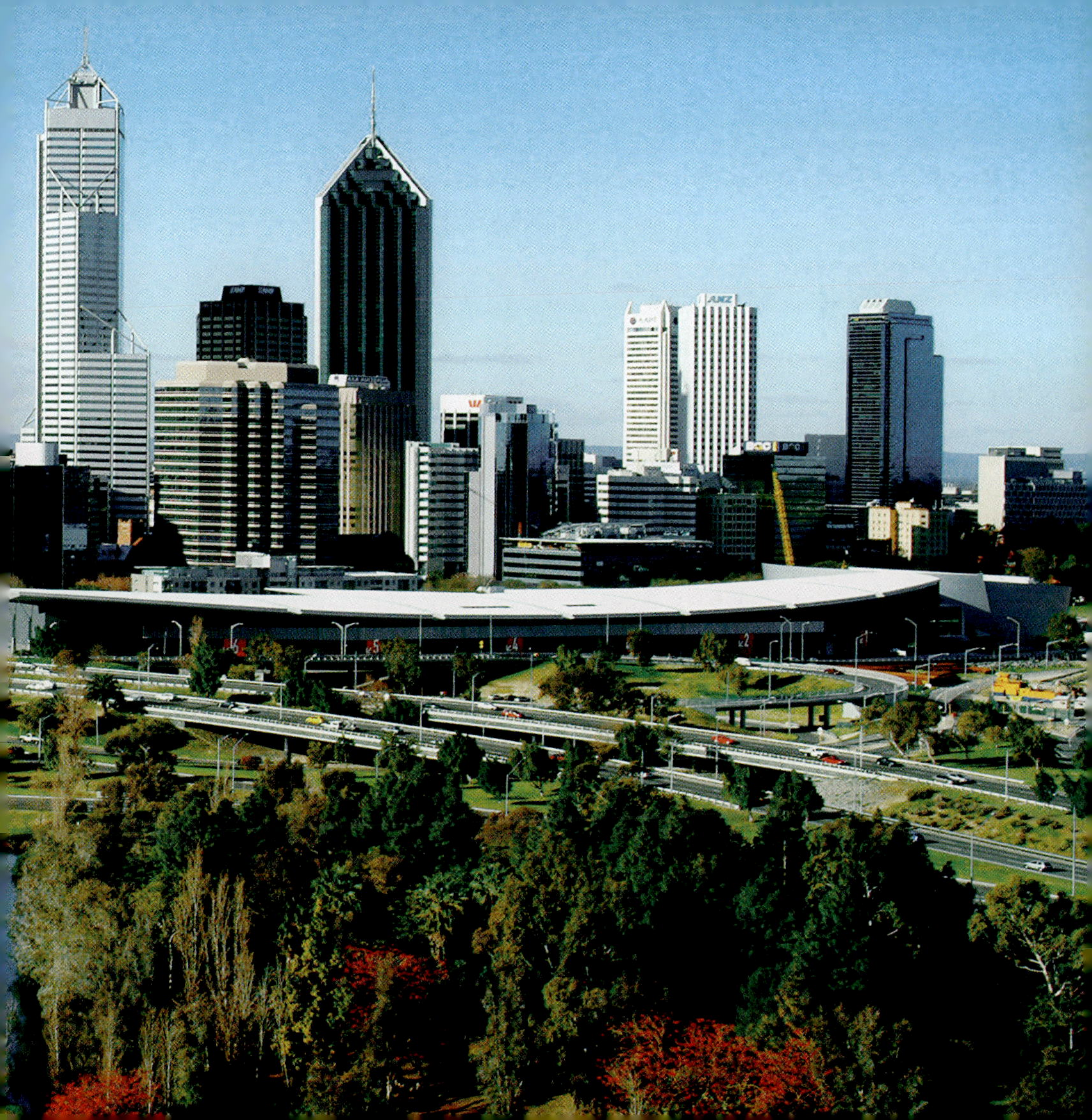
ANZ

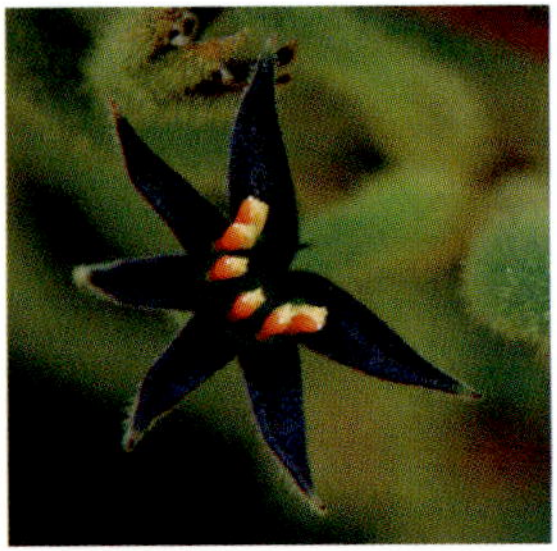
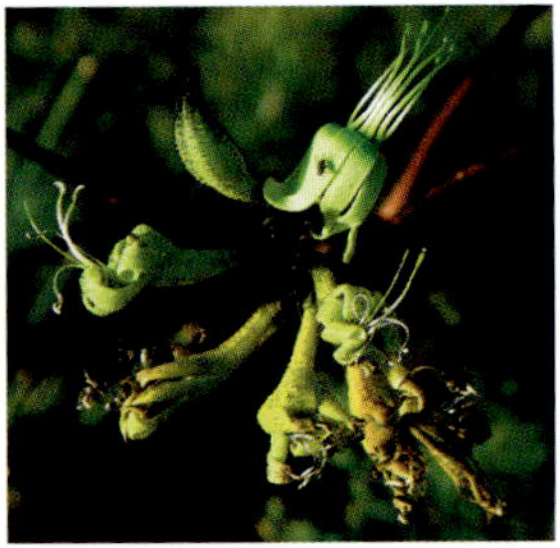
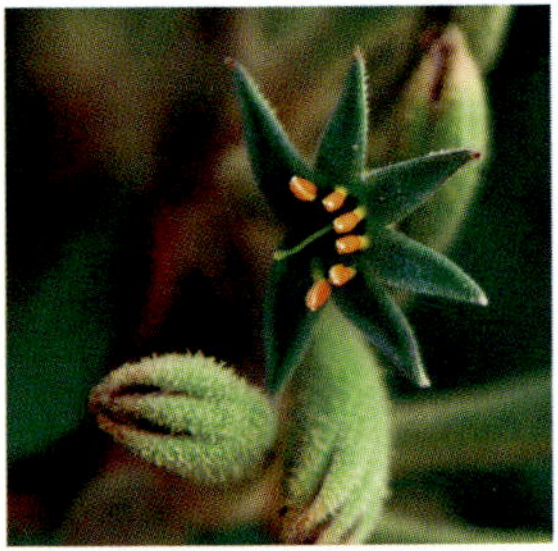
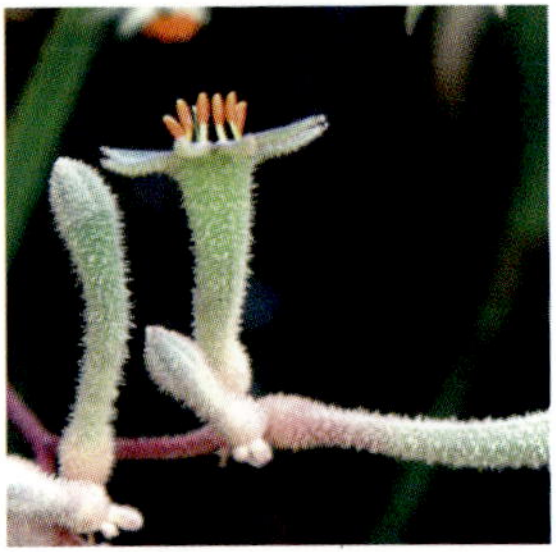
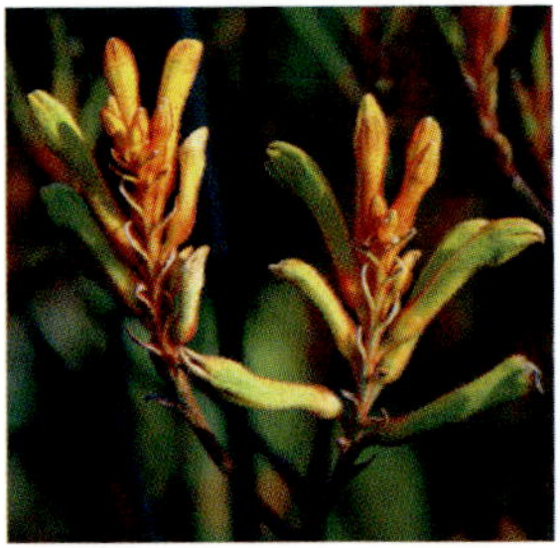
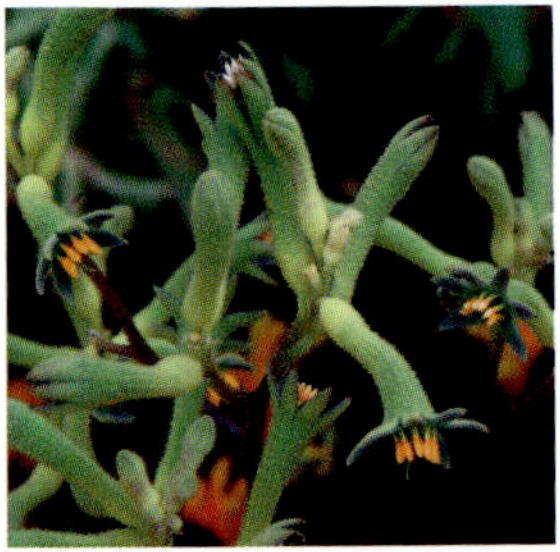
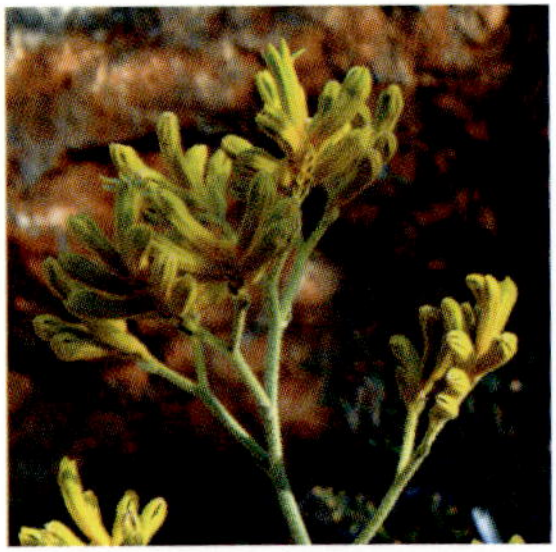
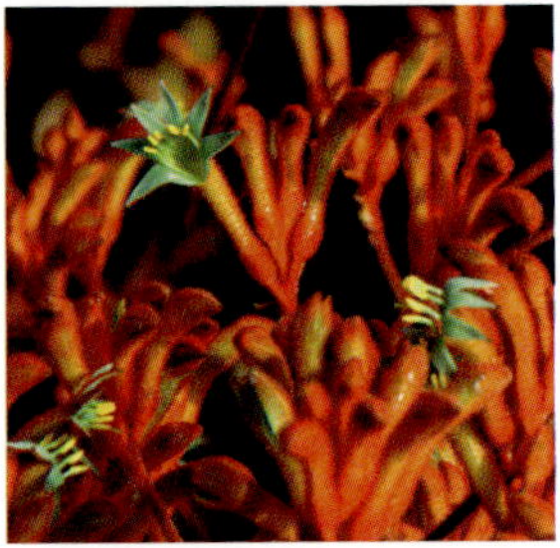
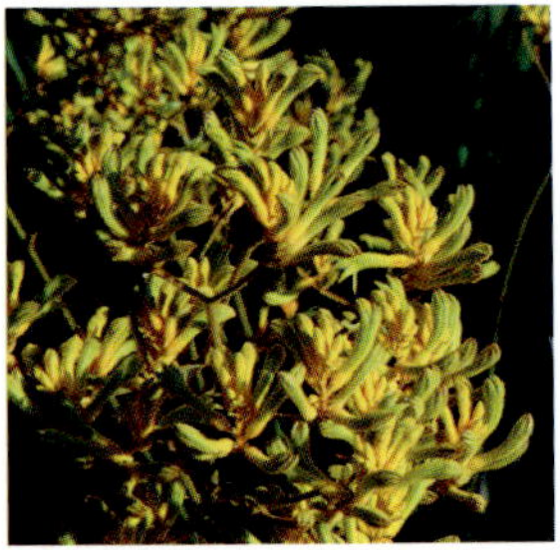

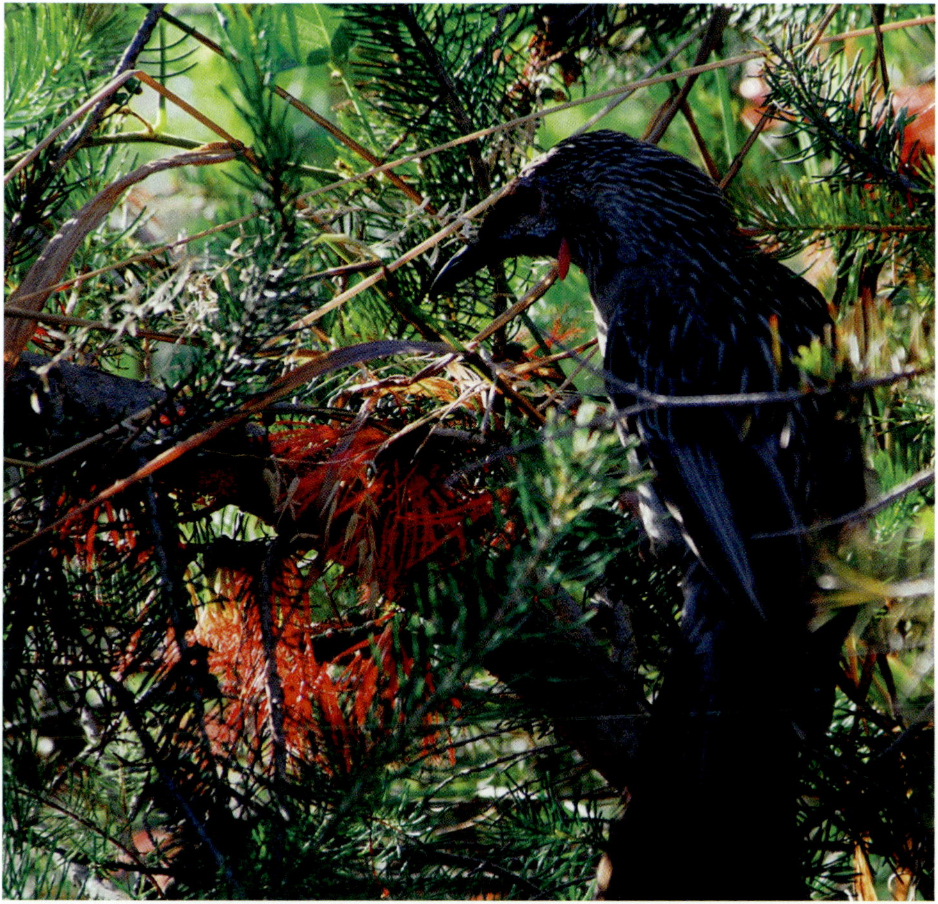

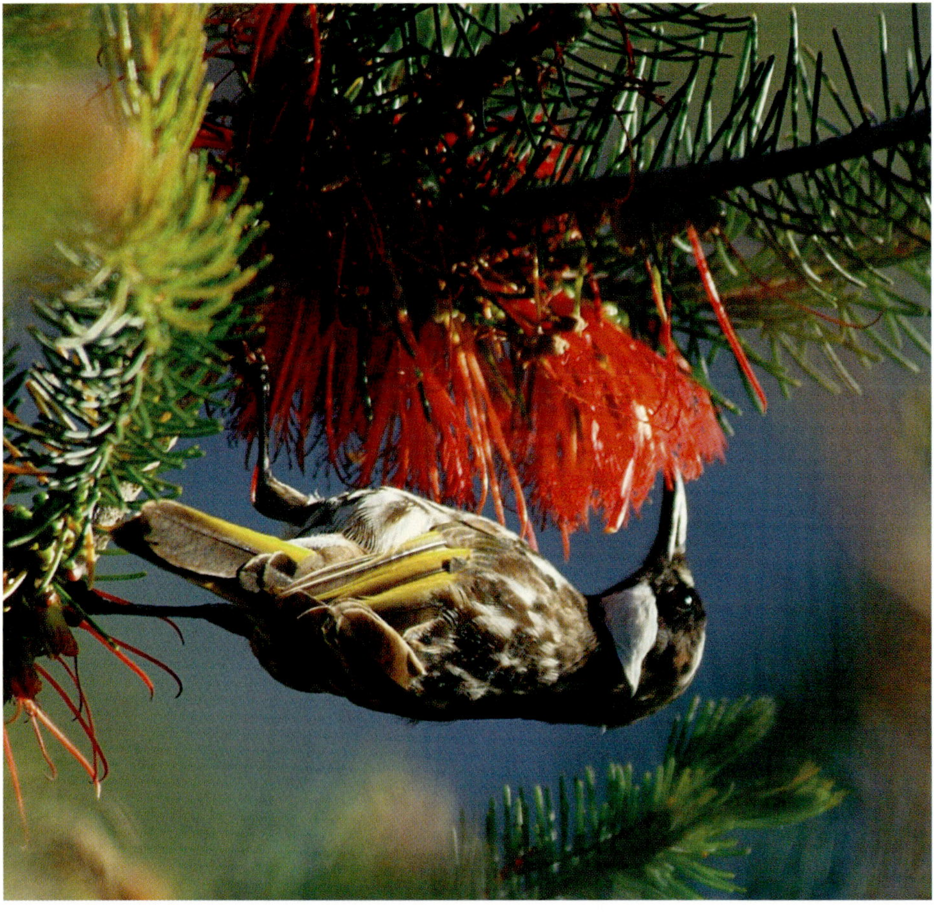

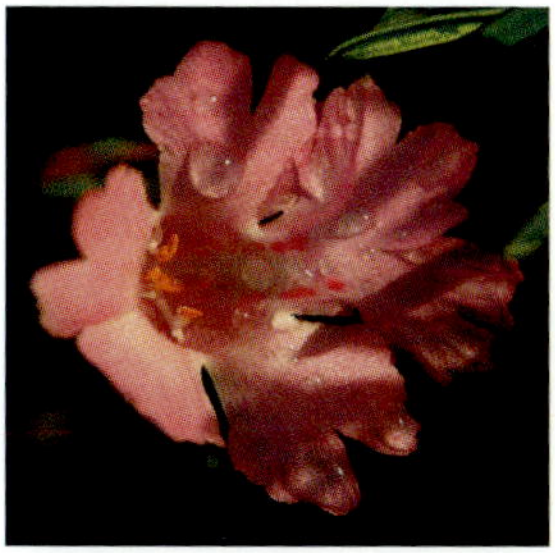
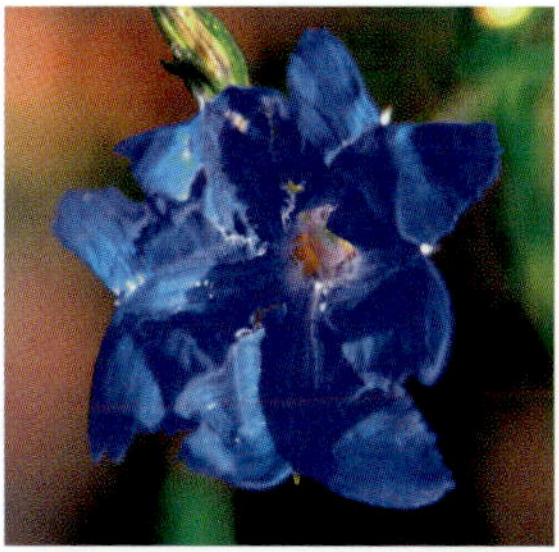
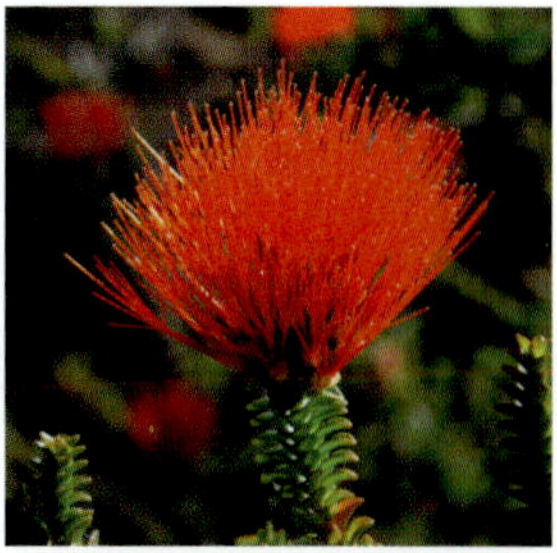
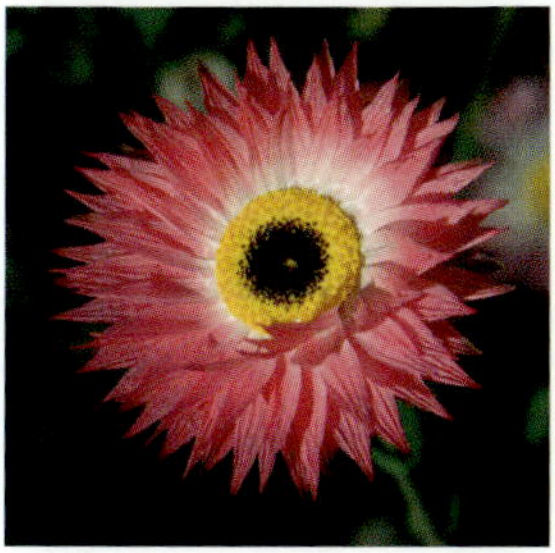
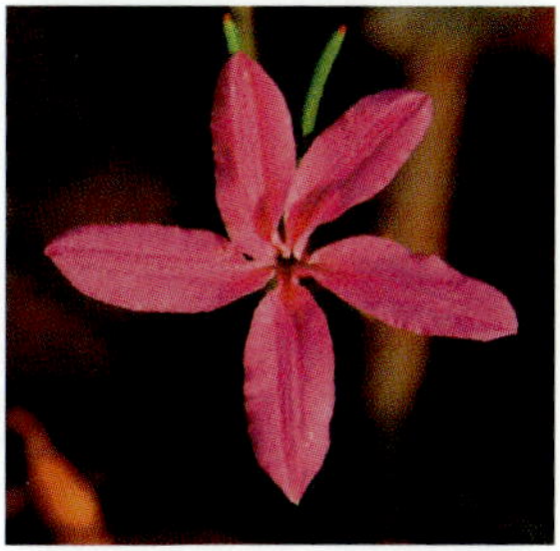
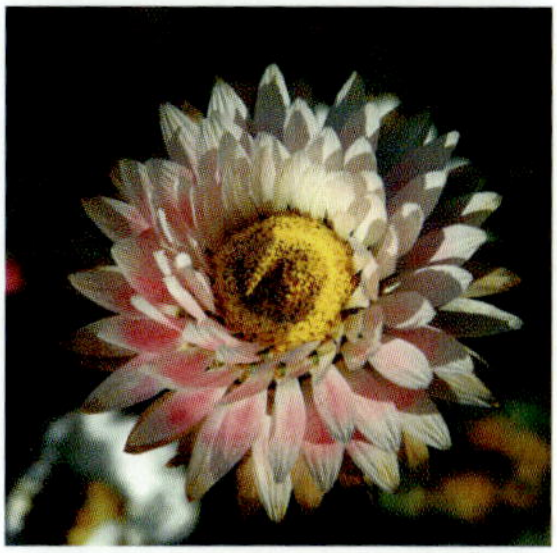
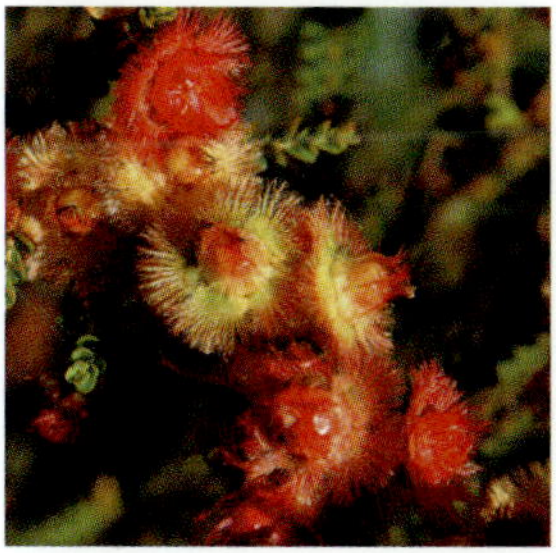
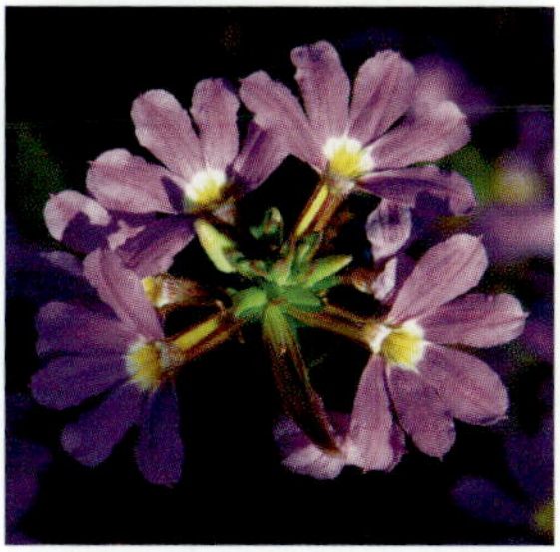
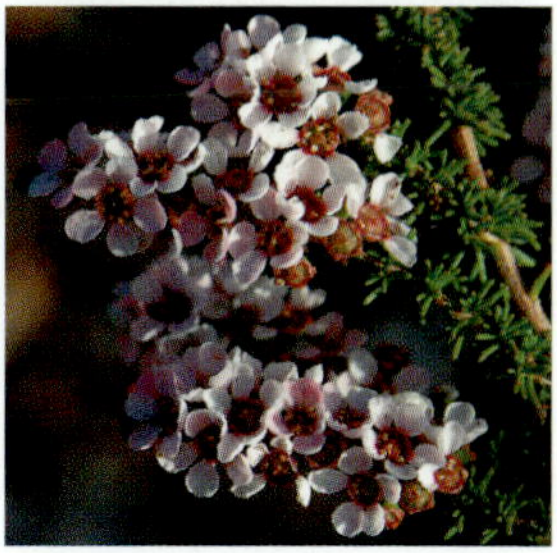

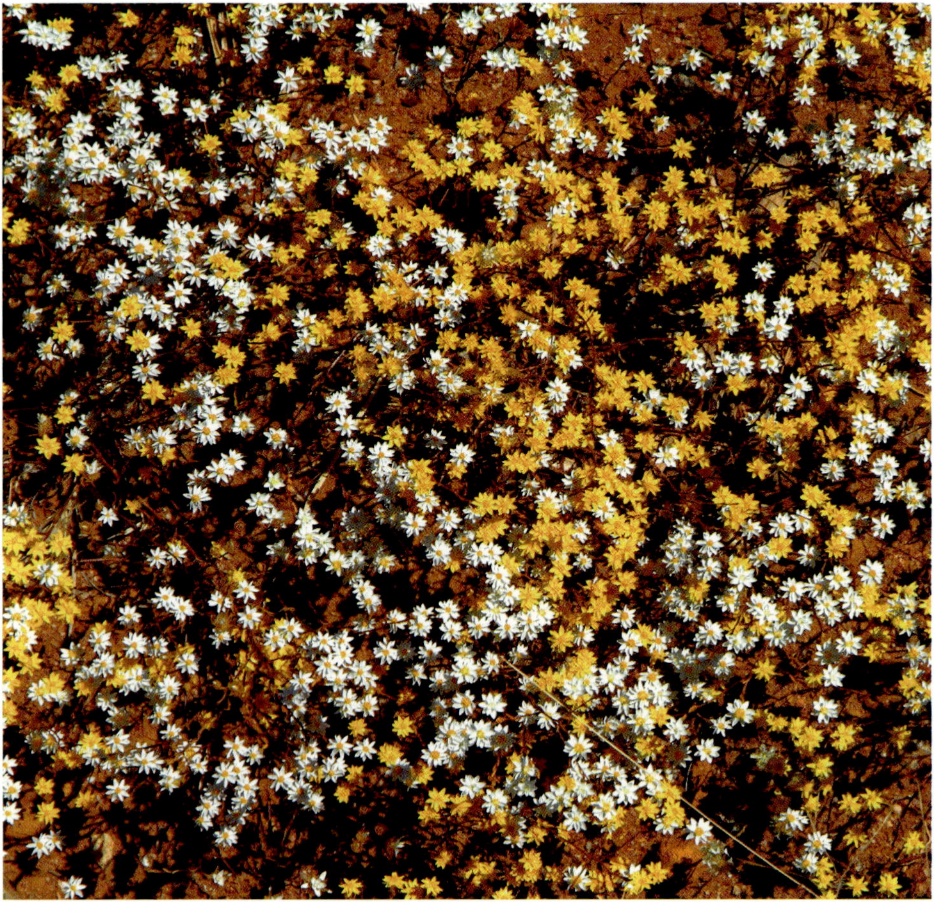

44. desert daisies

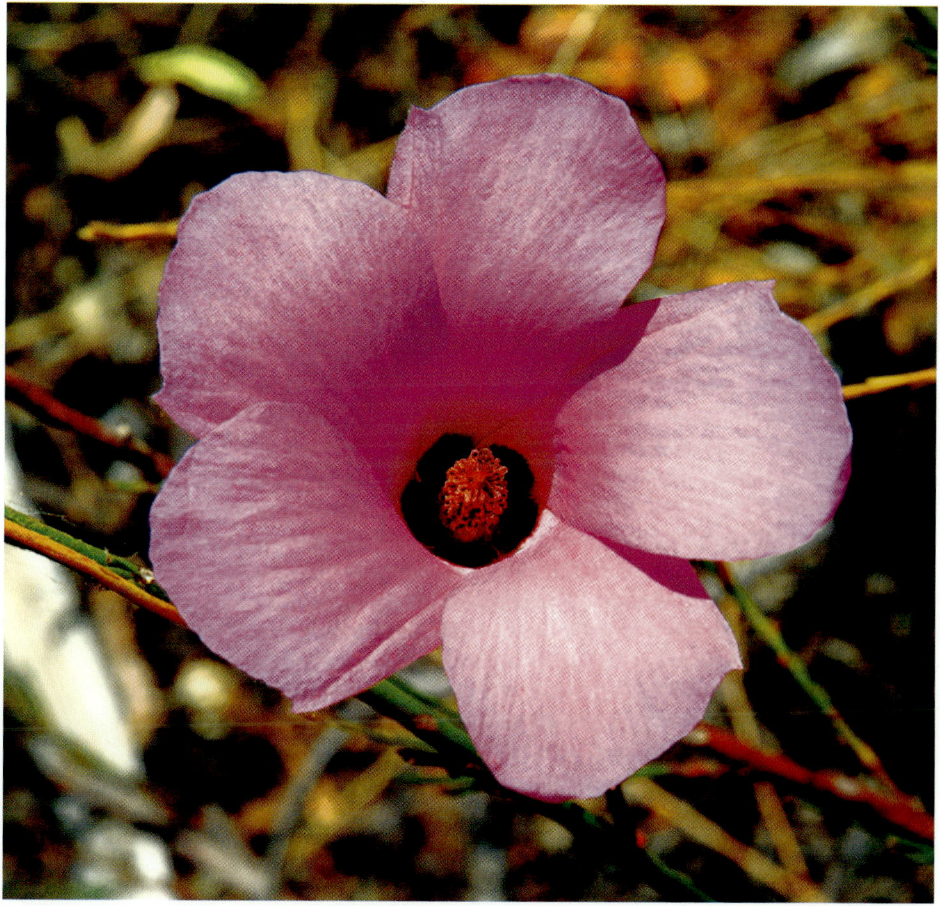

sturt desert rose

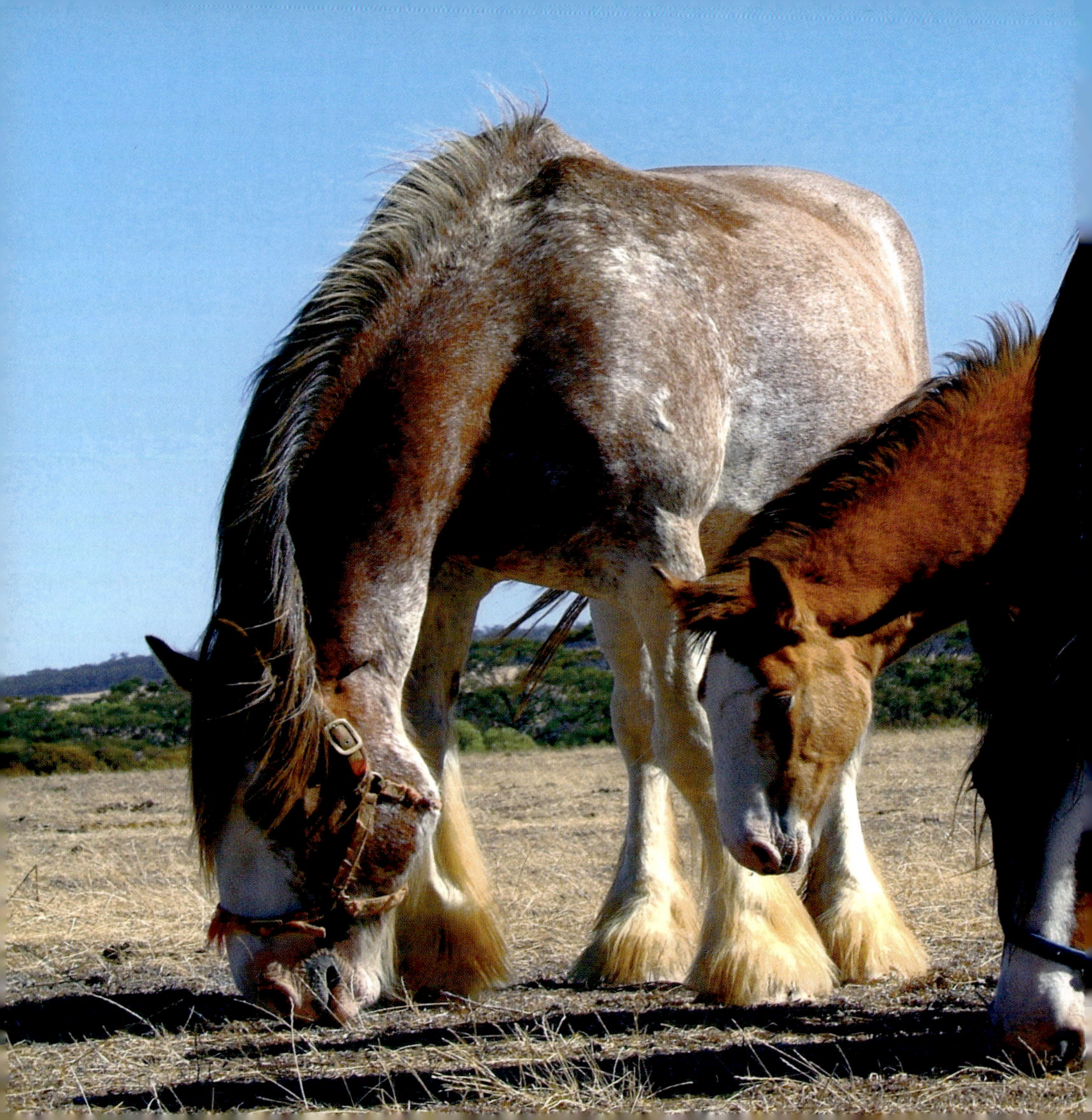

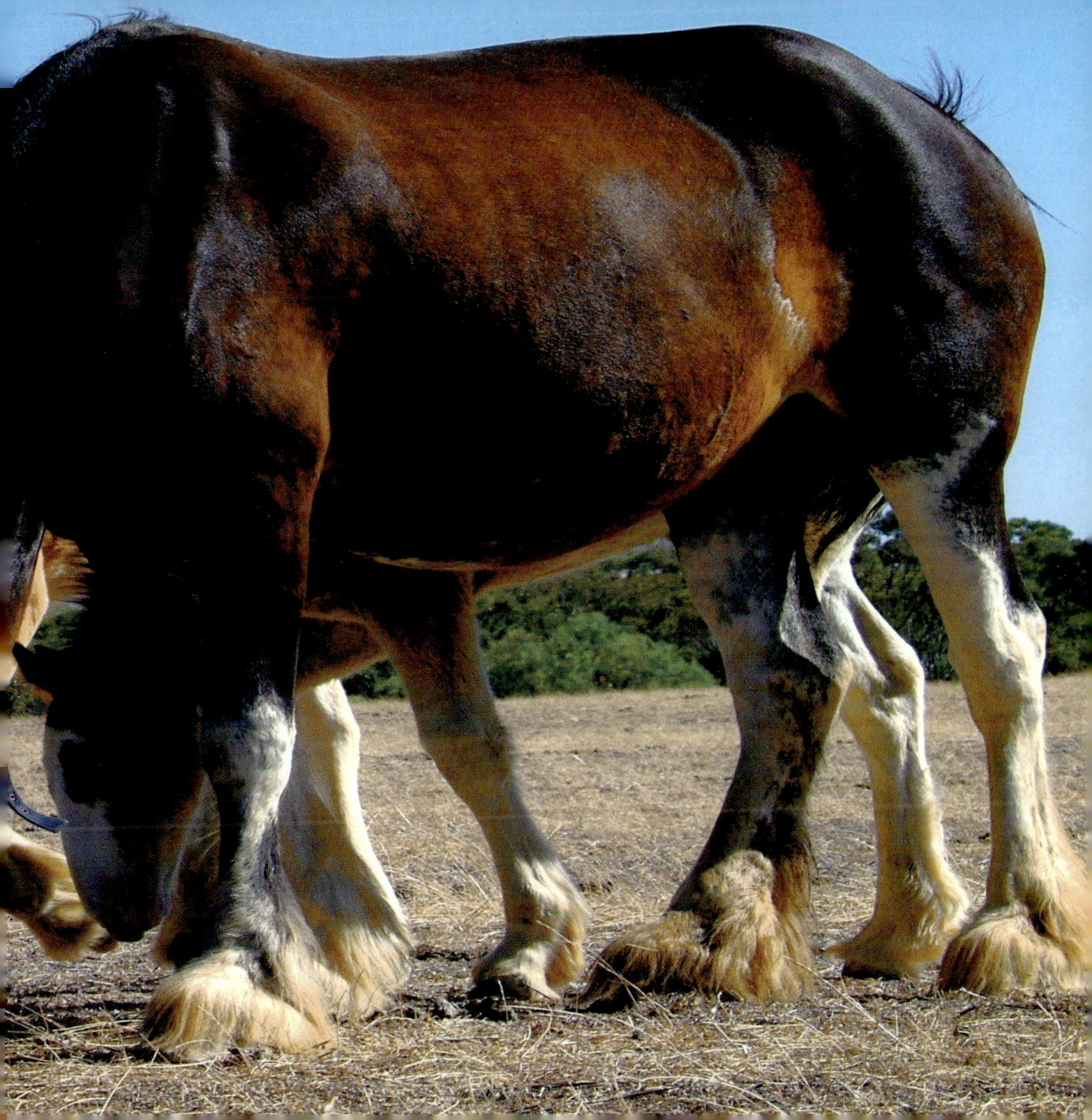

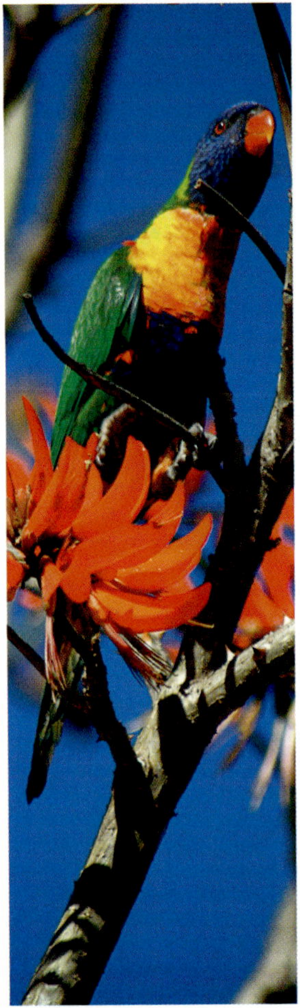

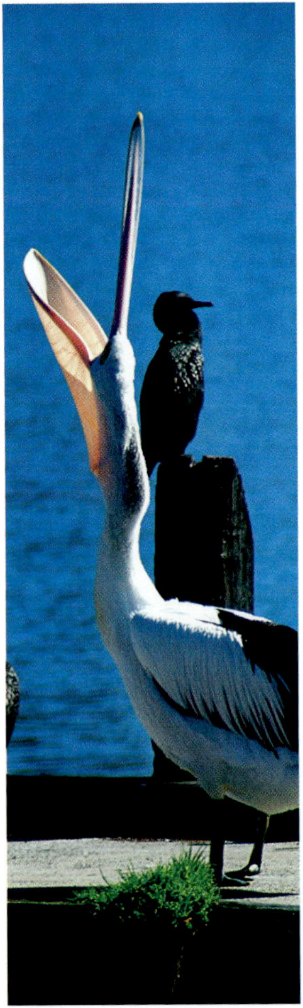

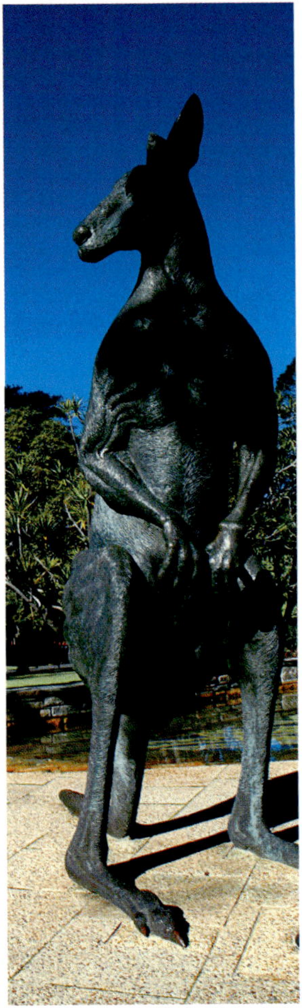

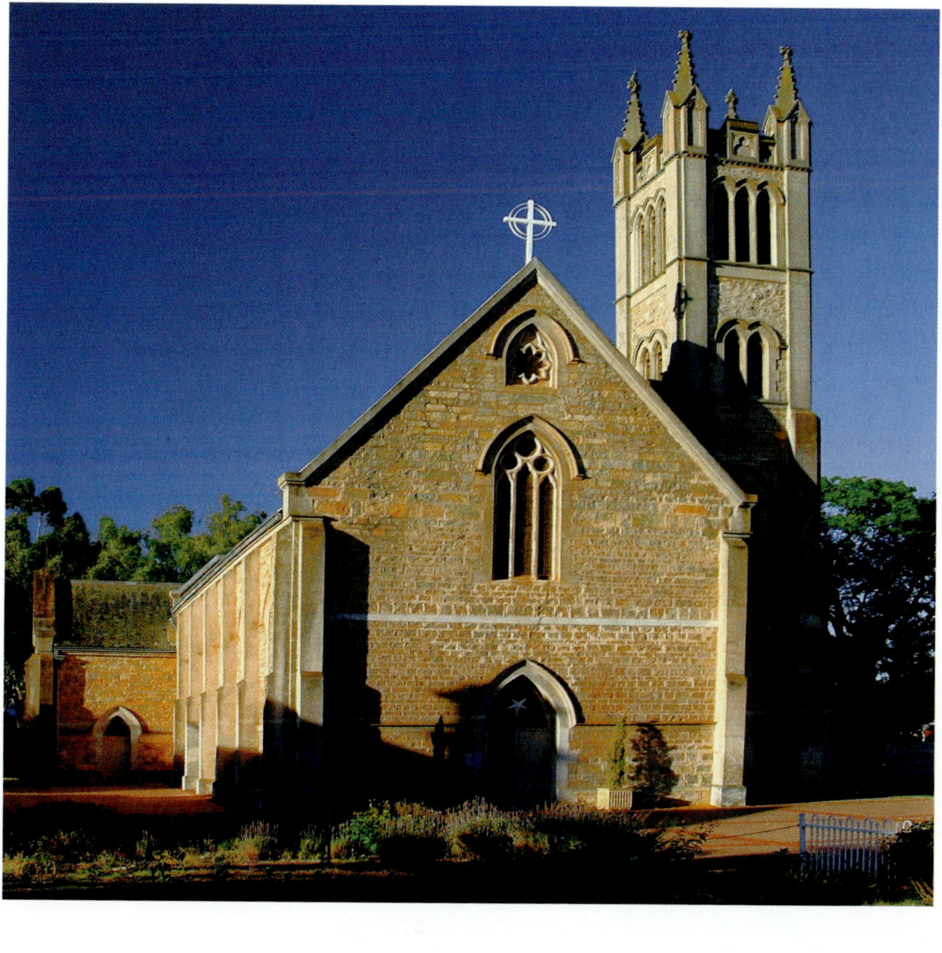

next page. pinnacles, north of perth

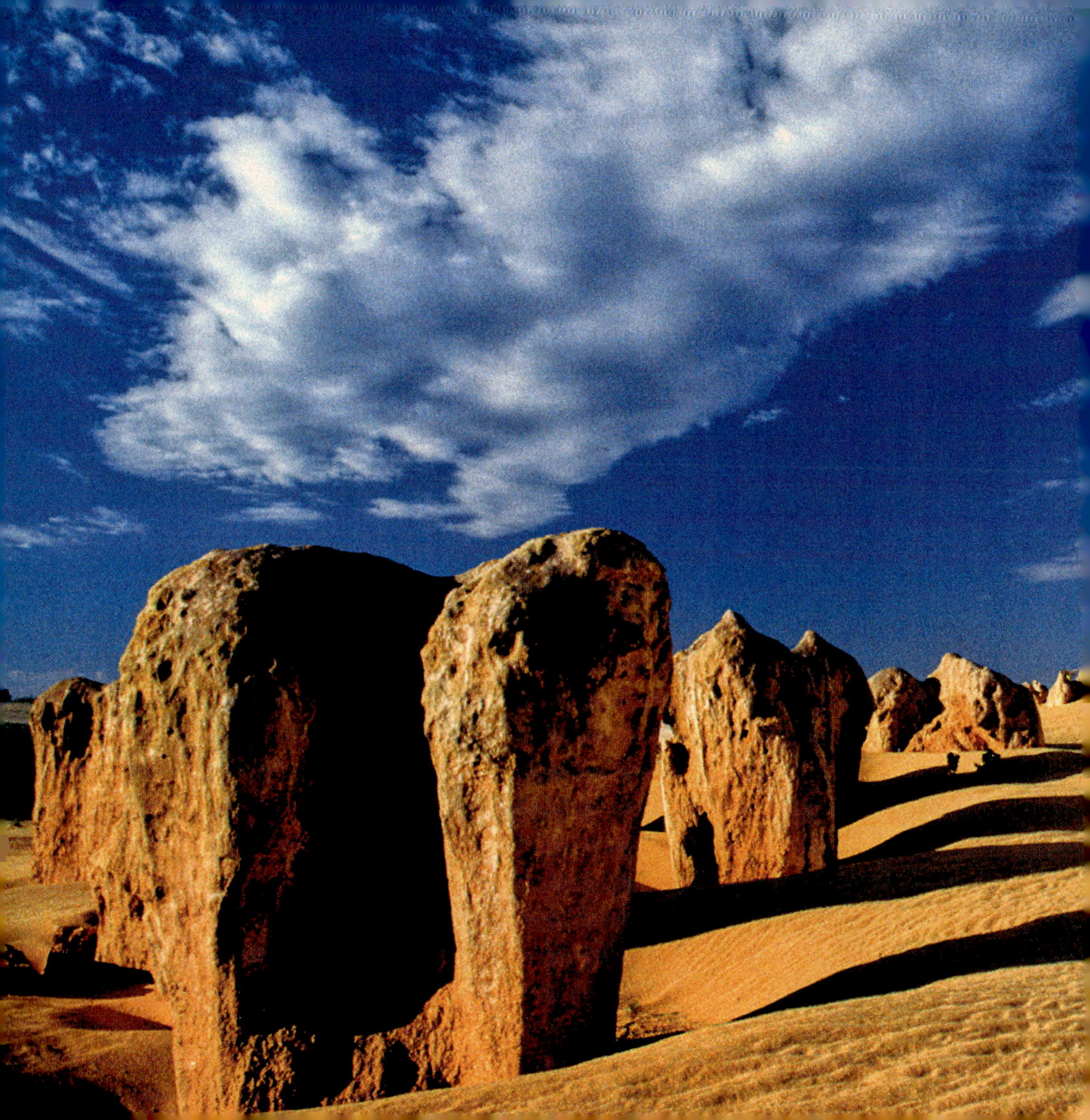

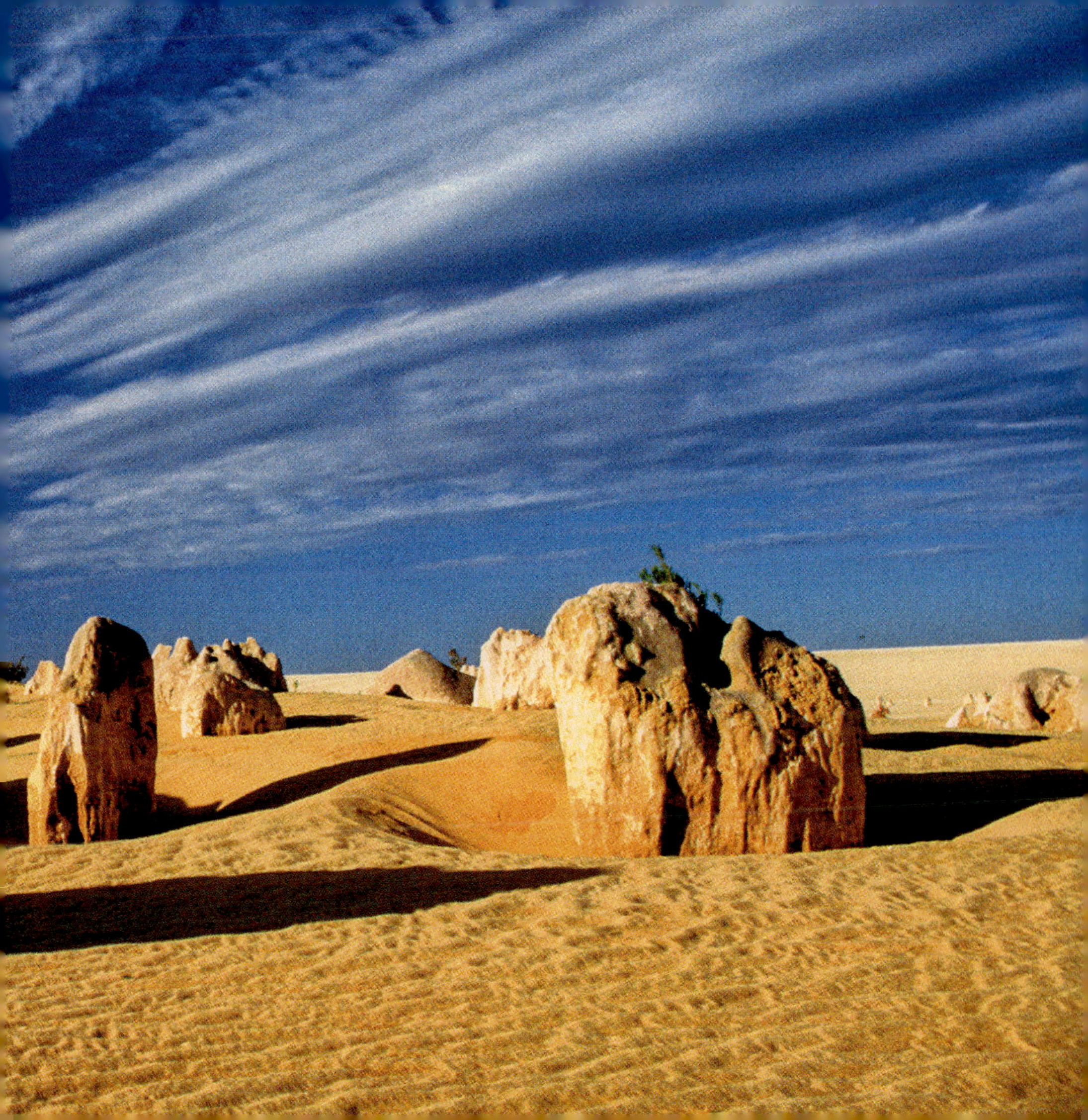

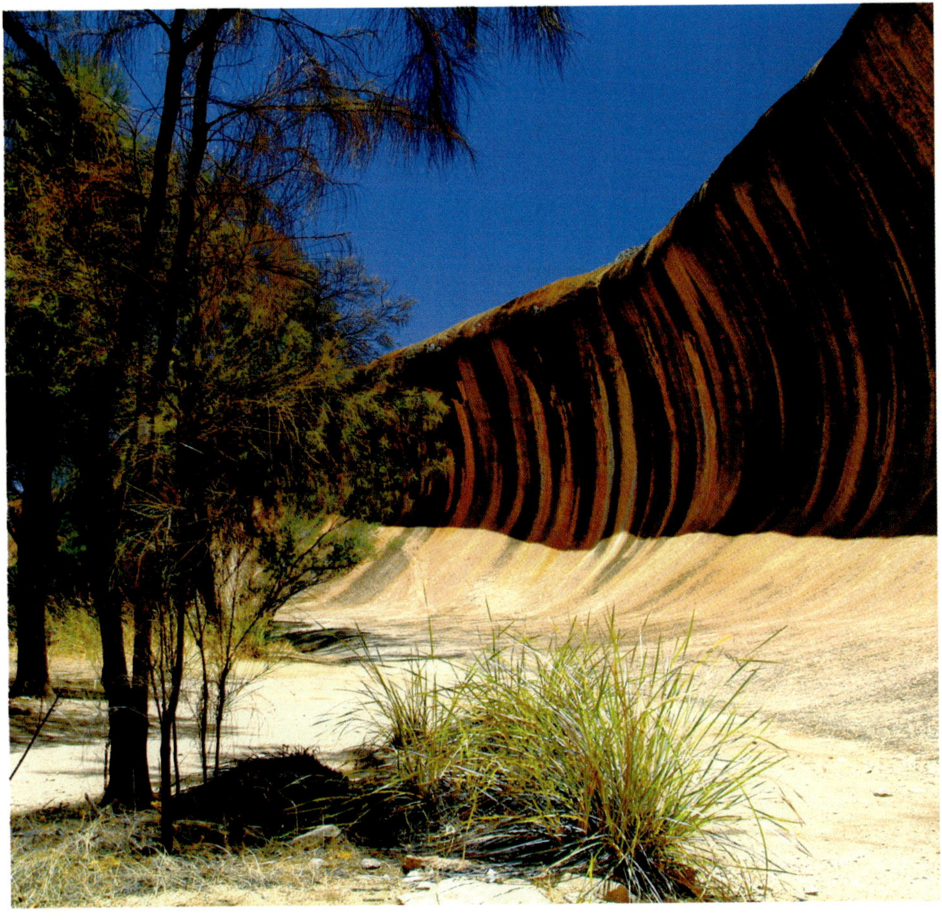

52. wave rock, east of perth

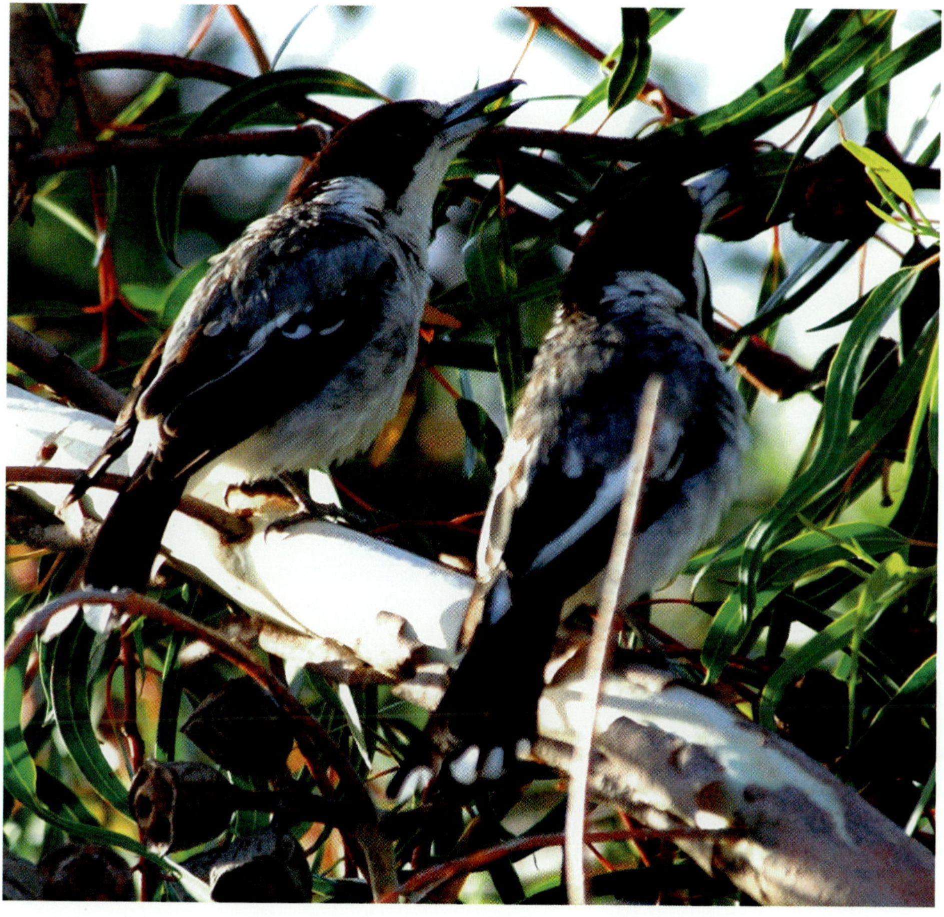

next page. perth railway station

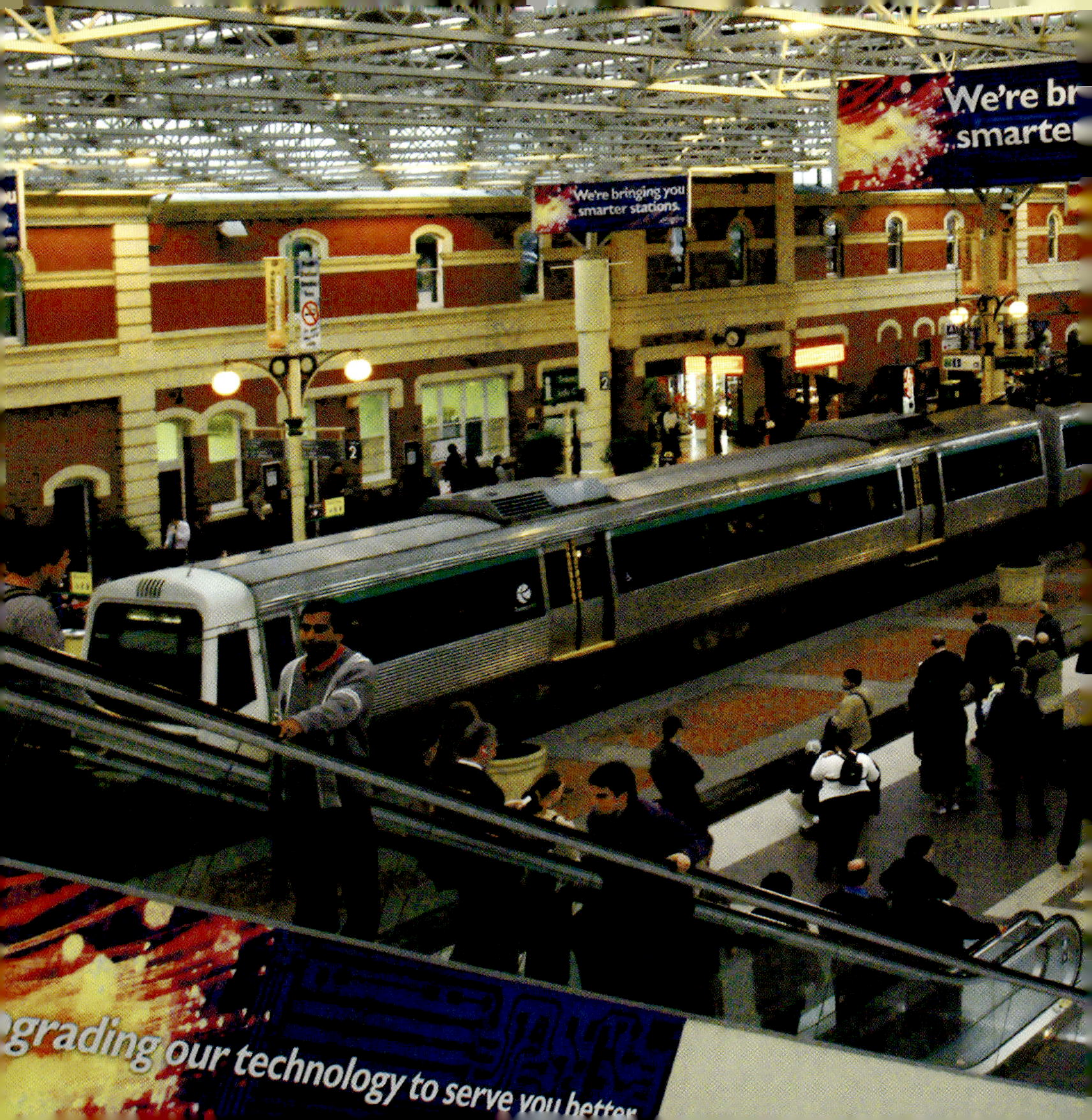
We're br
smarte
We're bringing you
smarter stations.
grading our technology to serve you better

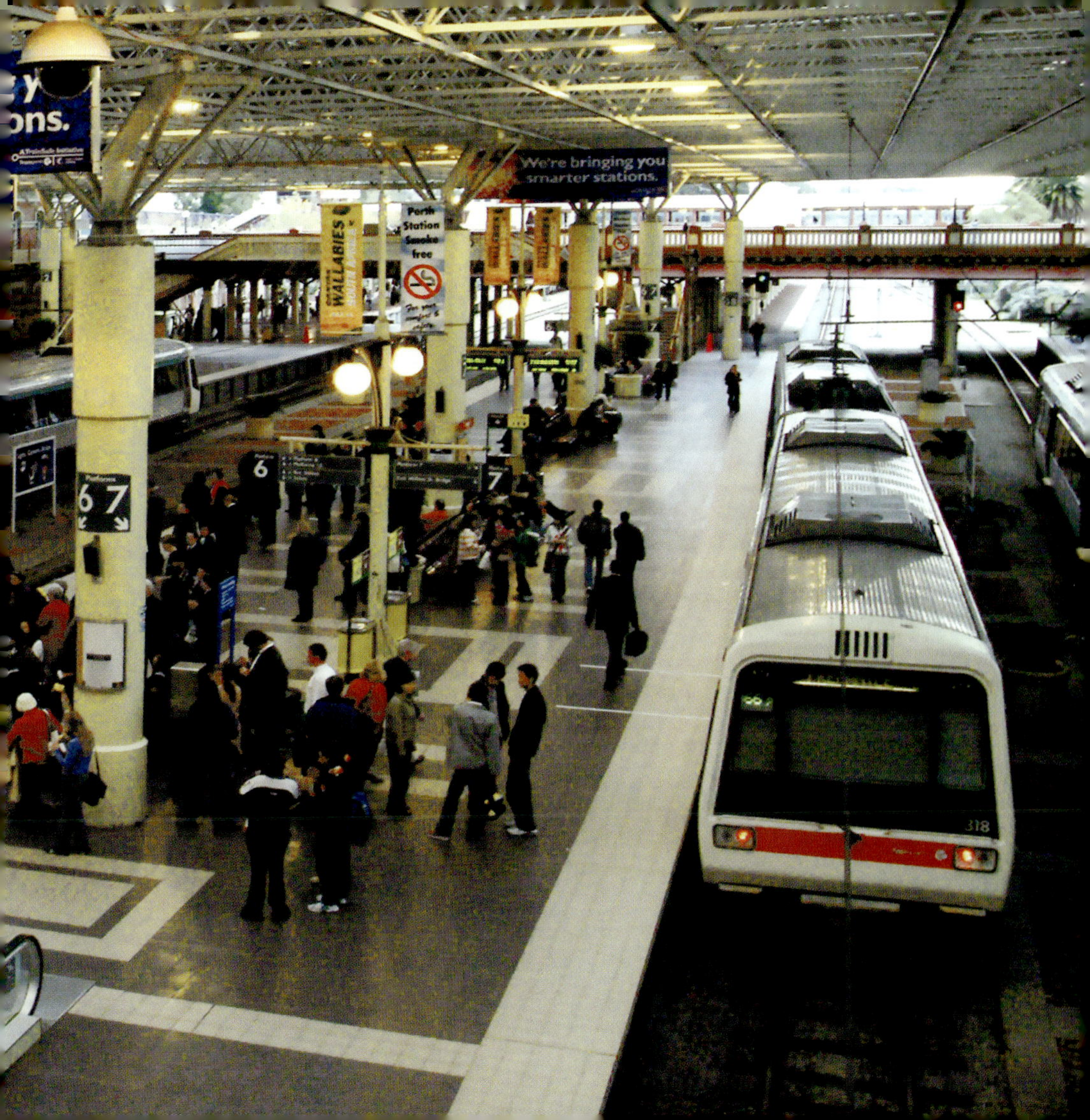
ons.
We're bringing you
smarter stations.
Perth
Station
Smoke
free
WALLABIES
6 7
6
7
318

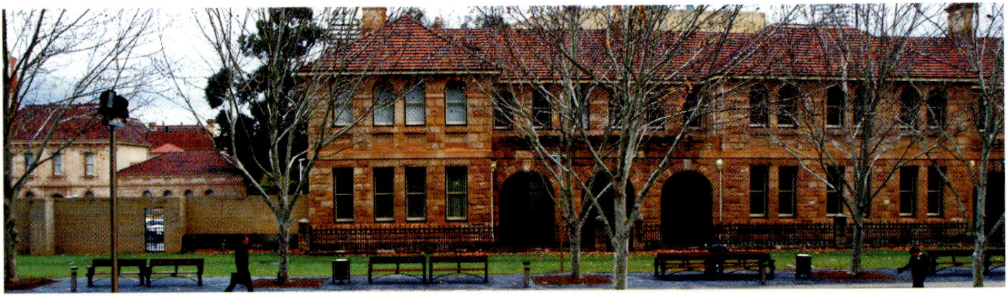

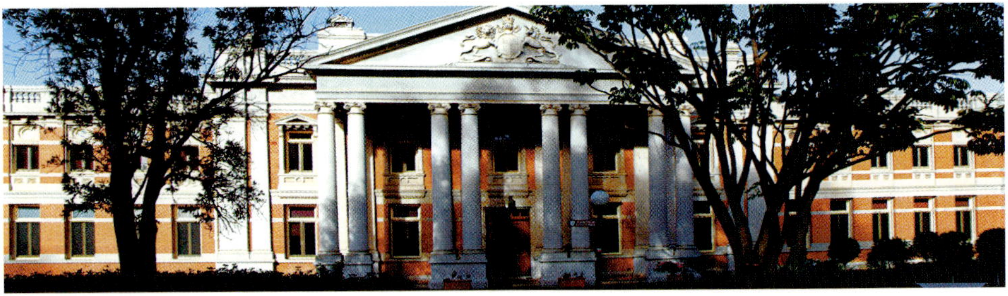

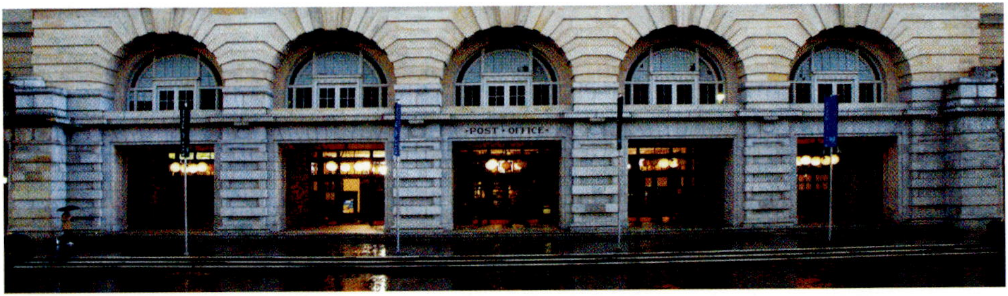
POST • OFFICE

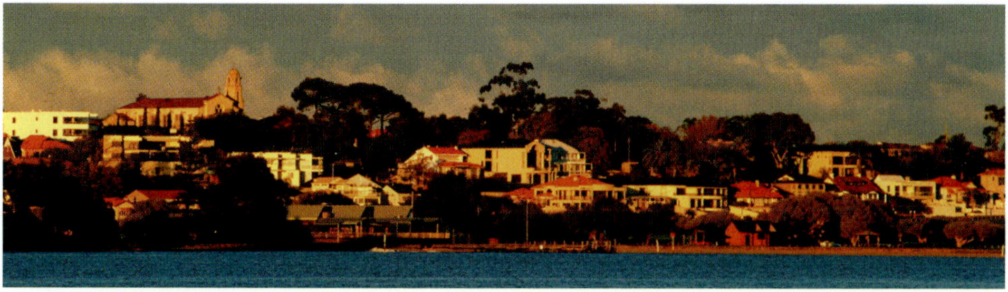

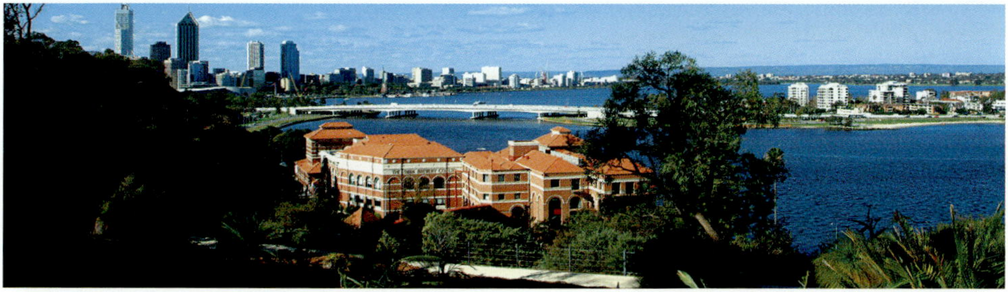

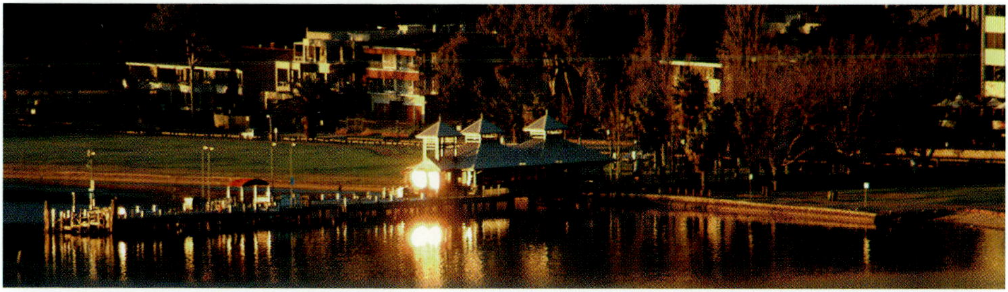

next page. james street mall

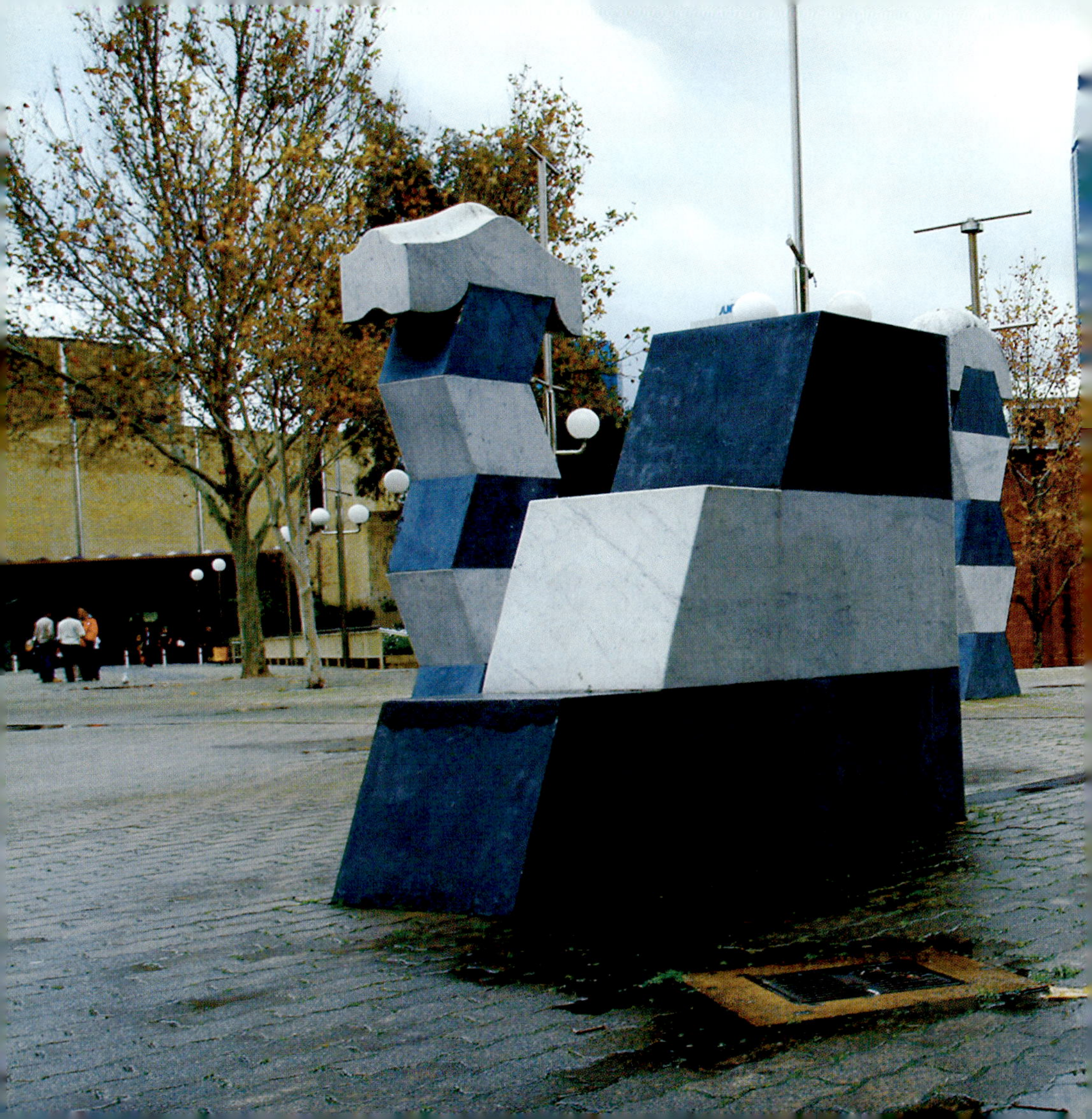

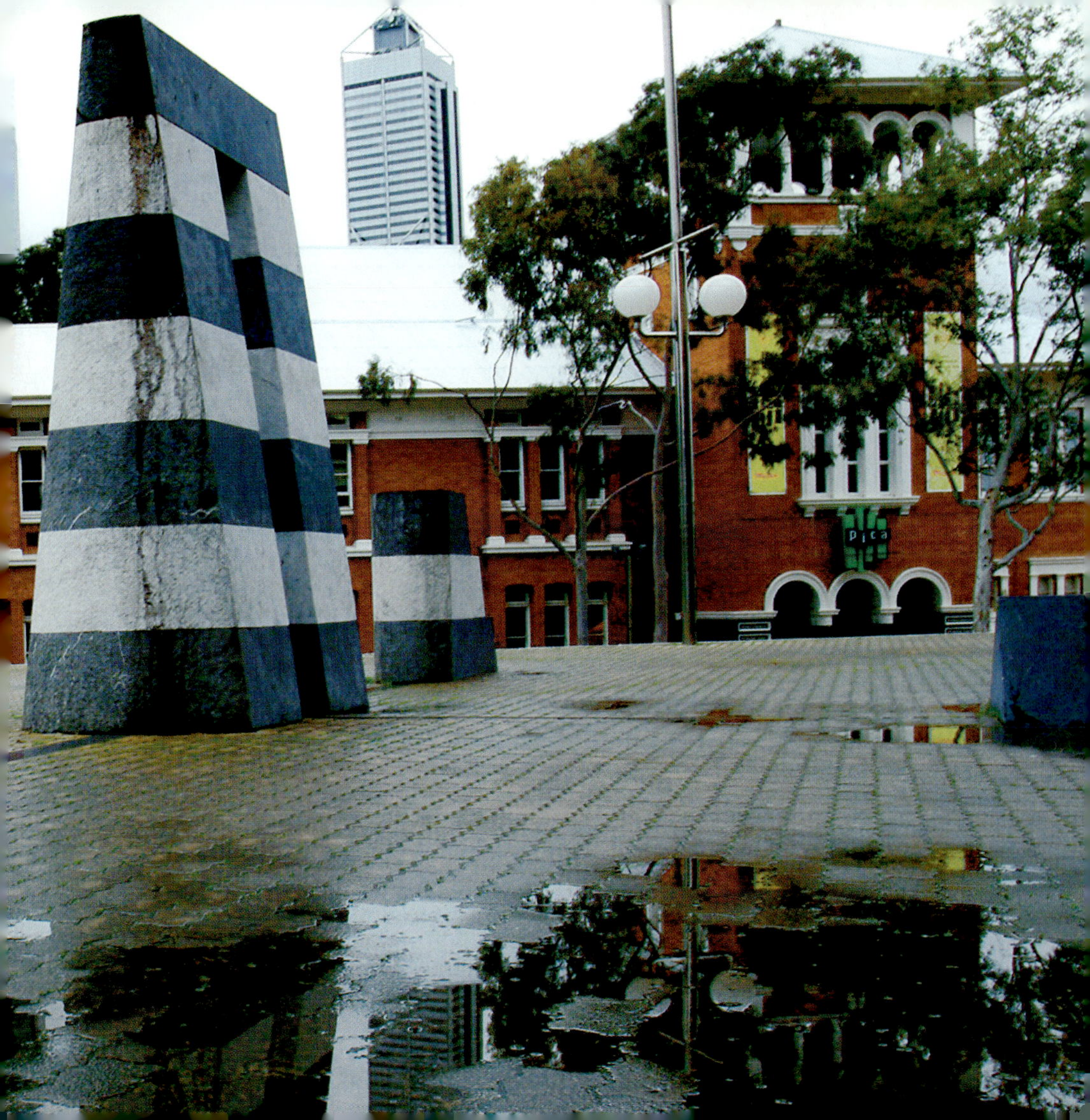
pica

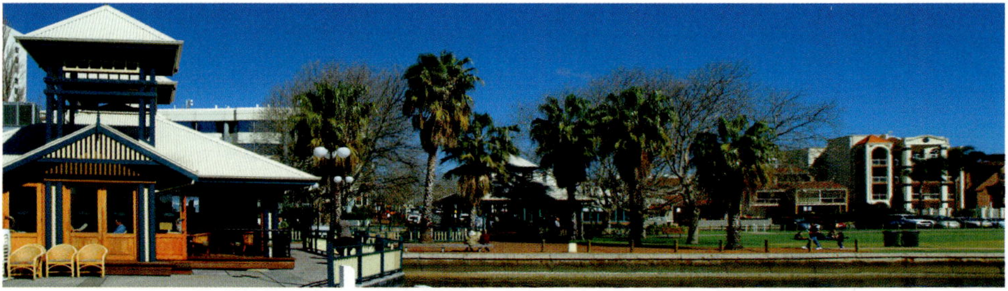

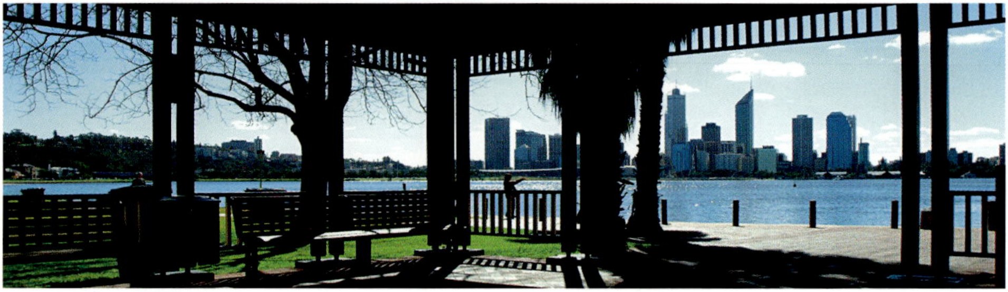

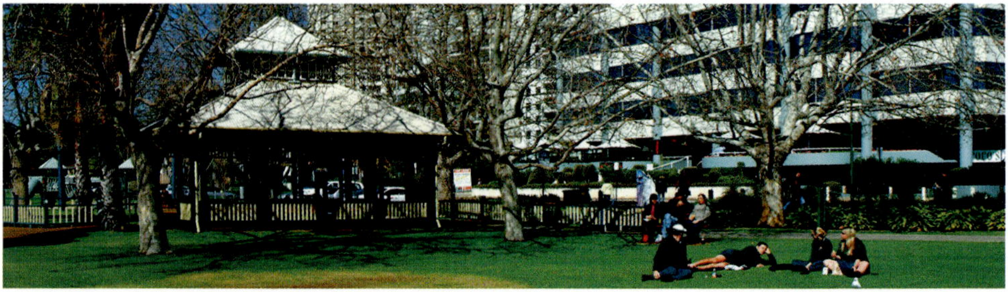

60. mends street jetty, south perth

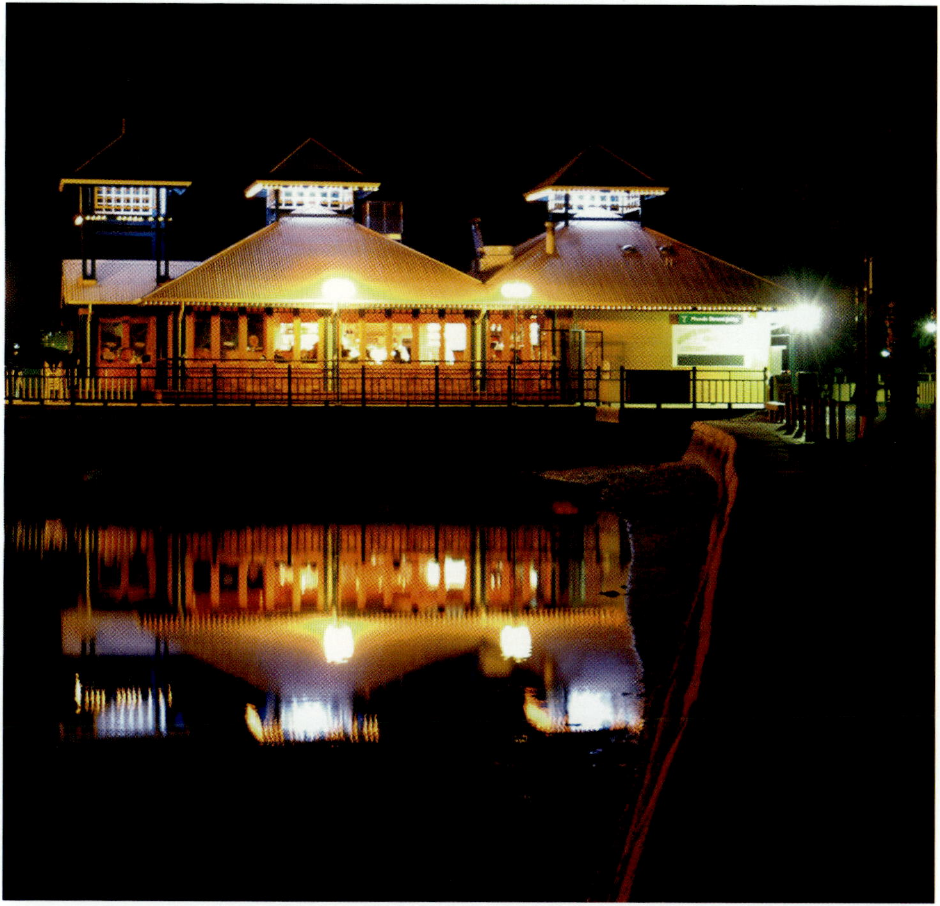

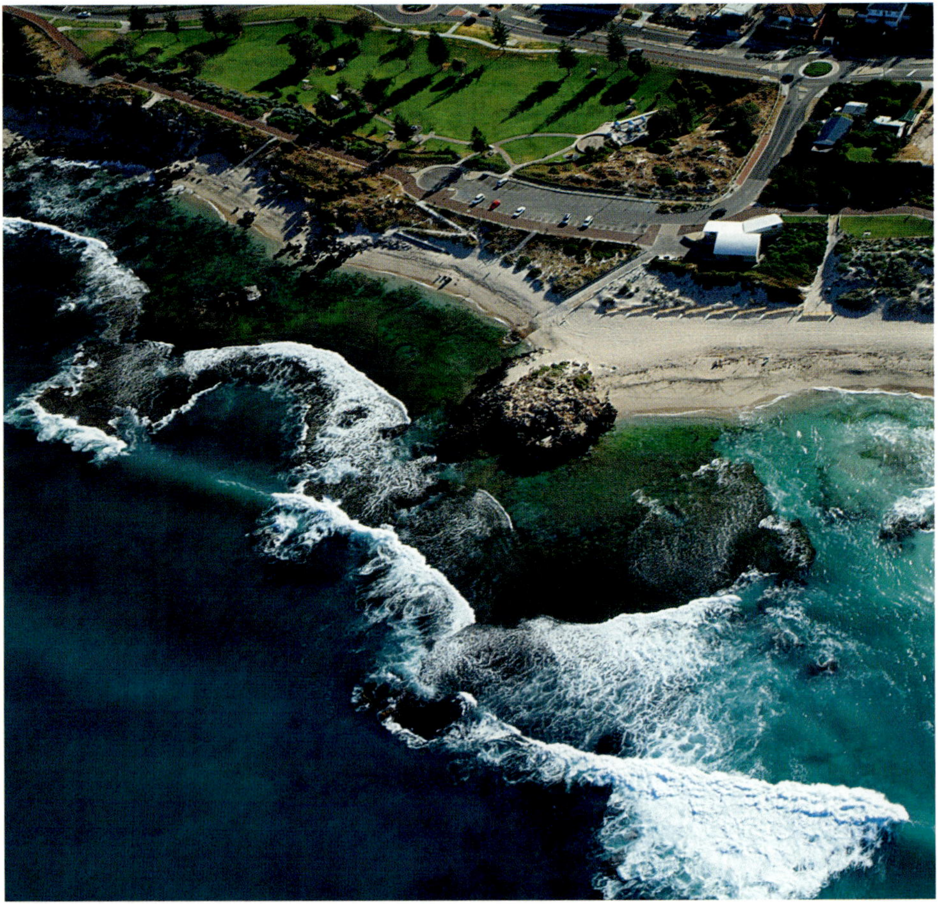

62. trigg island

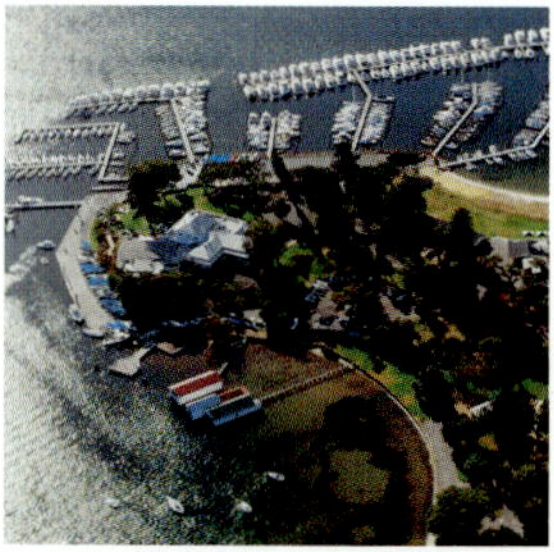
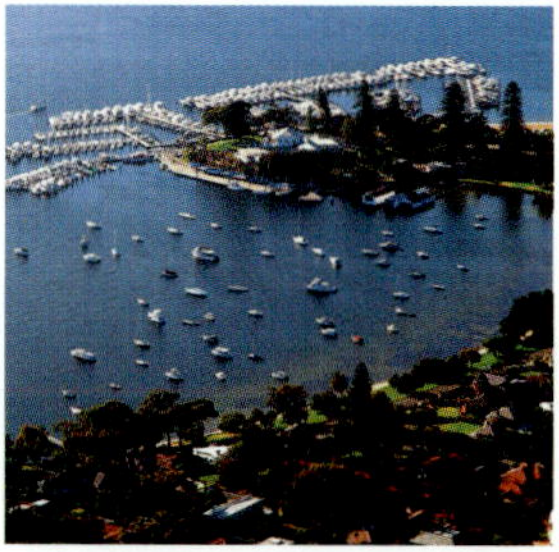
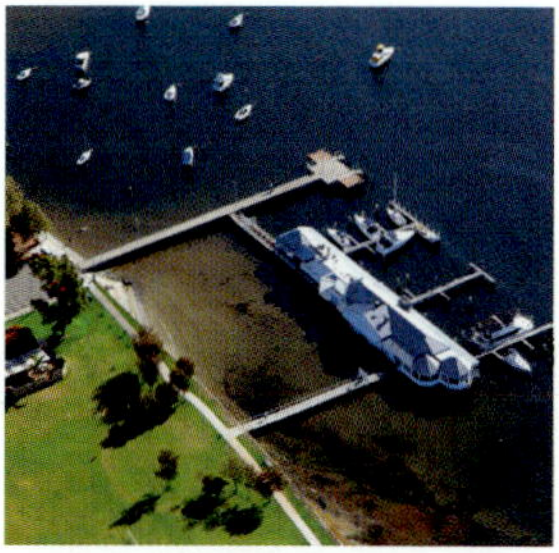

next page. hillarys boat harbour

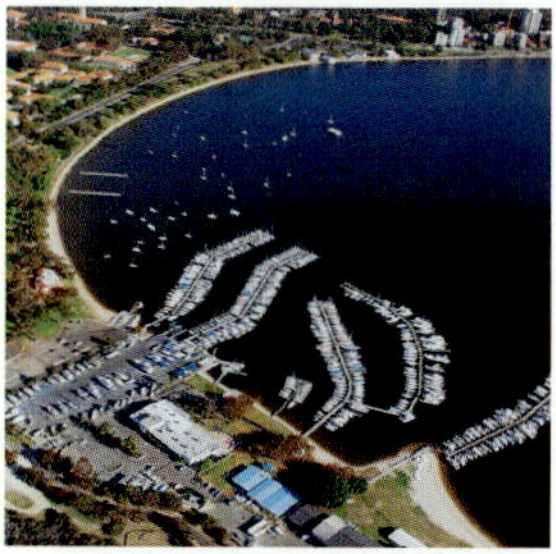
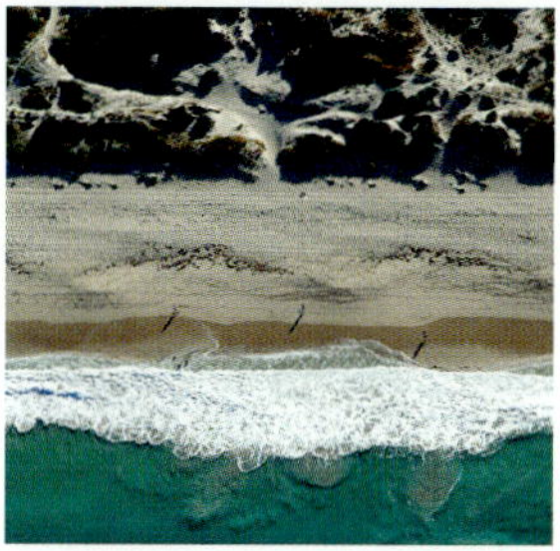
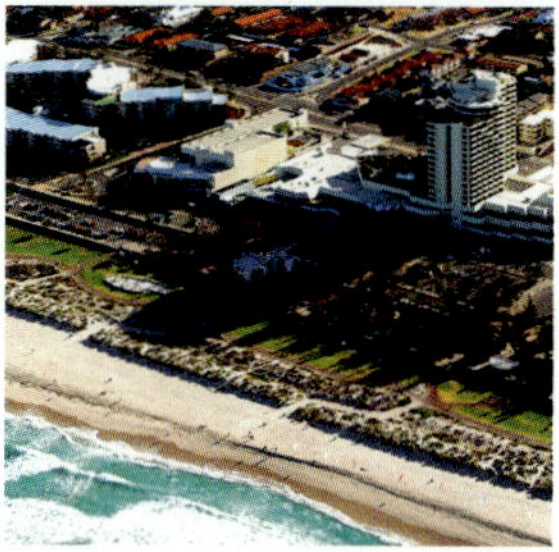
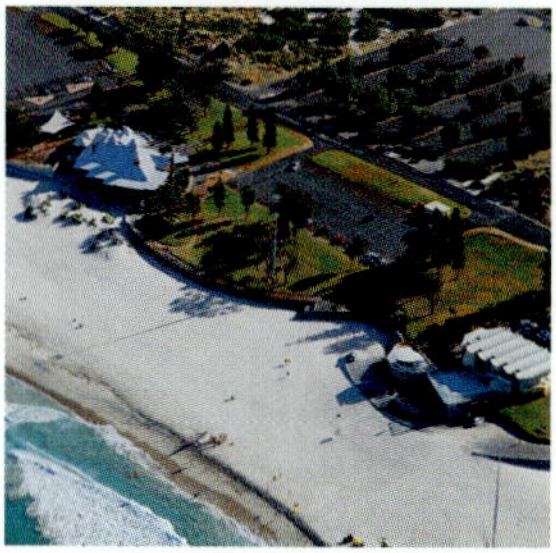
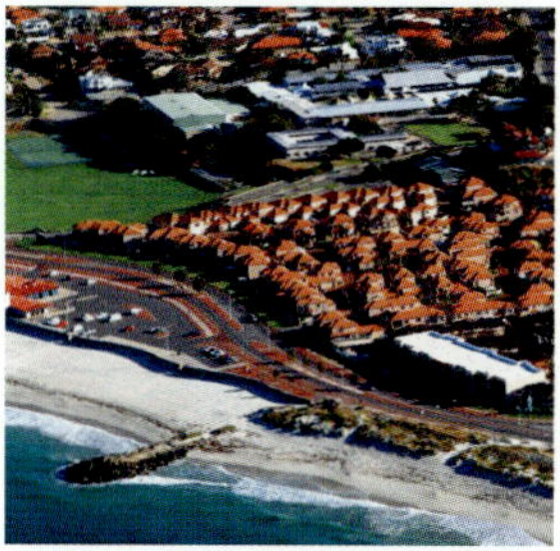
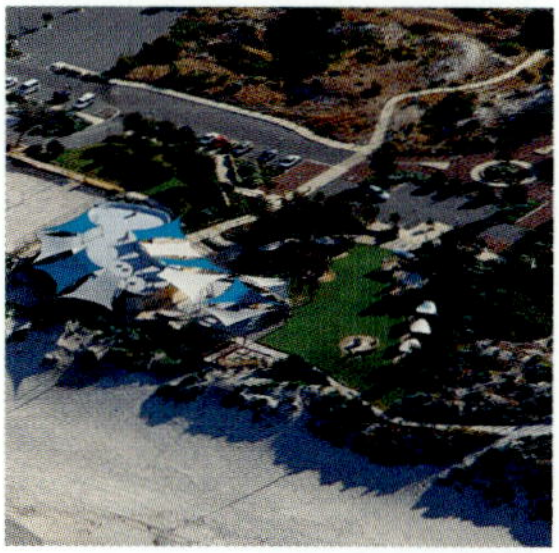

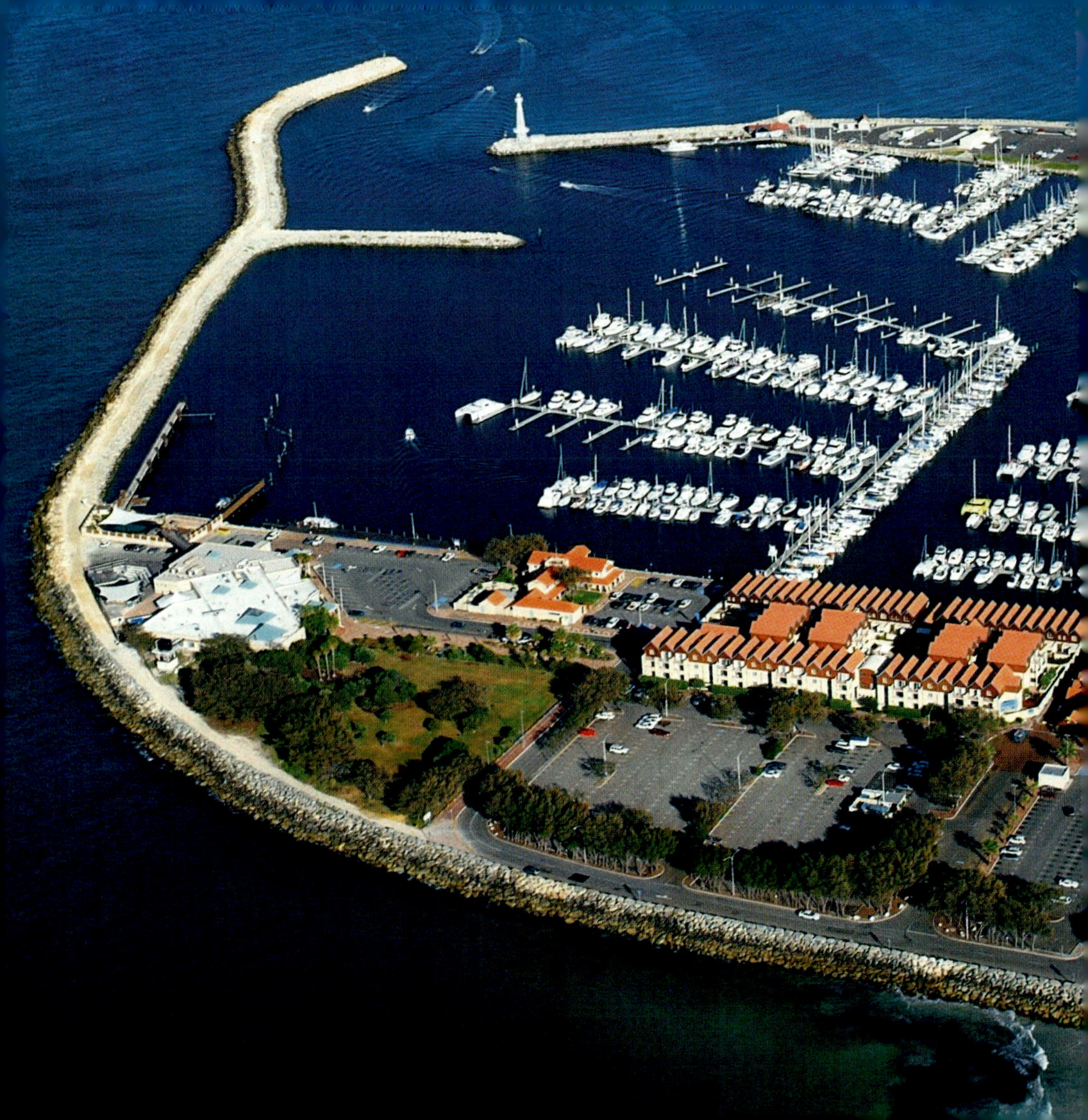

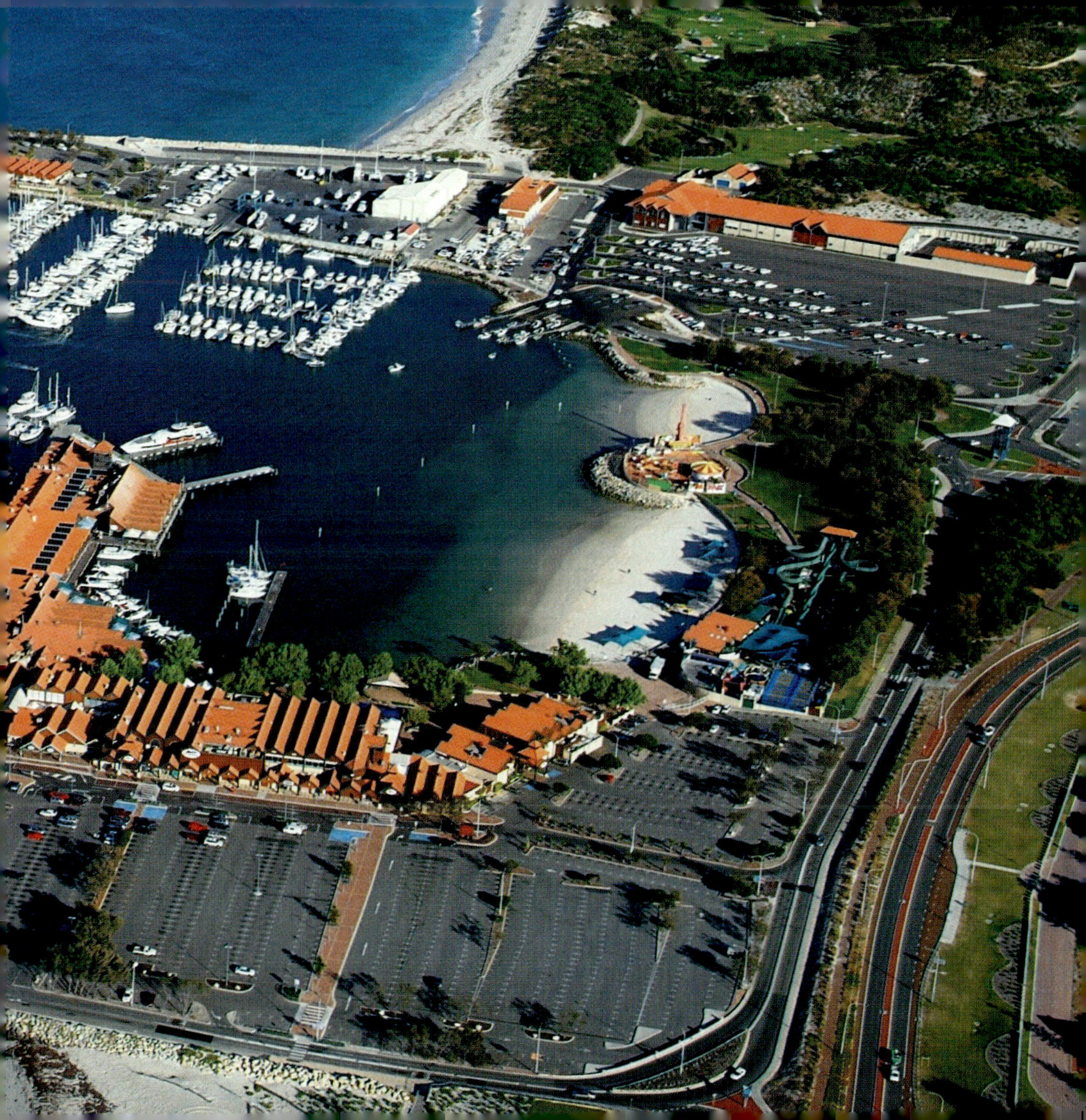

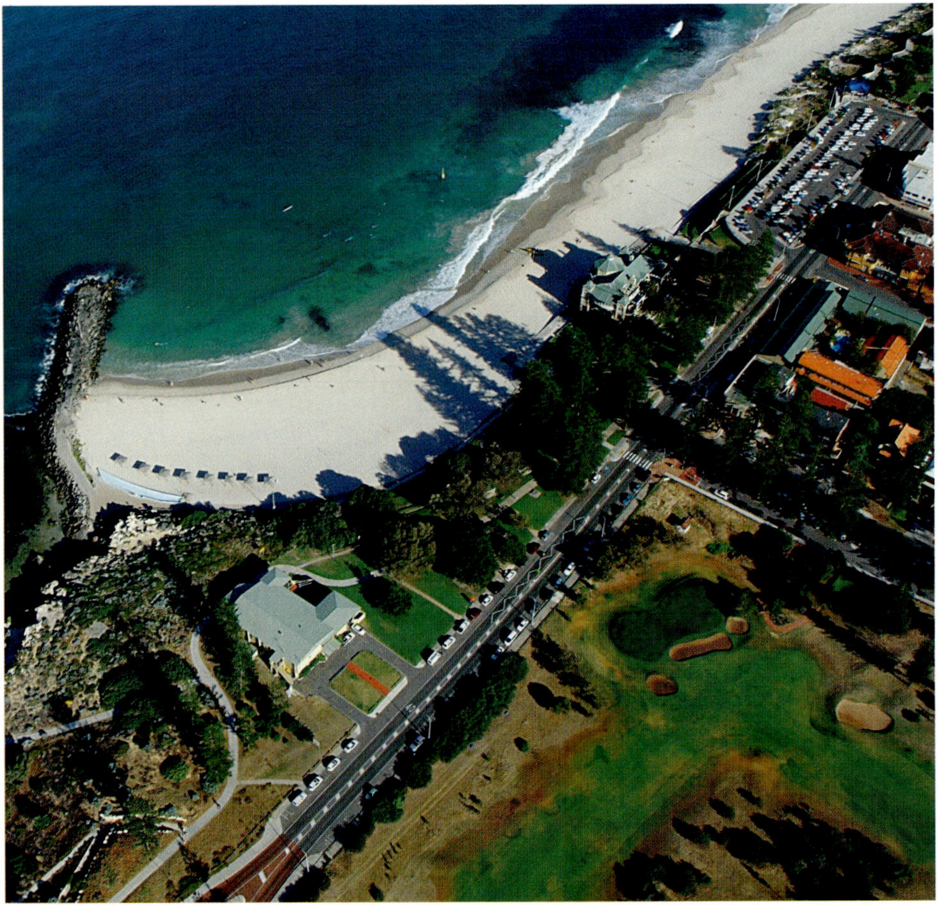

66. cottesloe beach

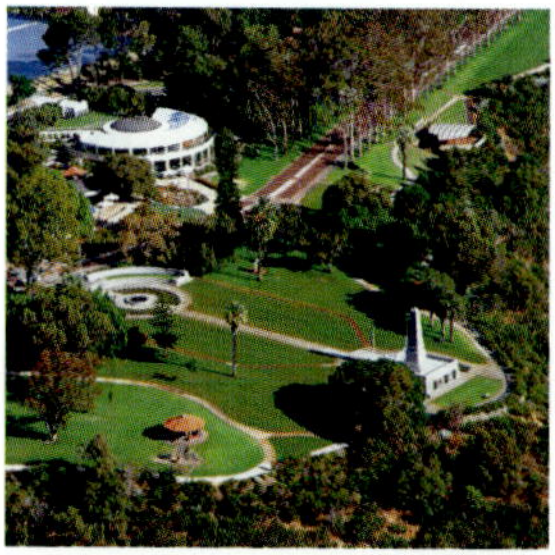
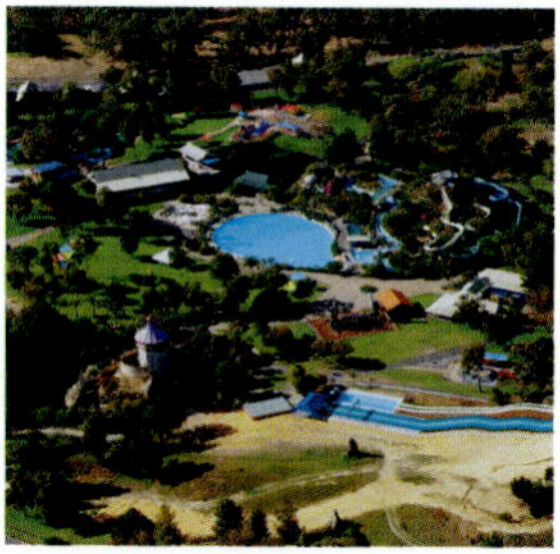
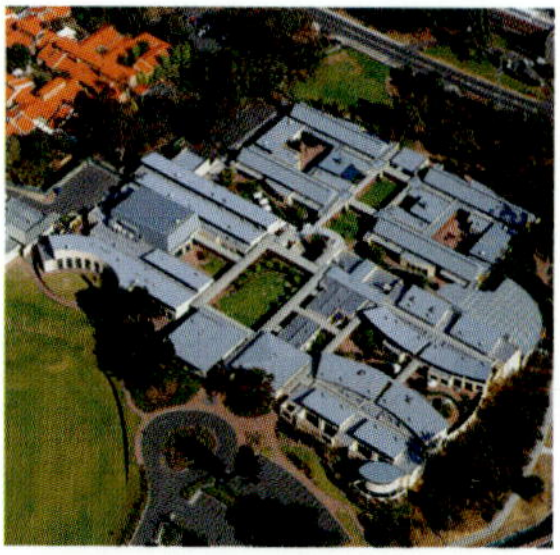
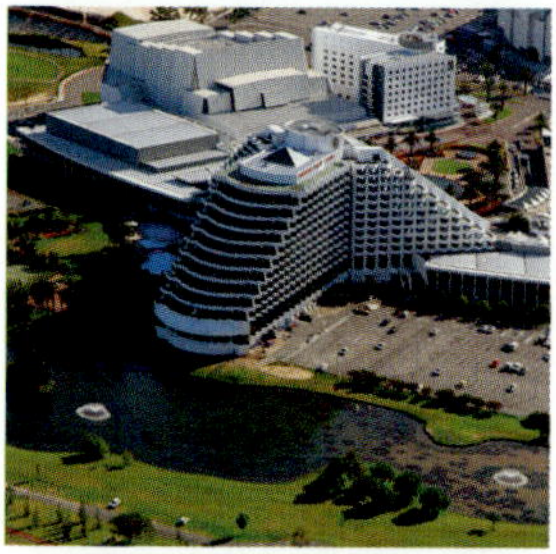
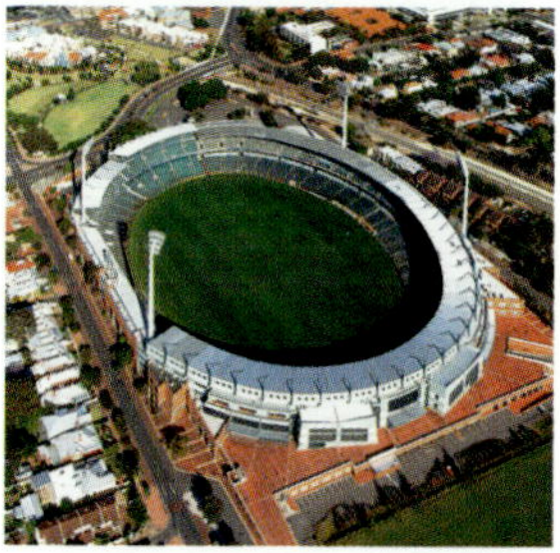
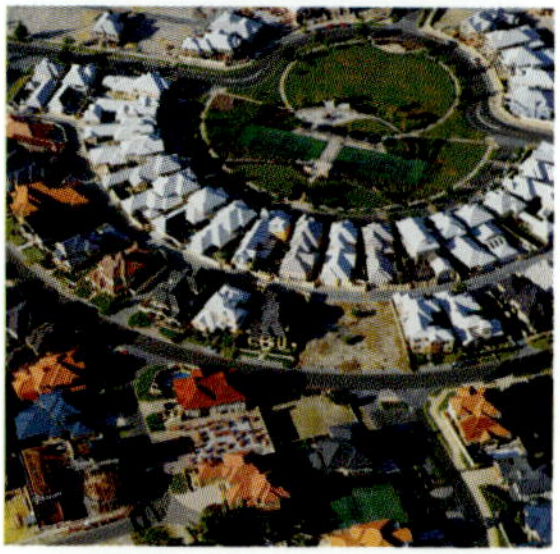
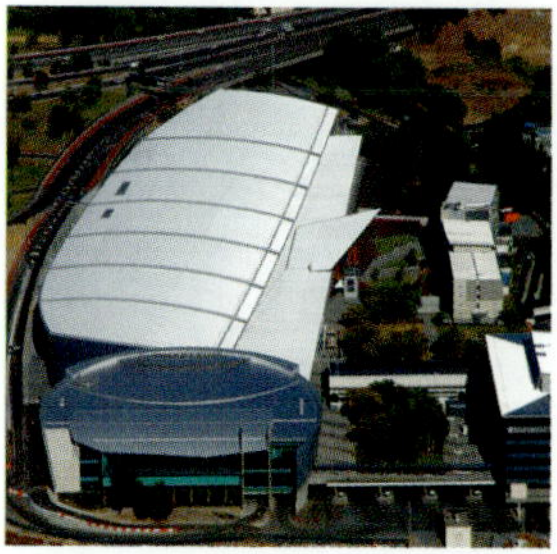
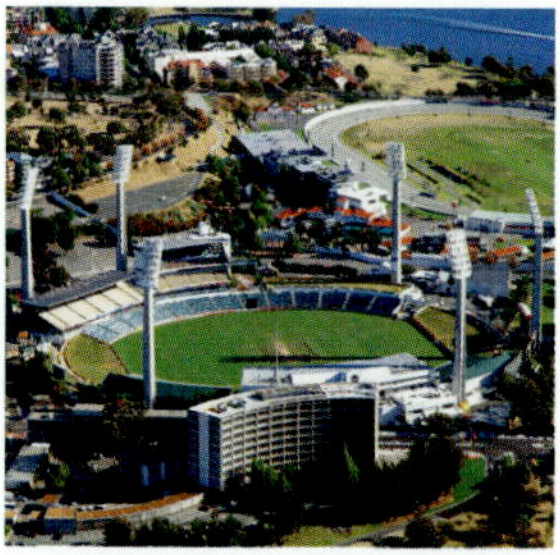
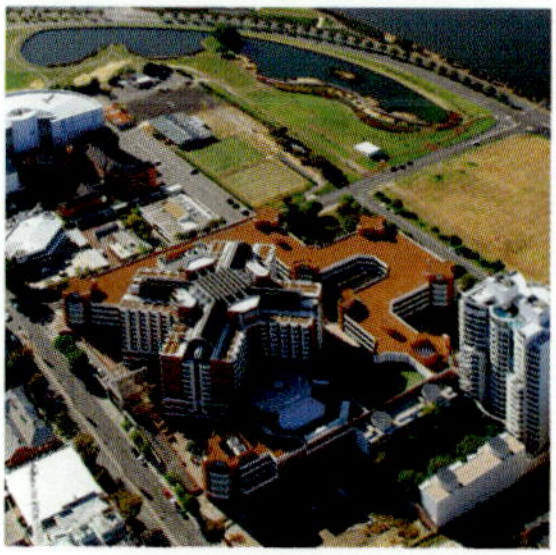

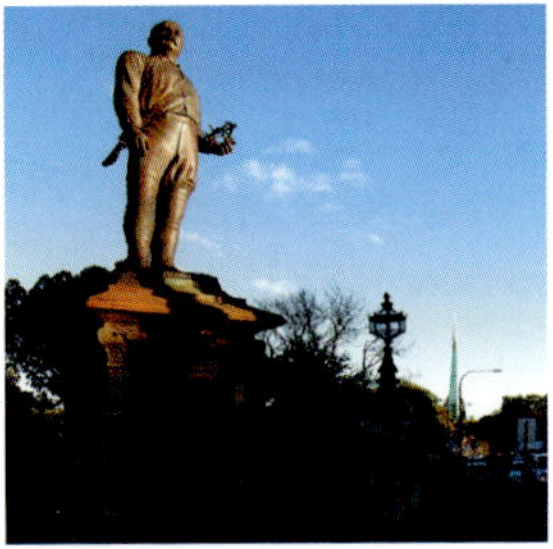
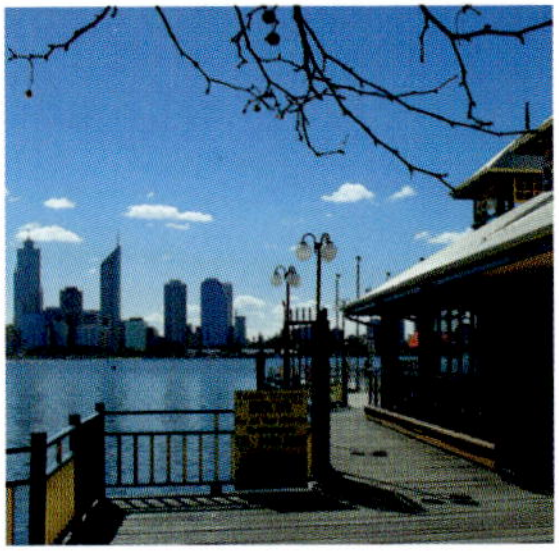
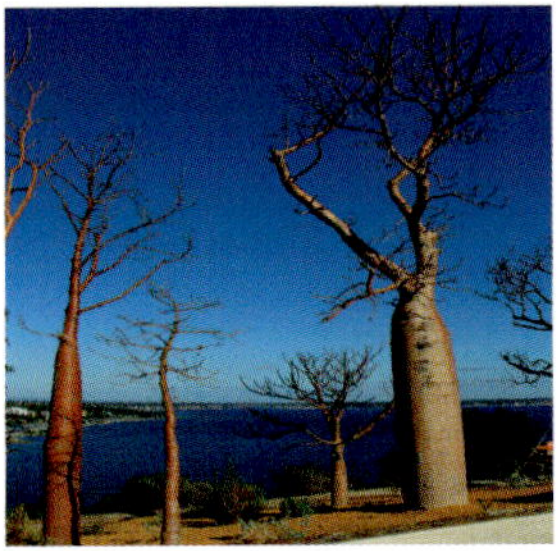
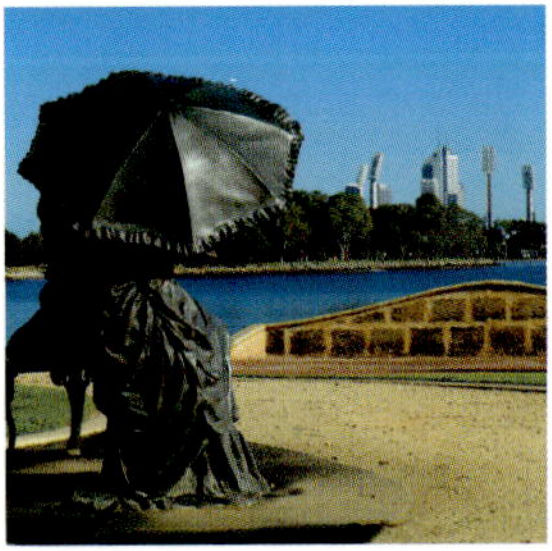
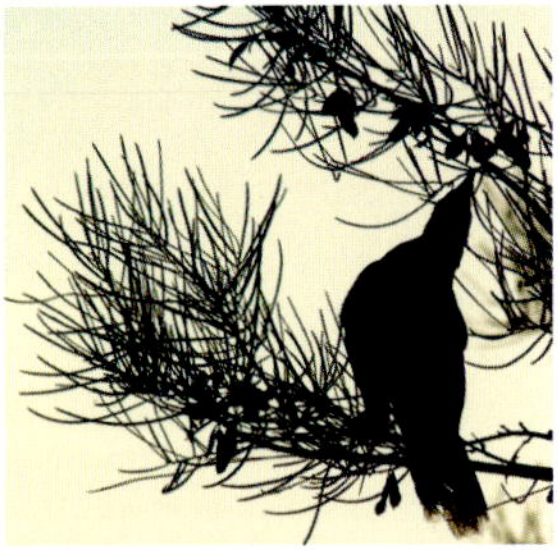
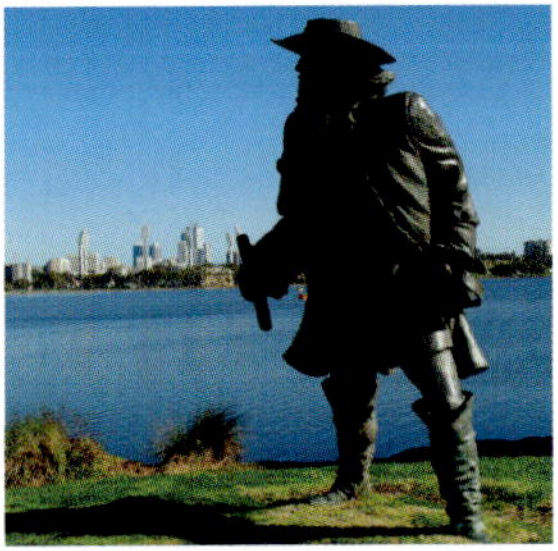
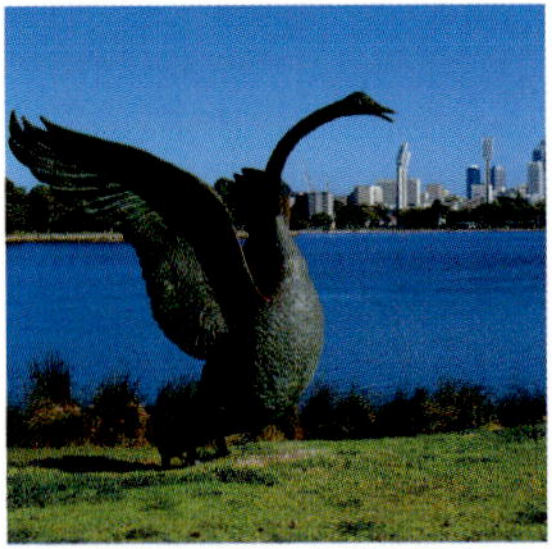
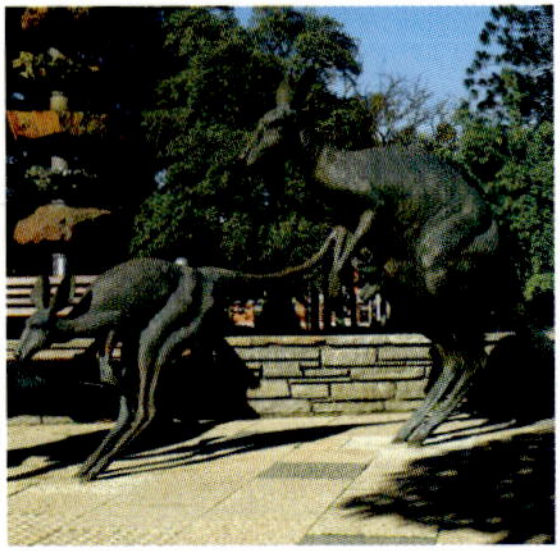
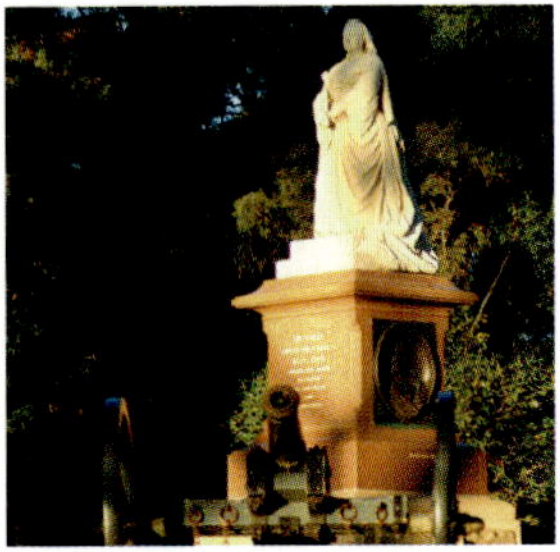

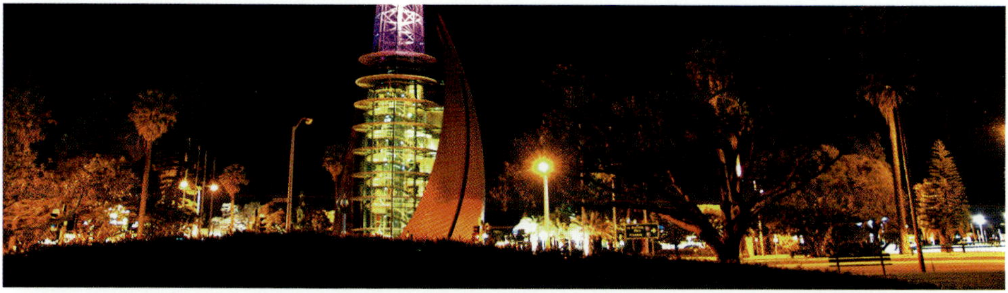

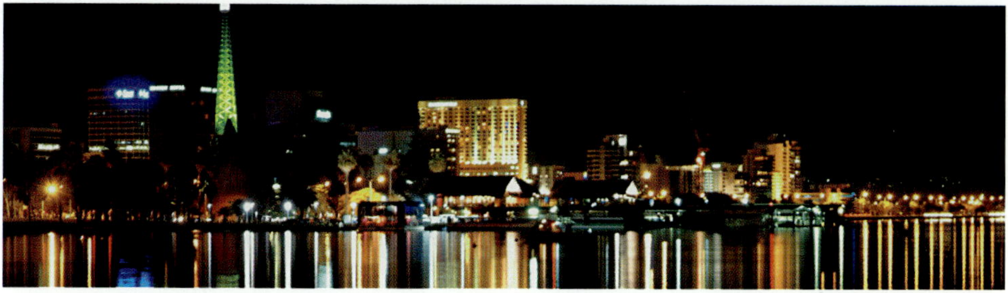

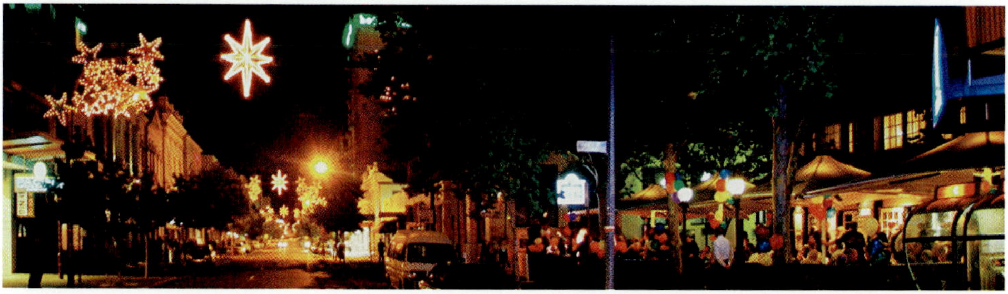

next page. forrest place

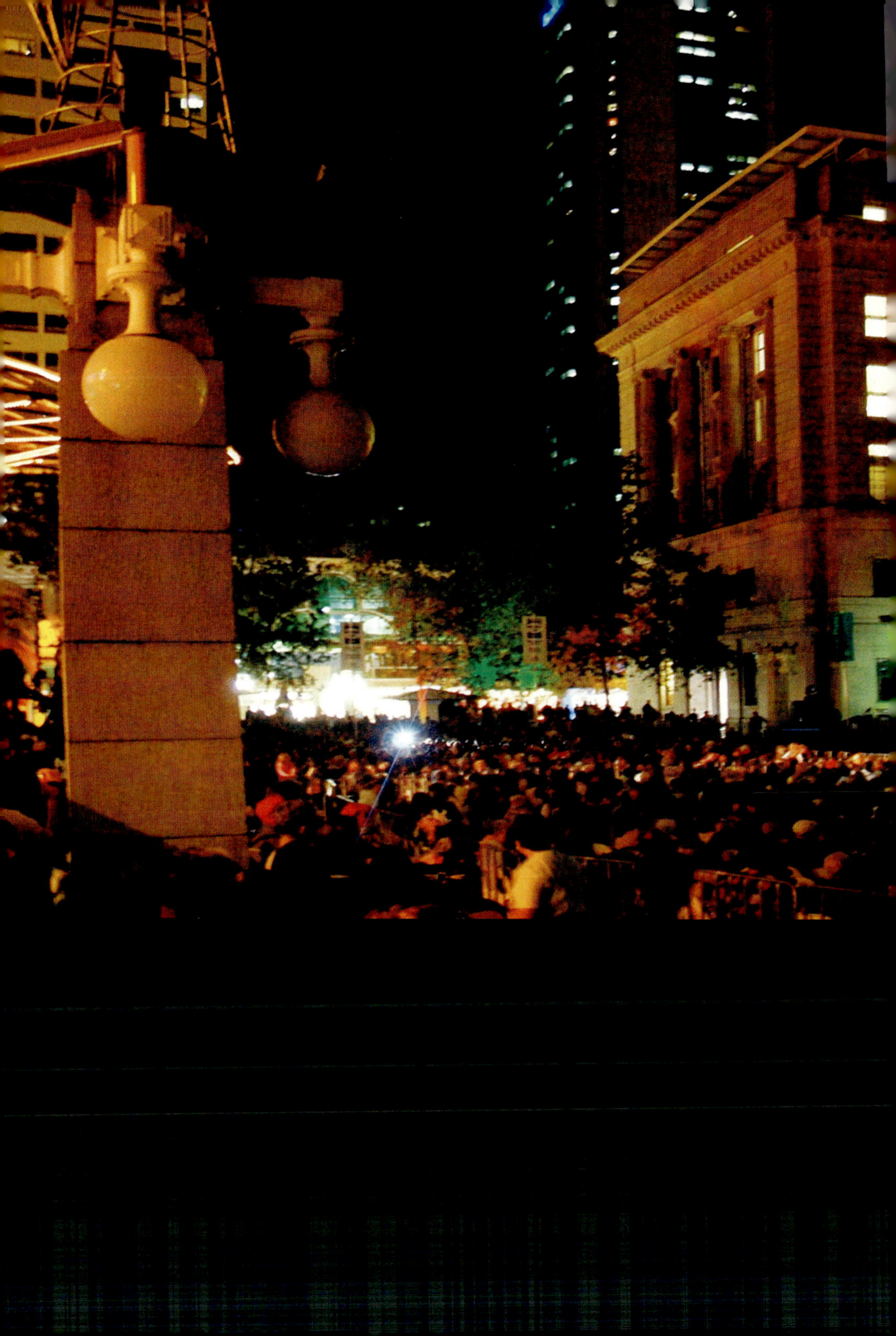

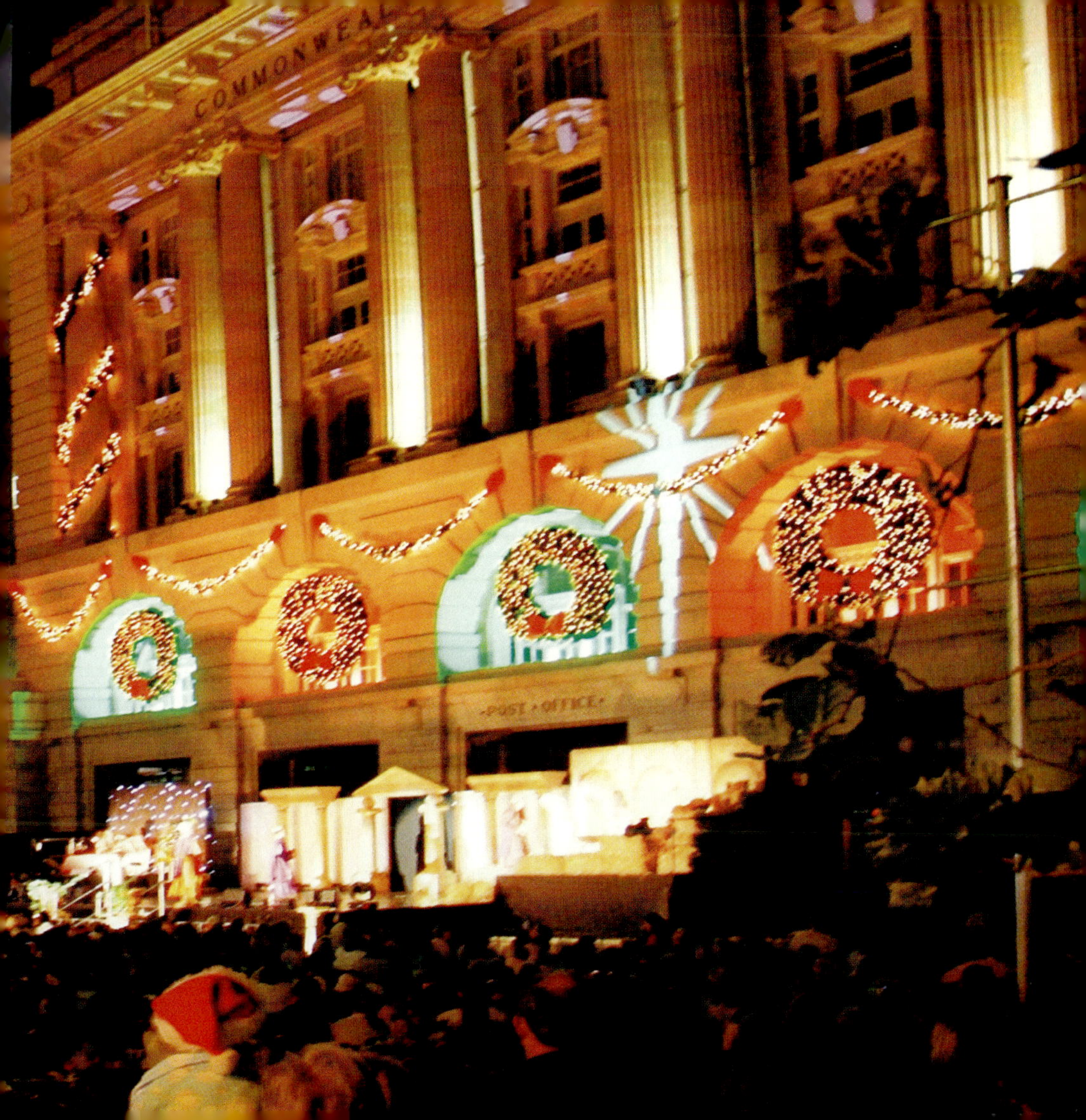
POST OFFICE

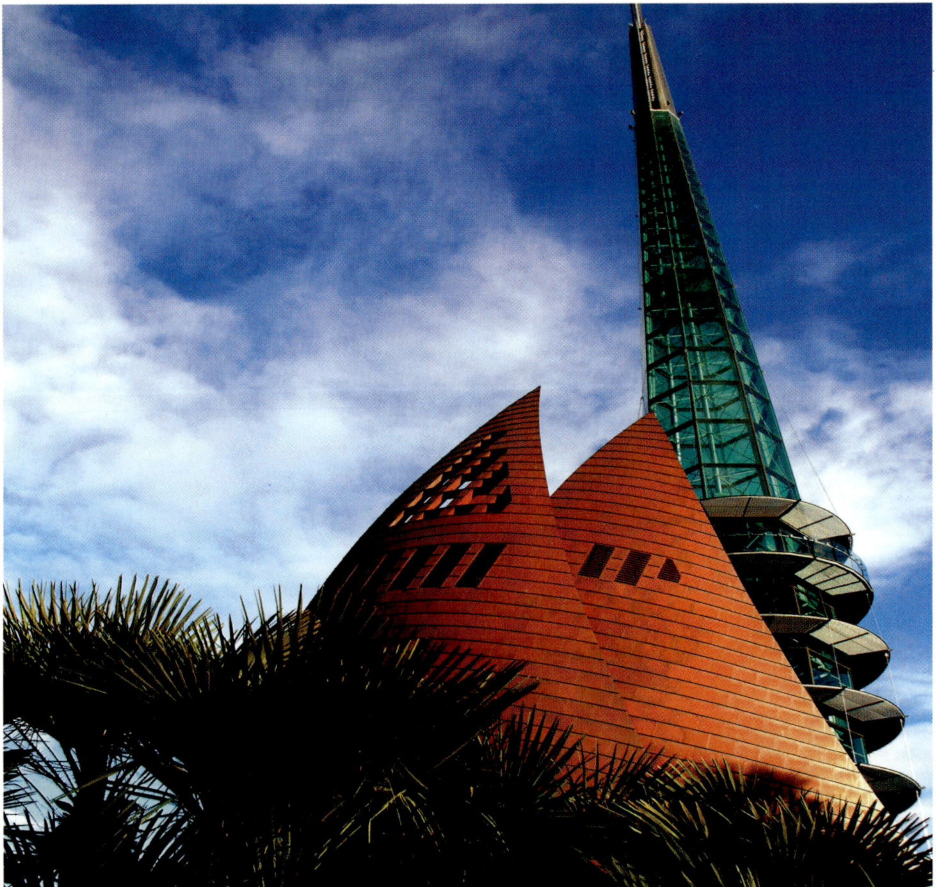

72. swan bells

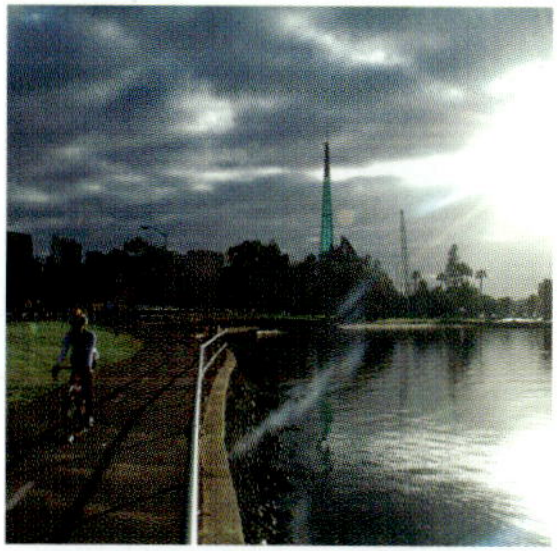

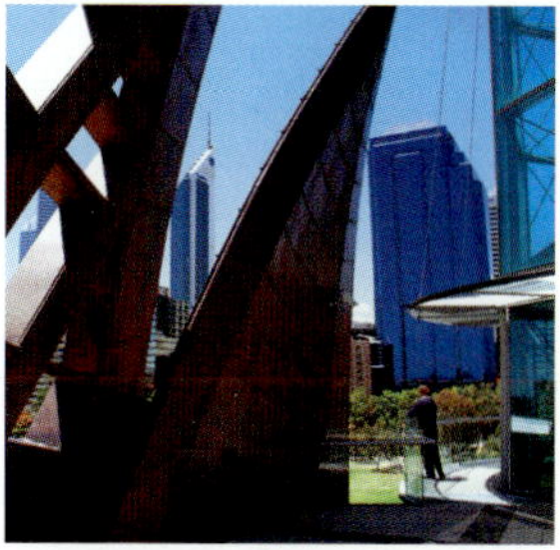

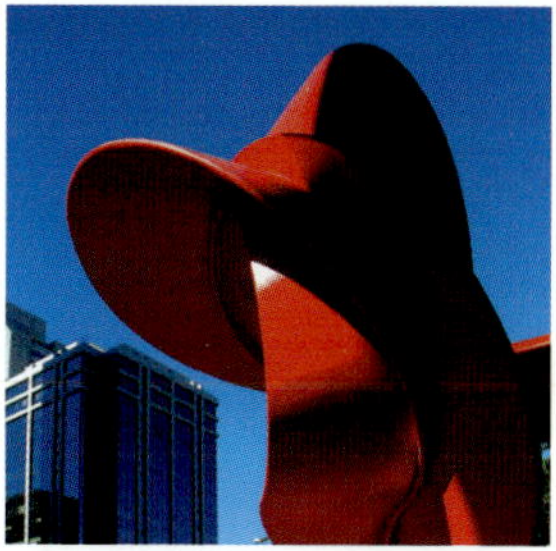

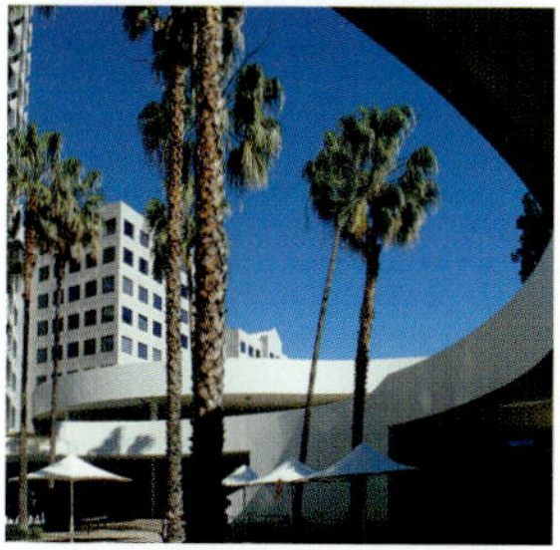

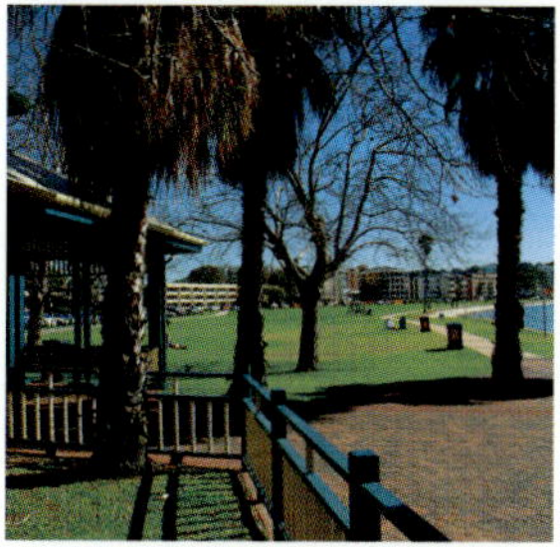

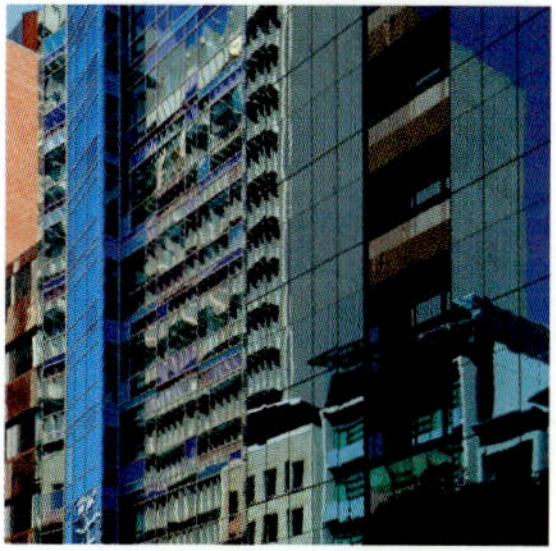

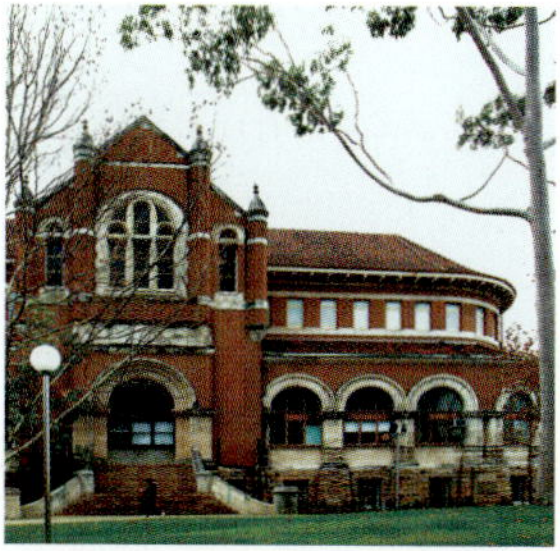

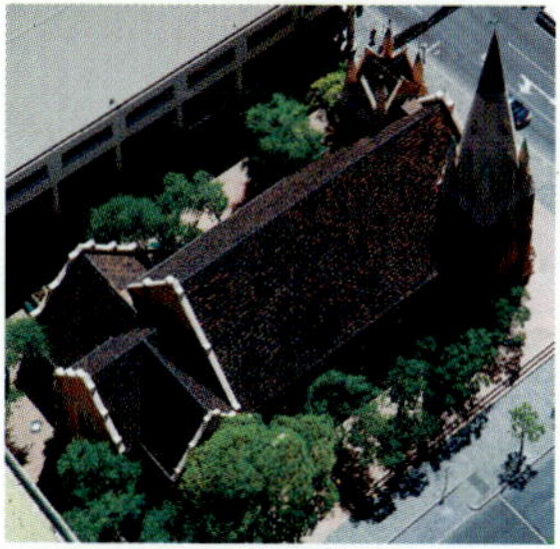

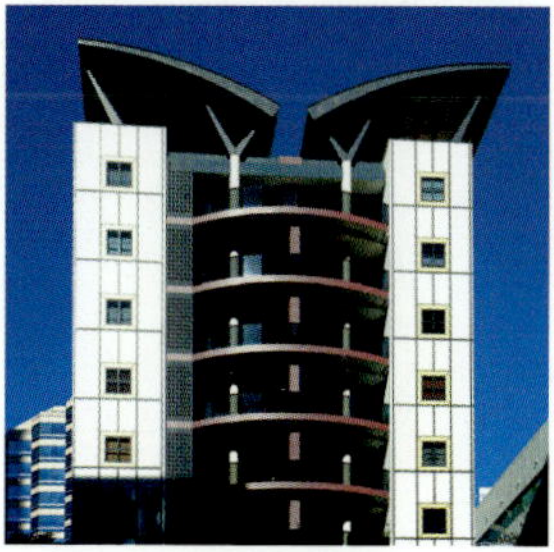

next page. barrack square jetty & swan bells

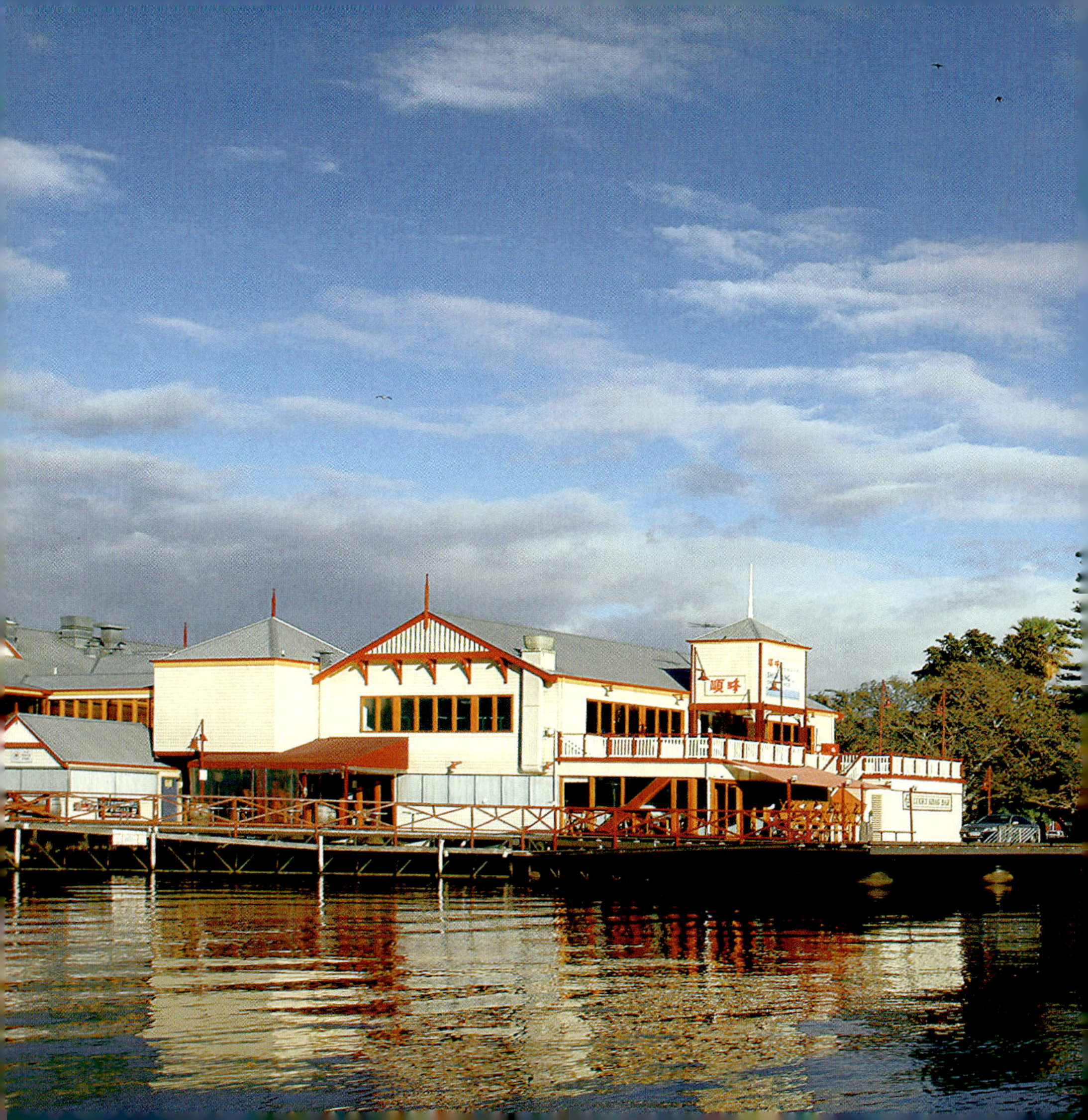

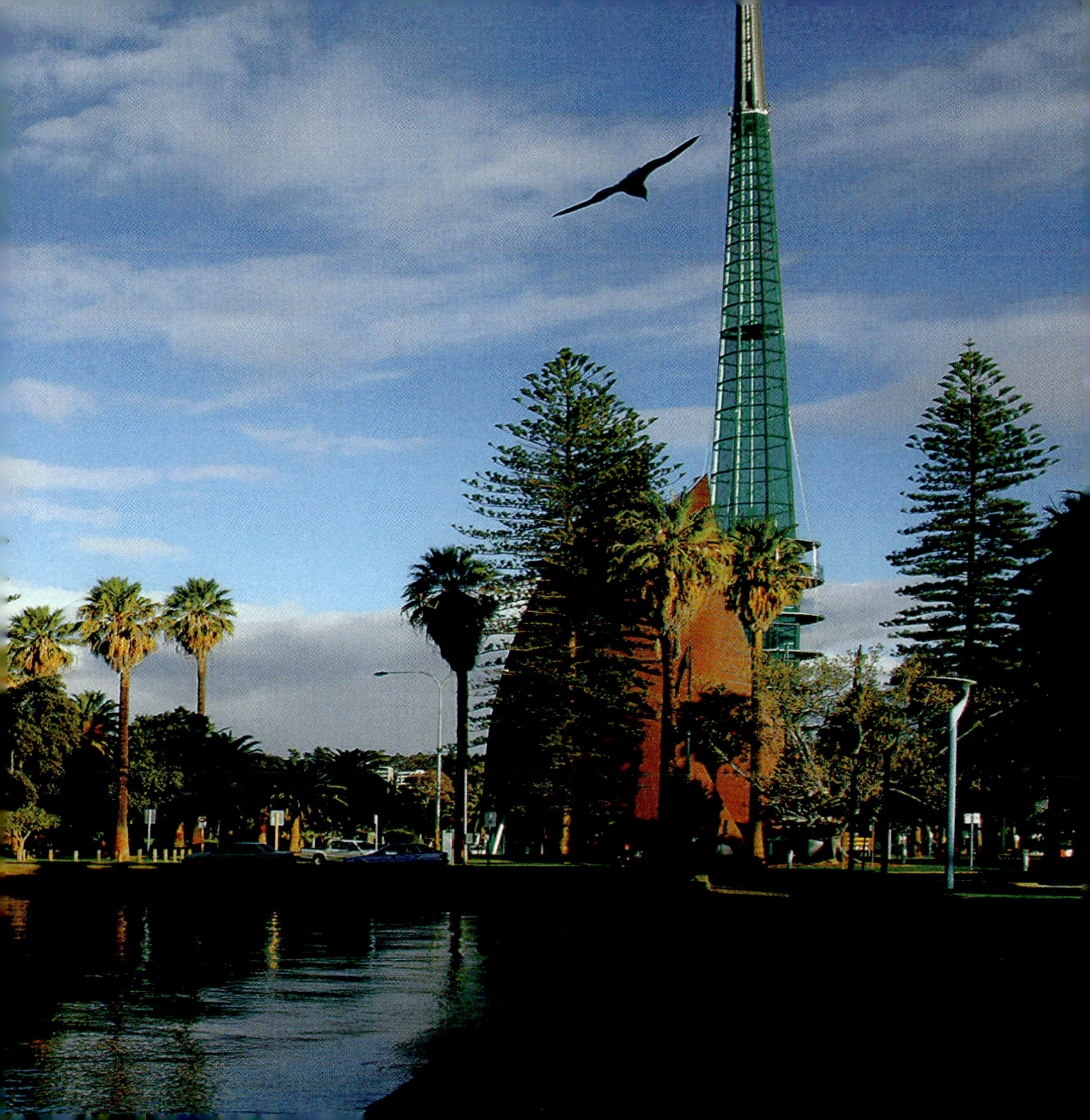

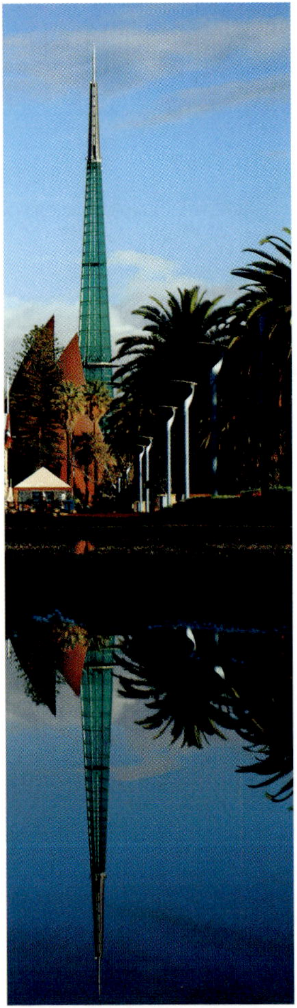

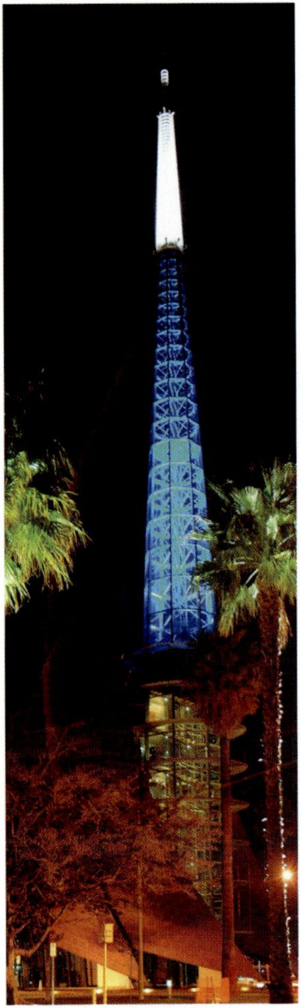

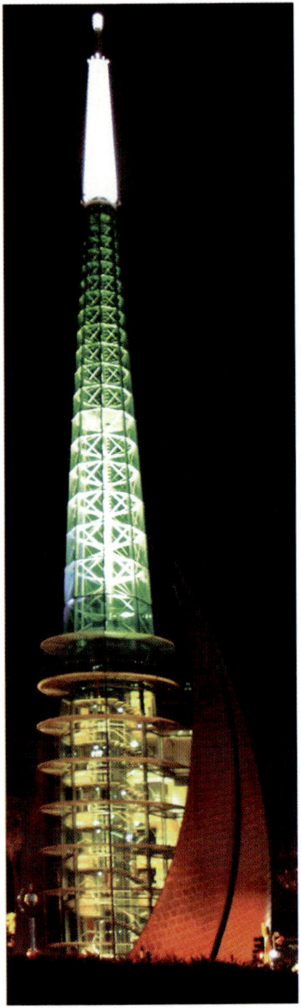

76. swan bells

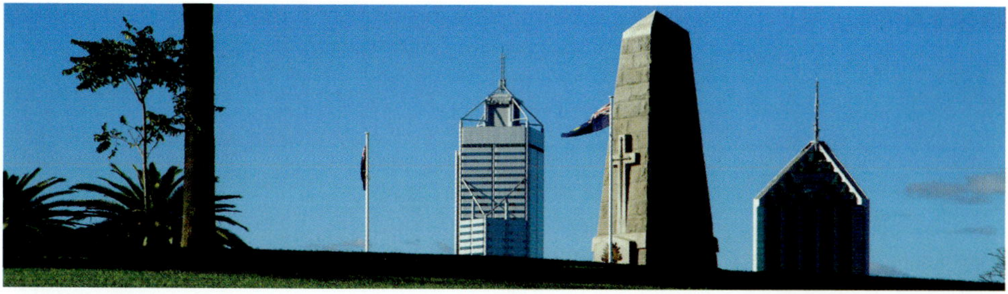

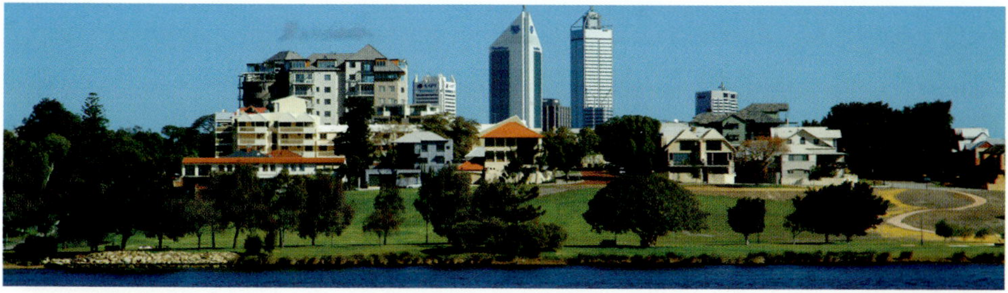

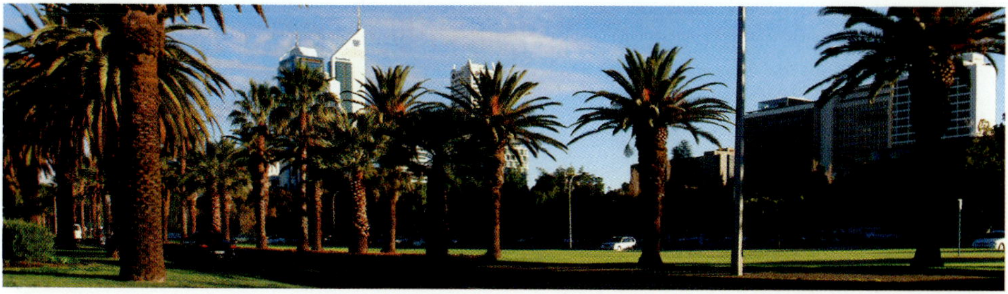

next page. perth city by the swan river

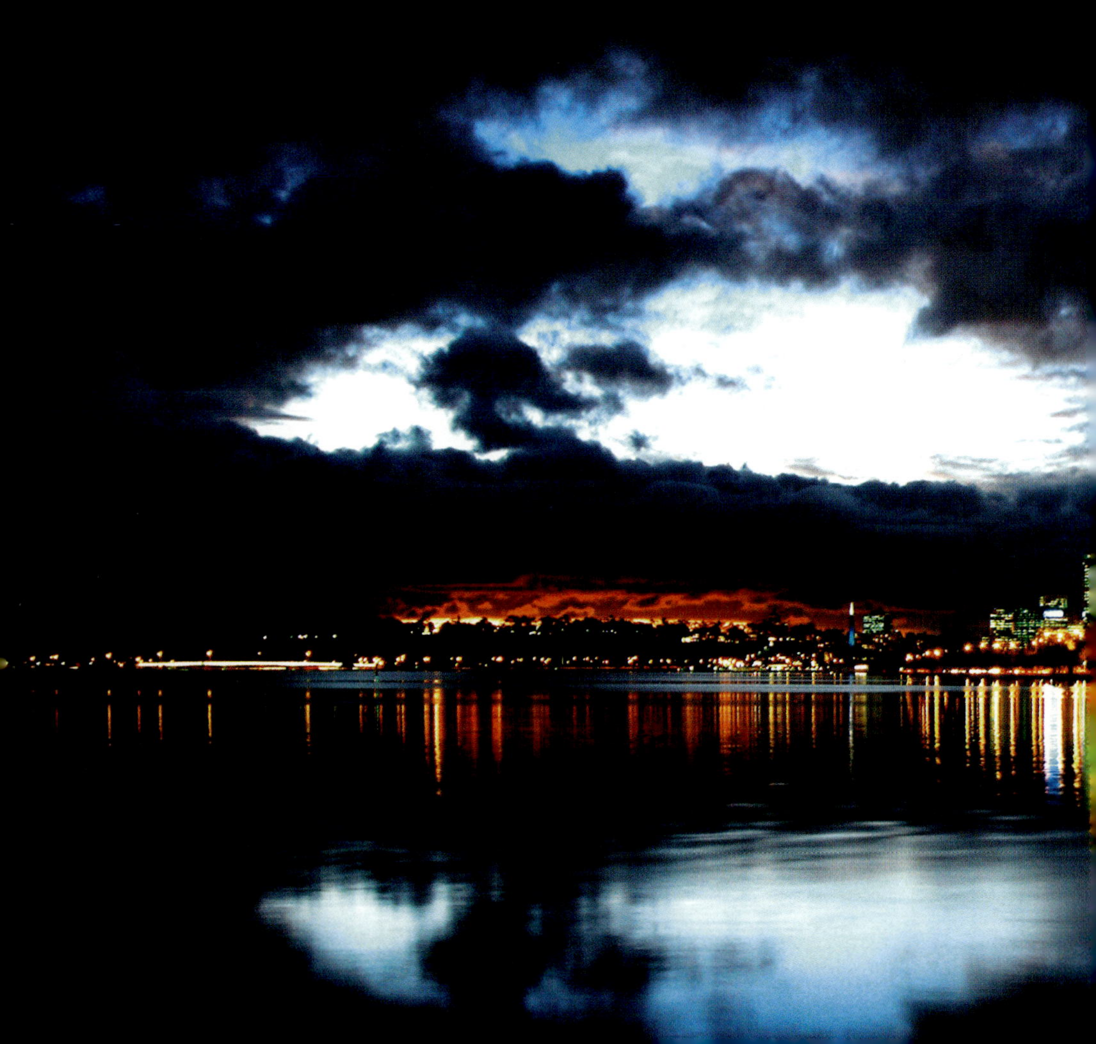

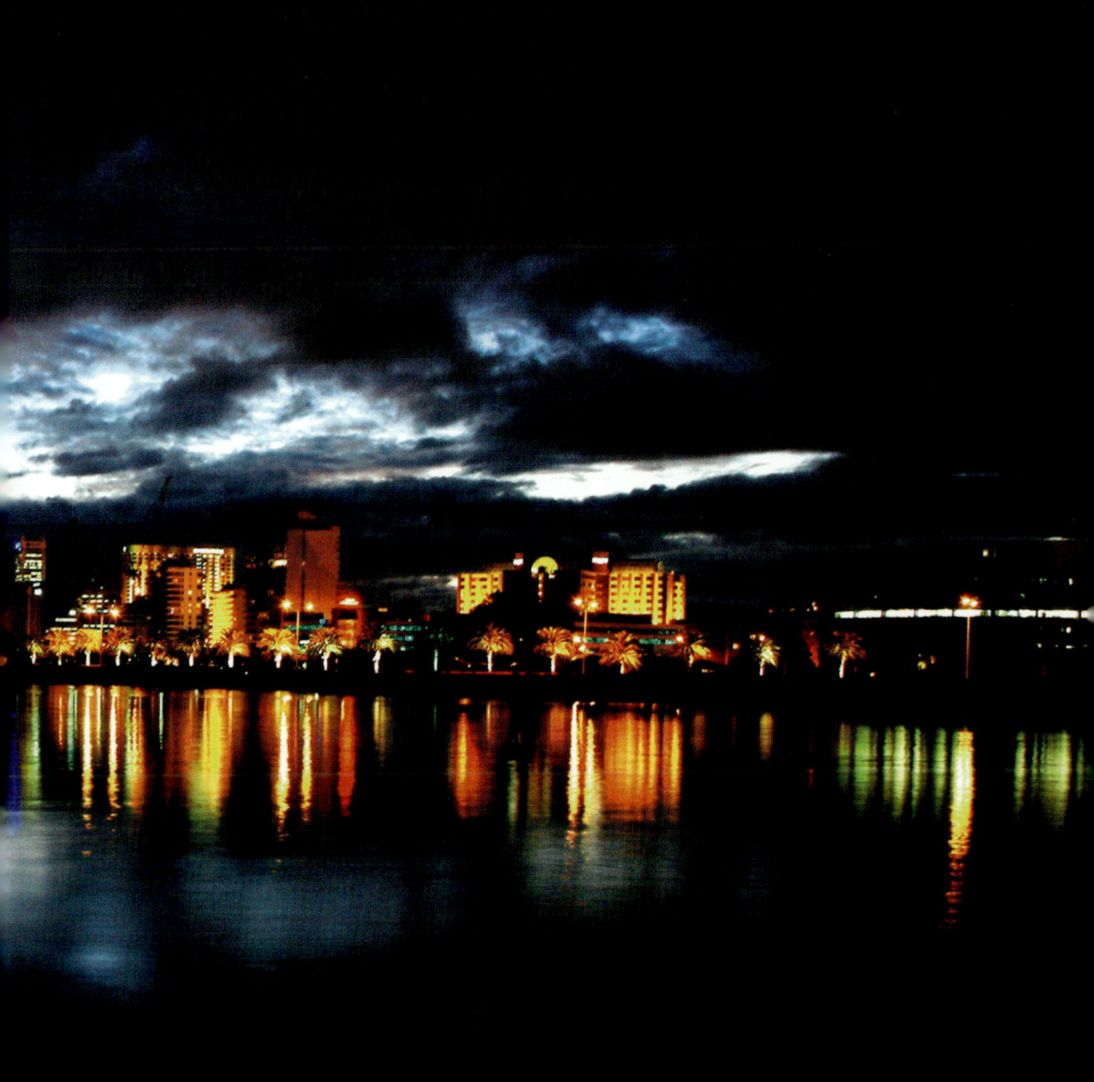

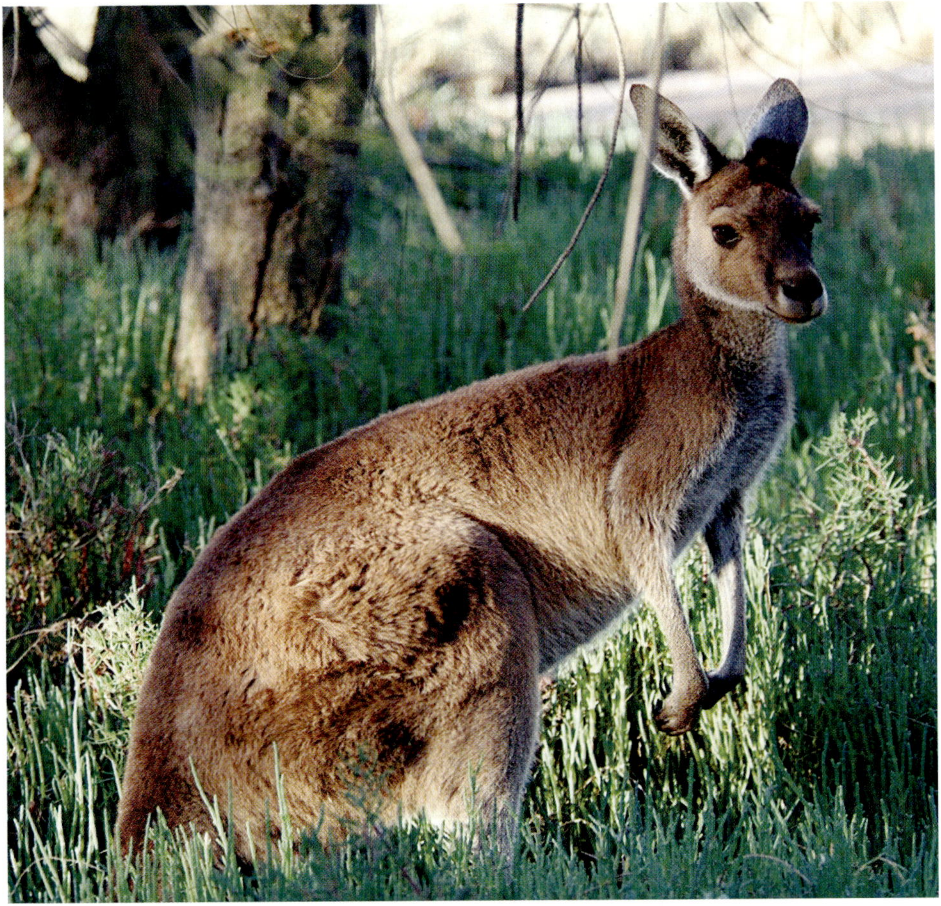

80. kangaroo on heirisson island

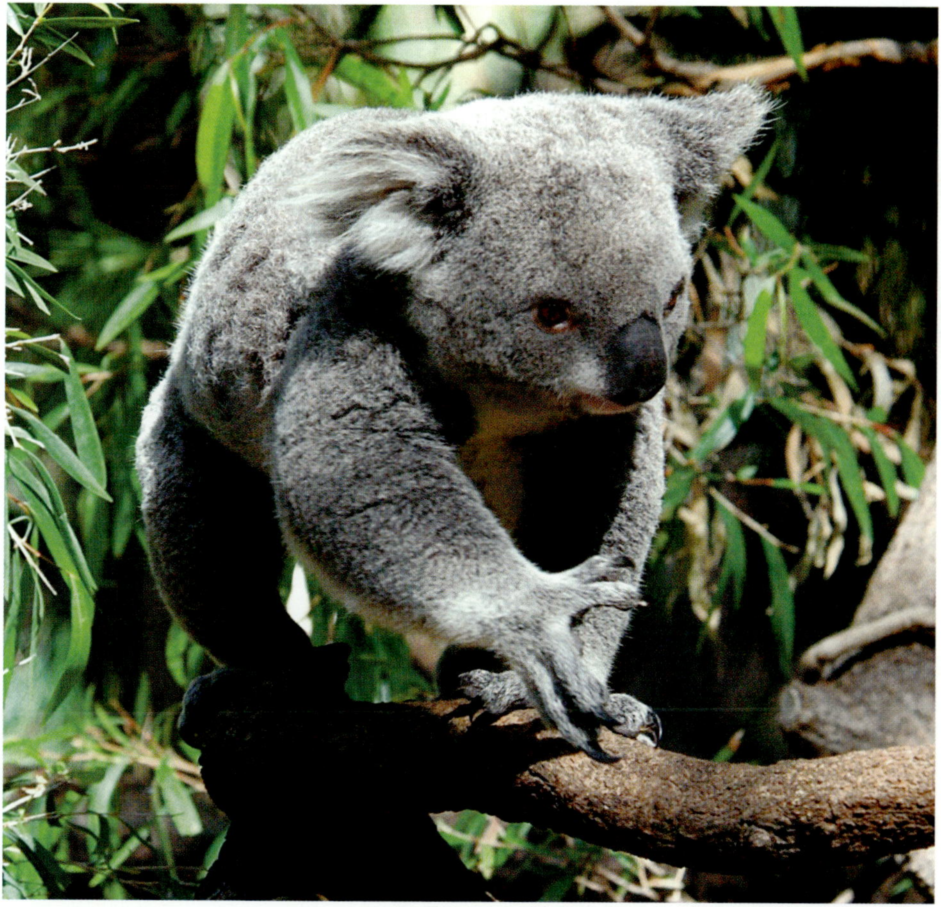

next page. pelicans on perth water

koala at perth zoo

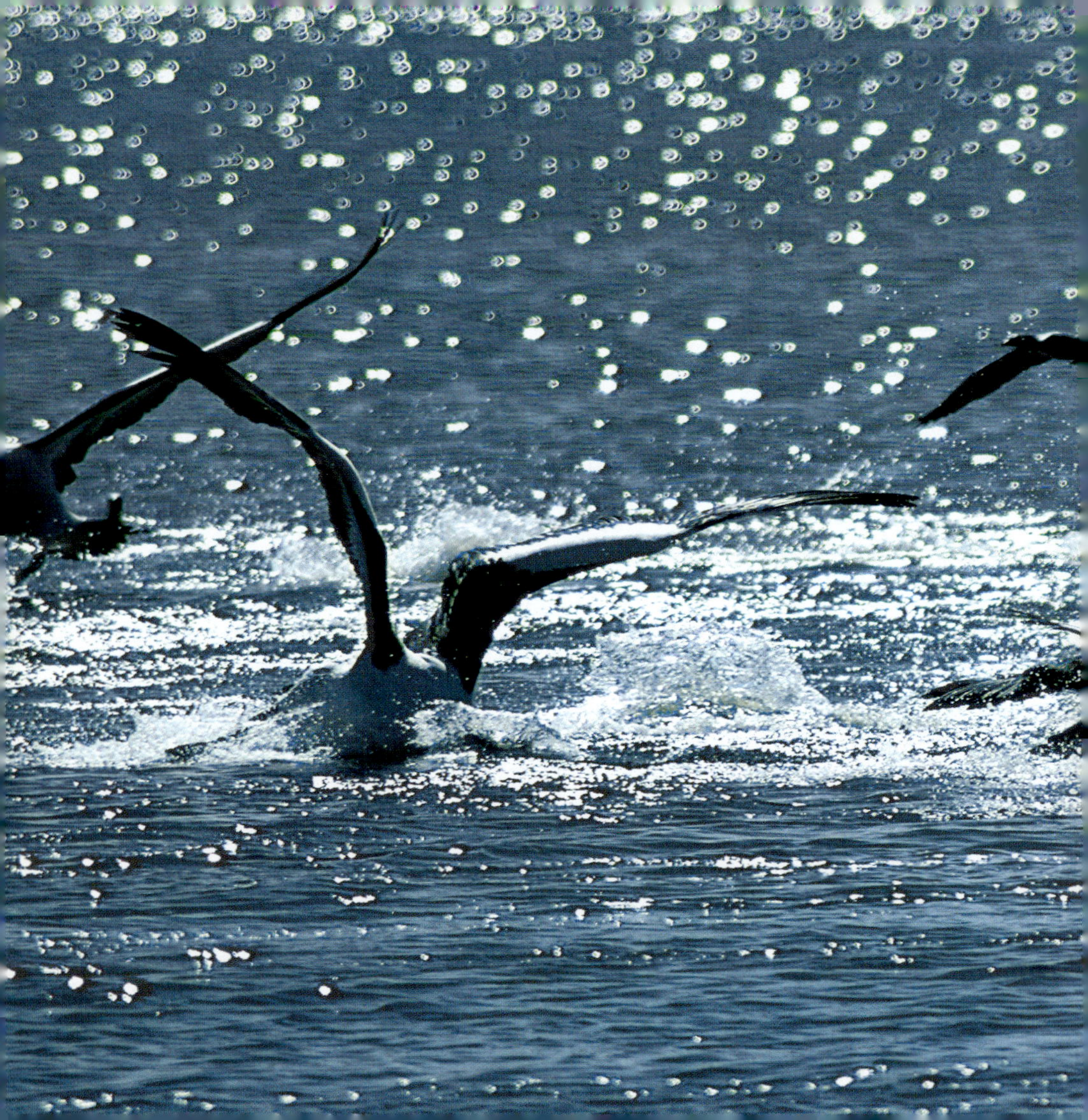

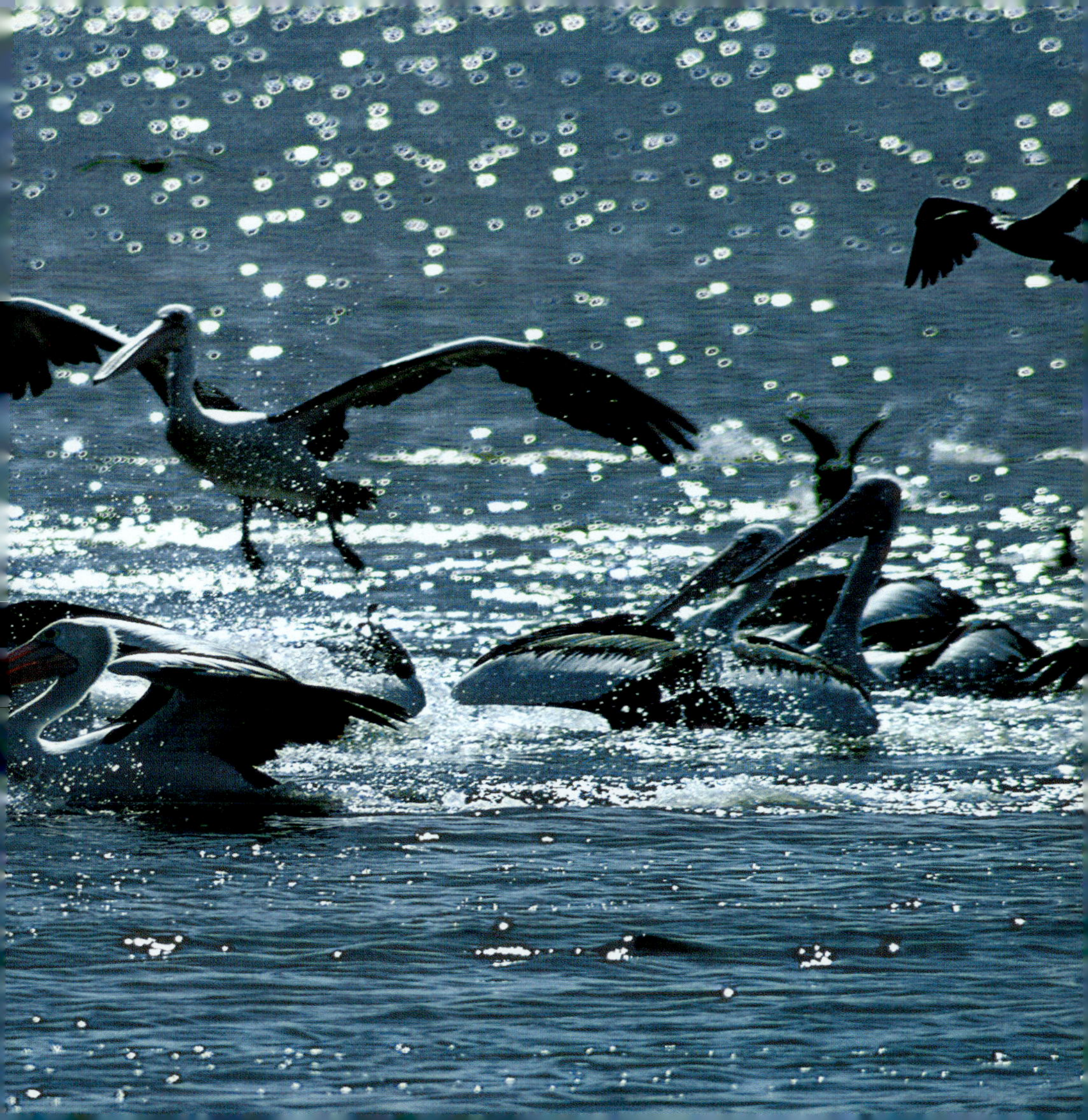

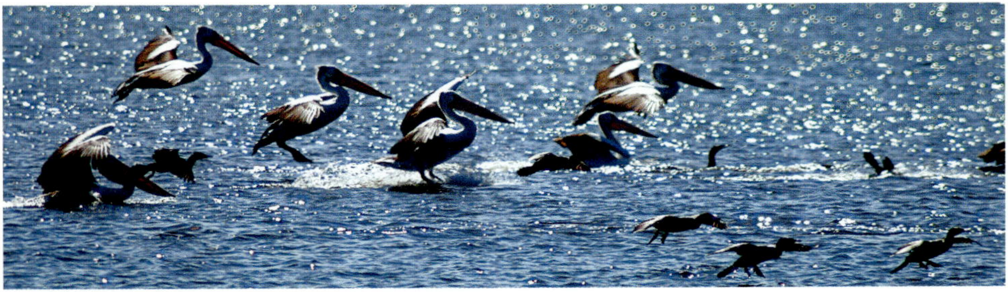

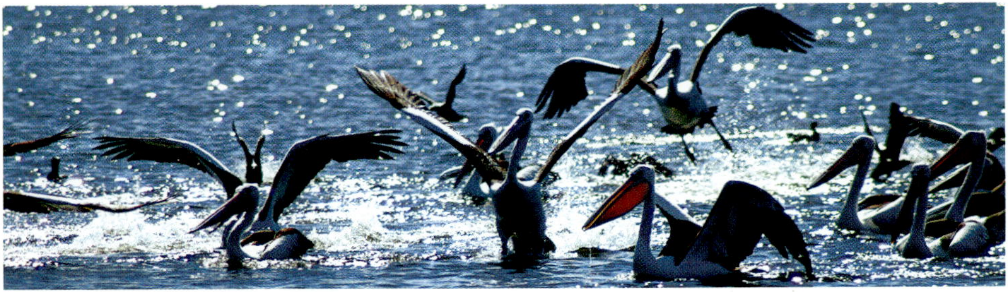

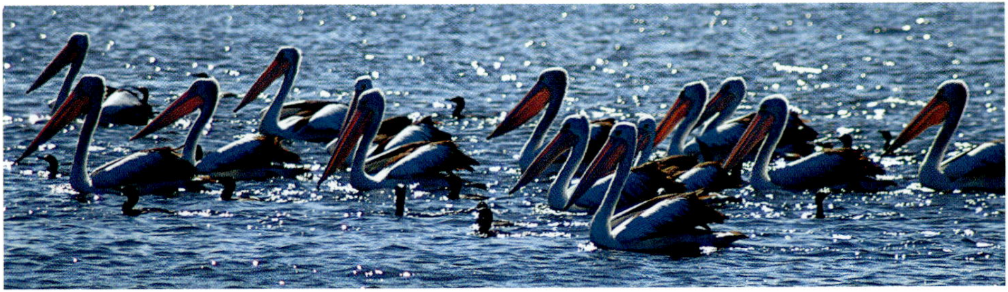

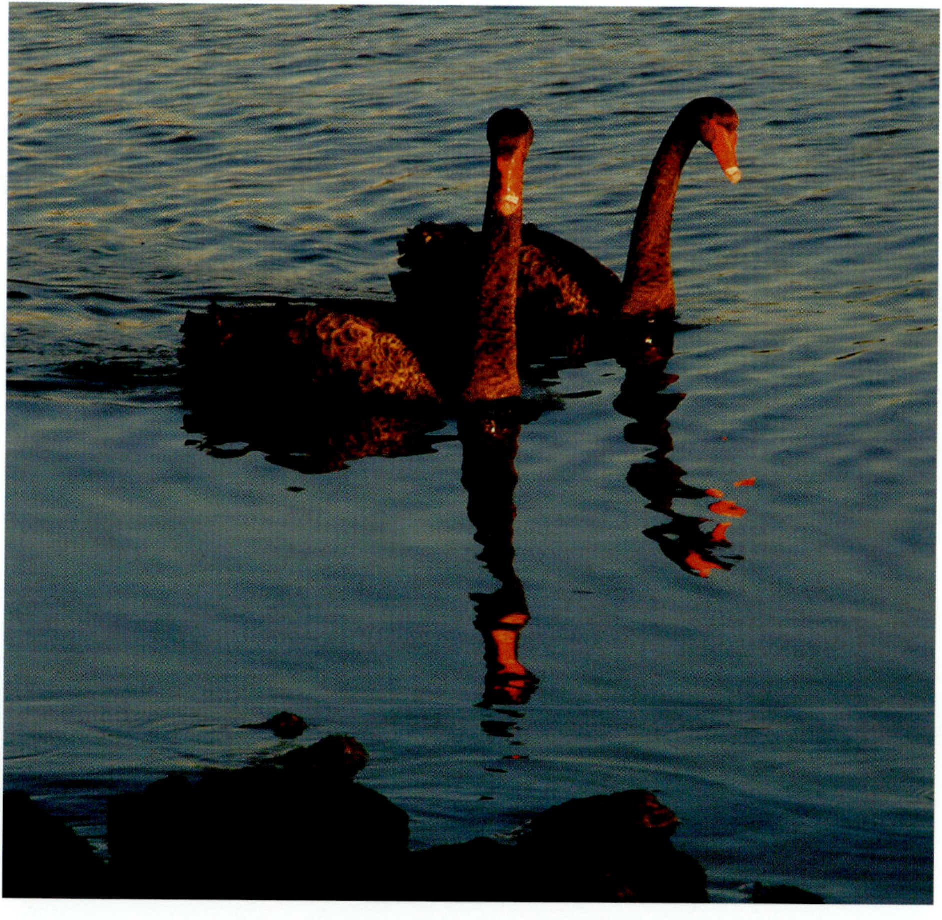

next page. success, challenger & fishing boat harbours, fremantle

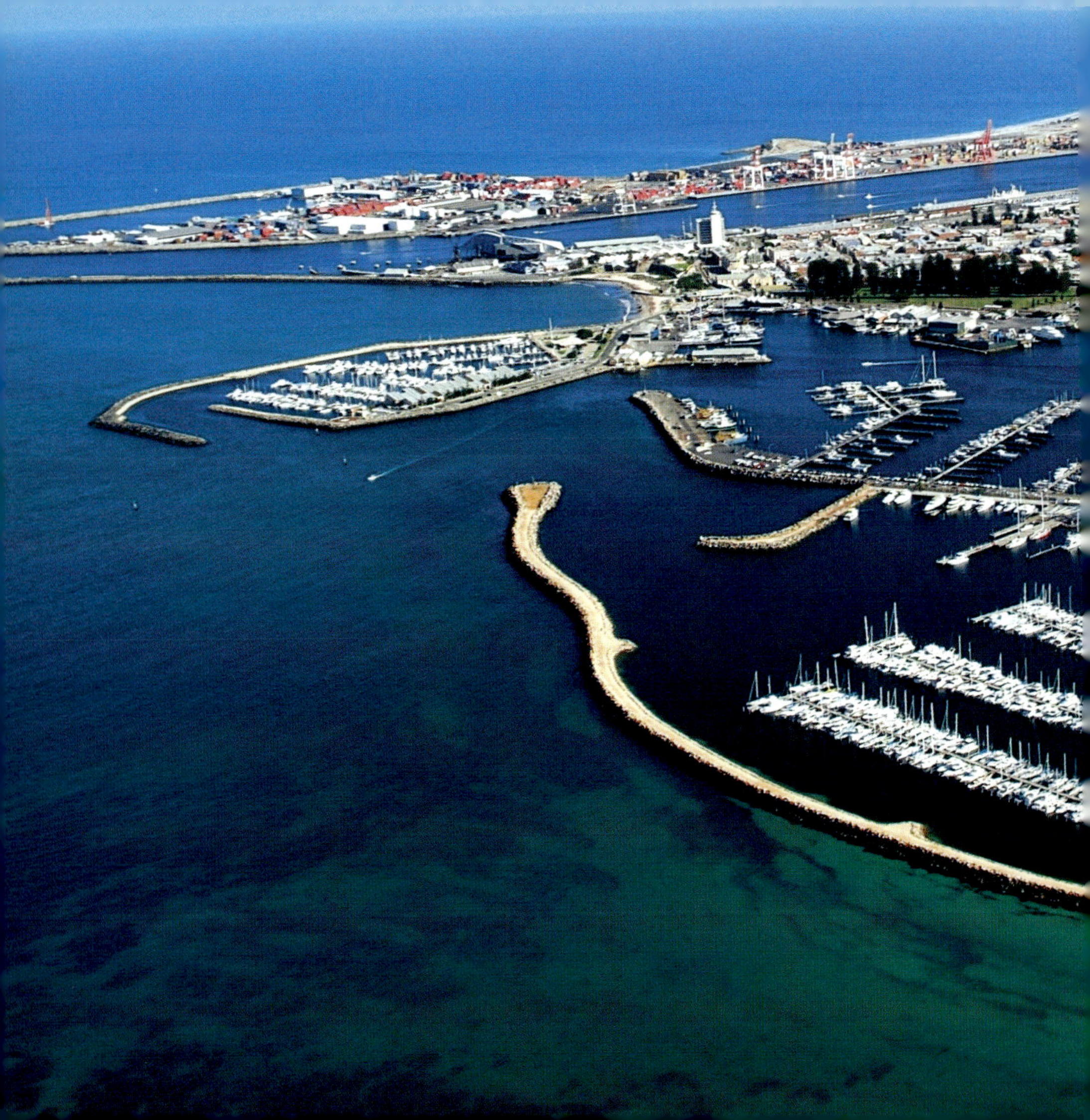

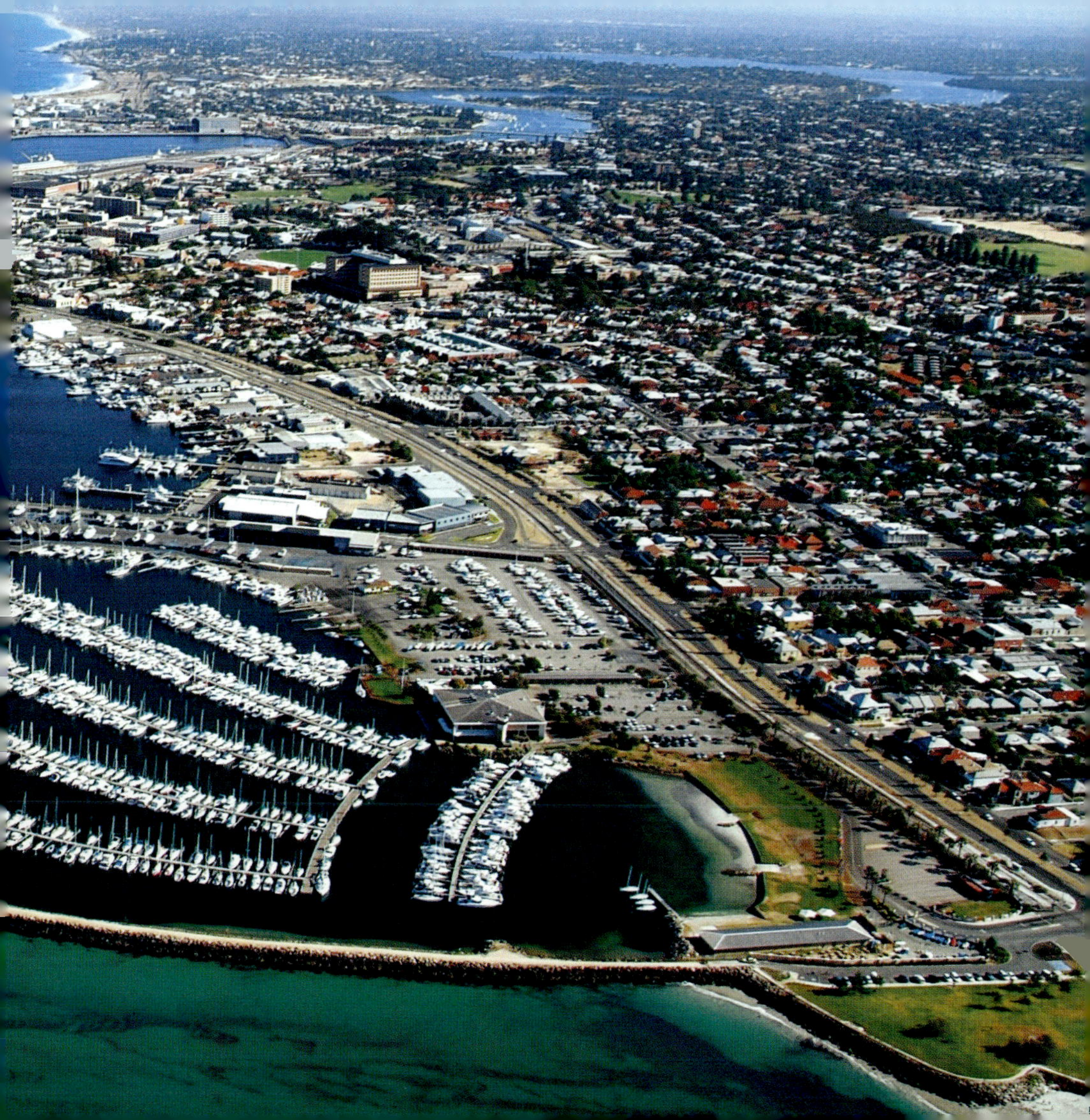

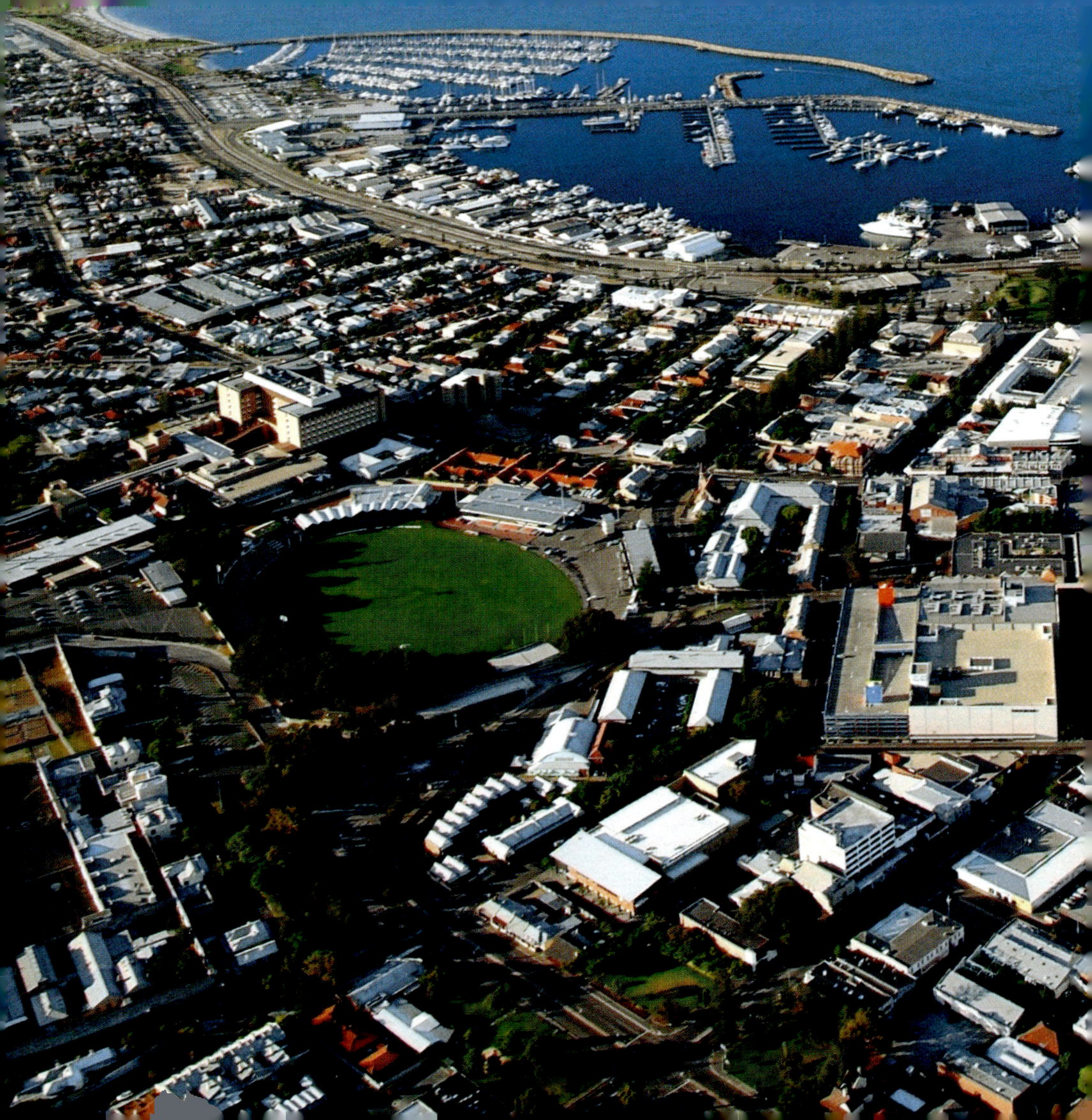

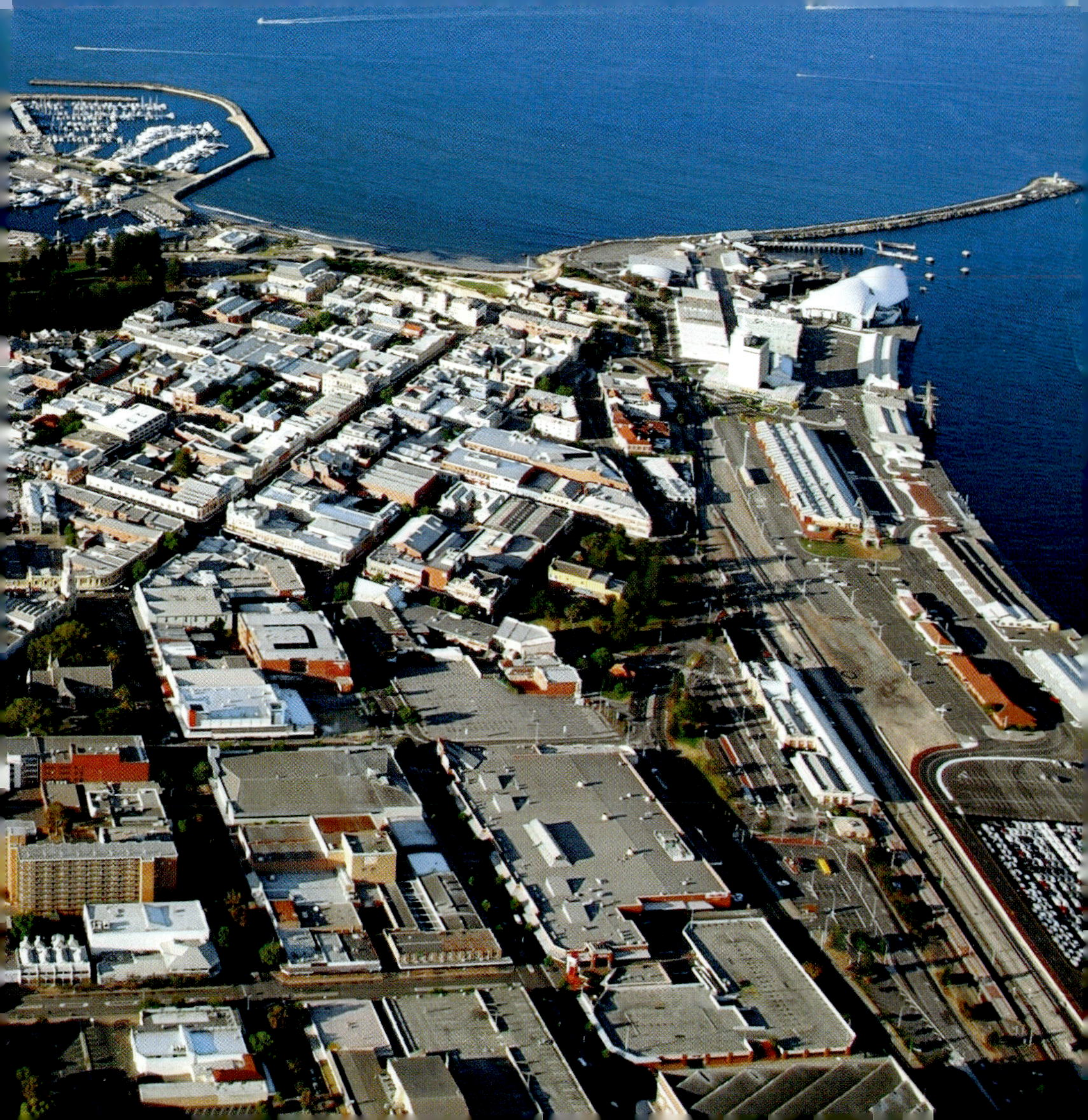

previous page. fremantle

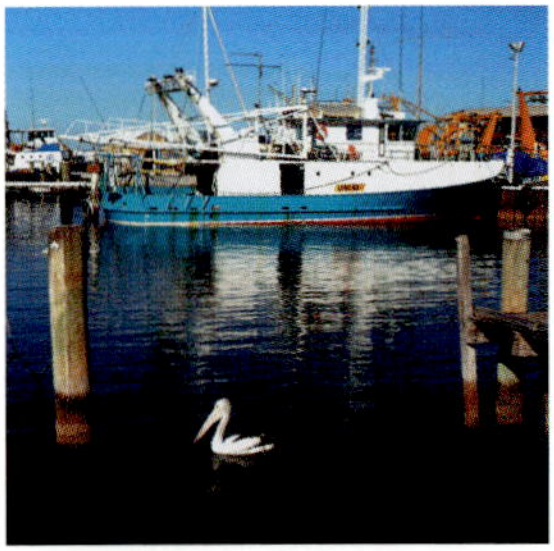
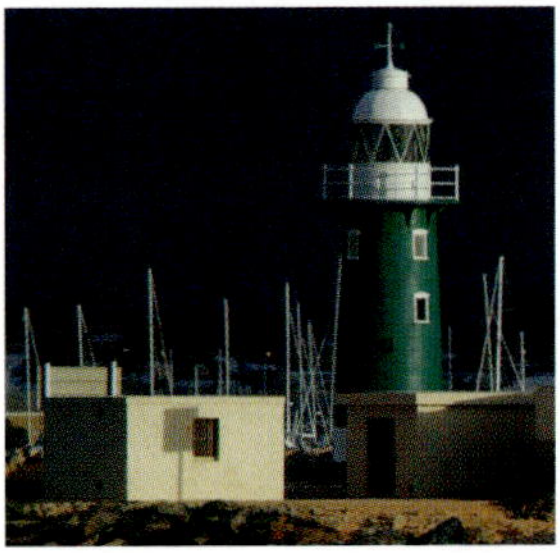
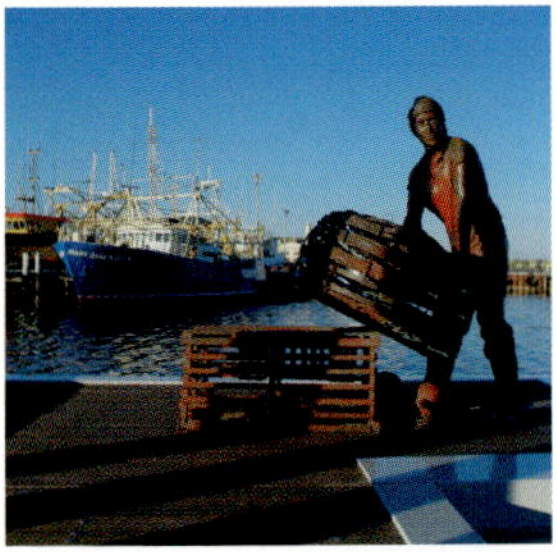
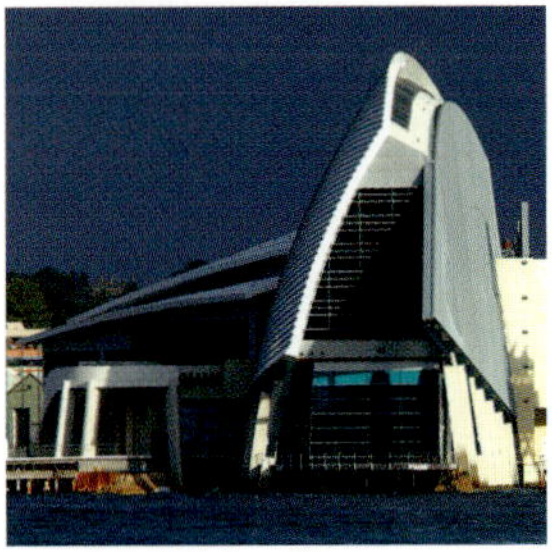
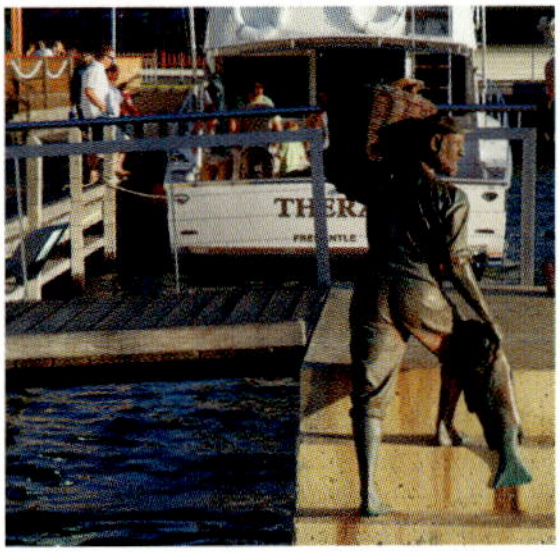
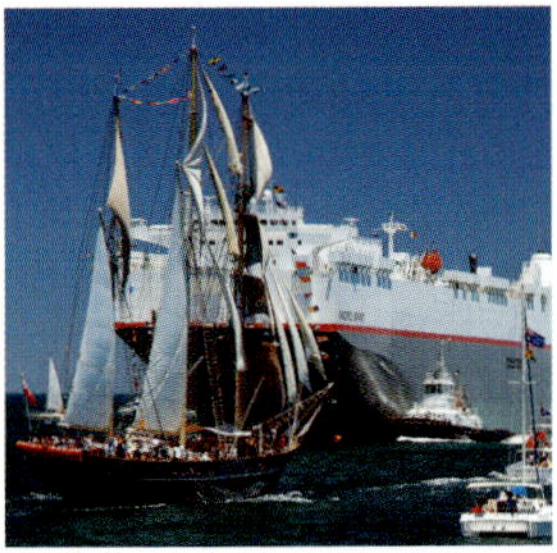
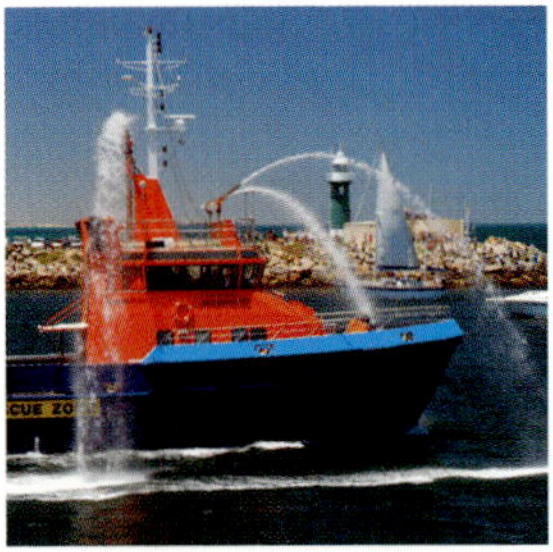
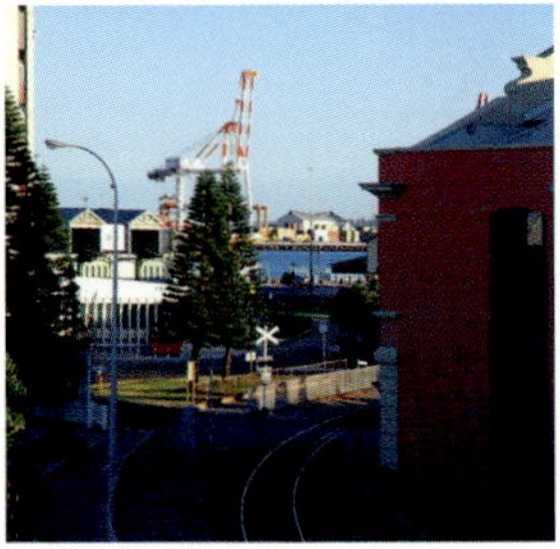
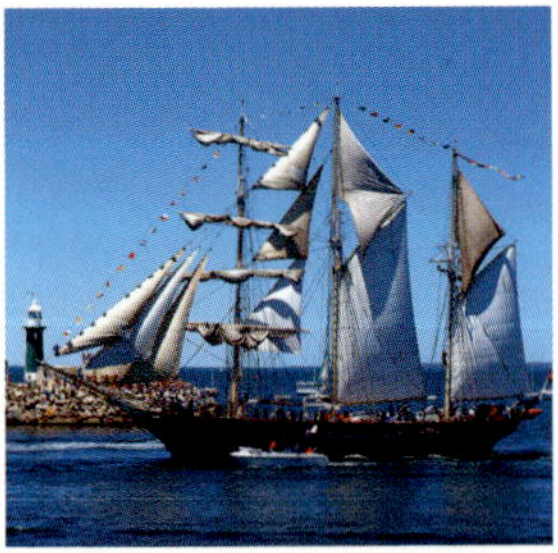

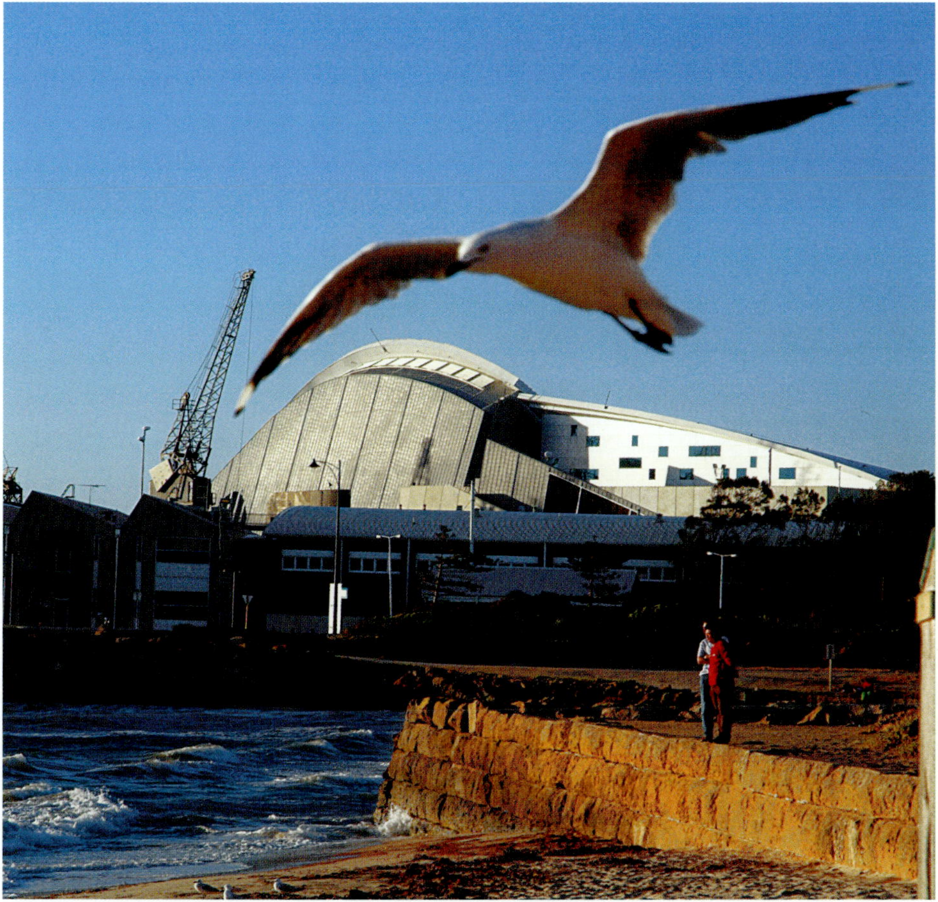

next page. the esplanade, fremantle

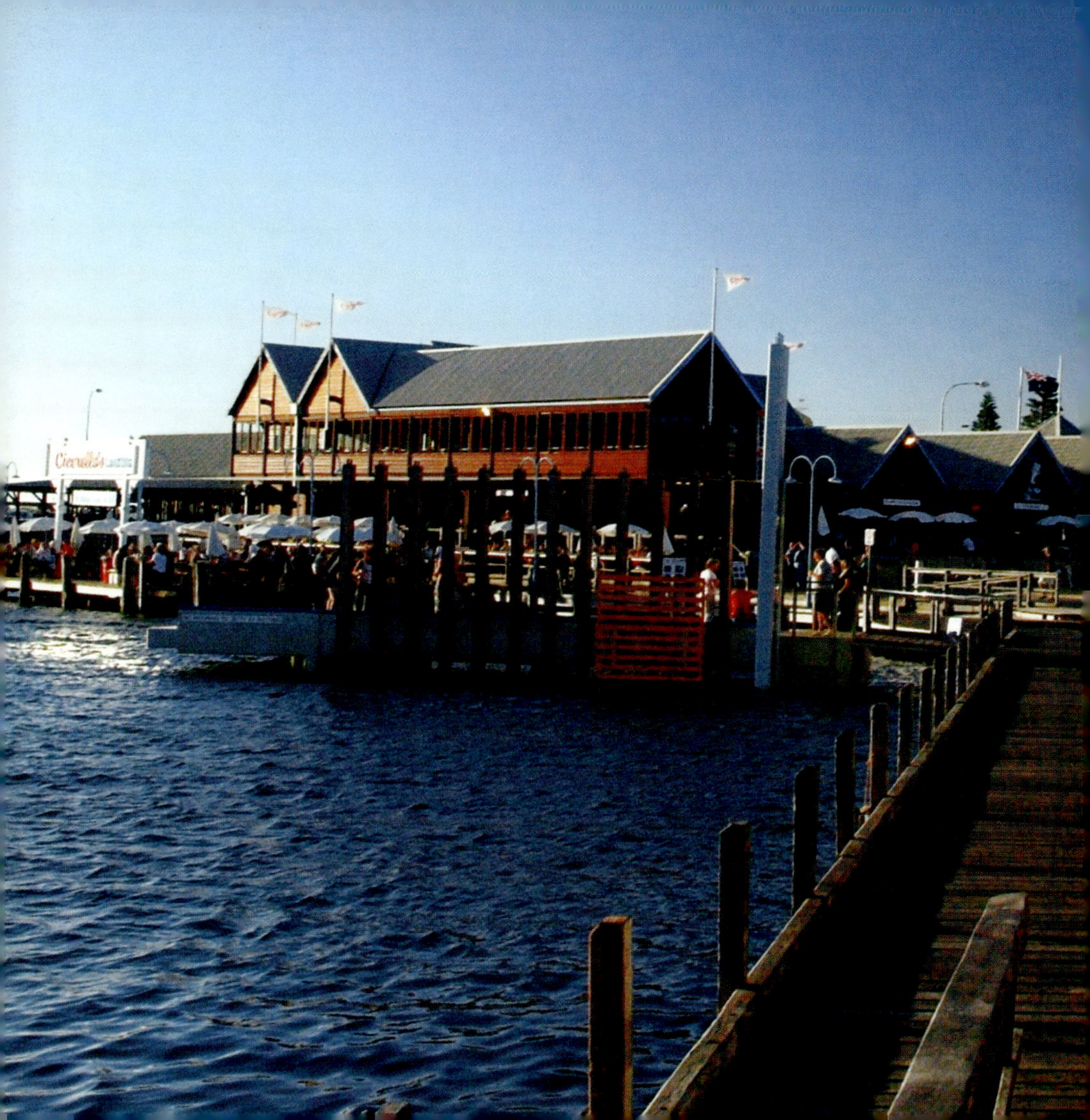

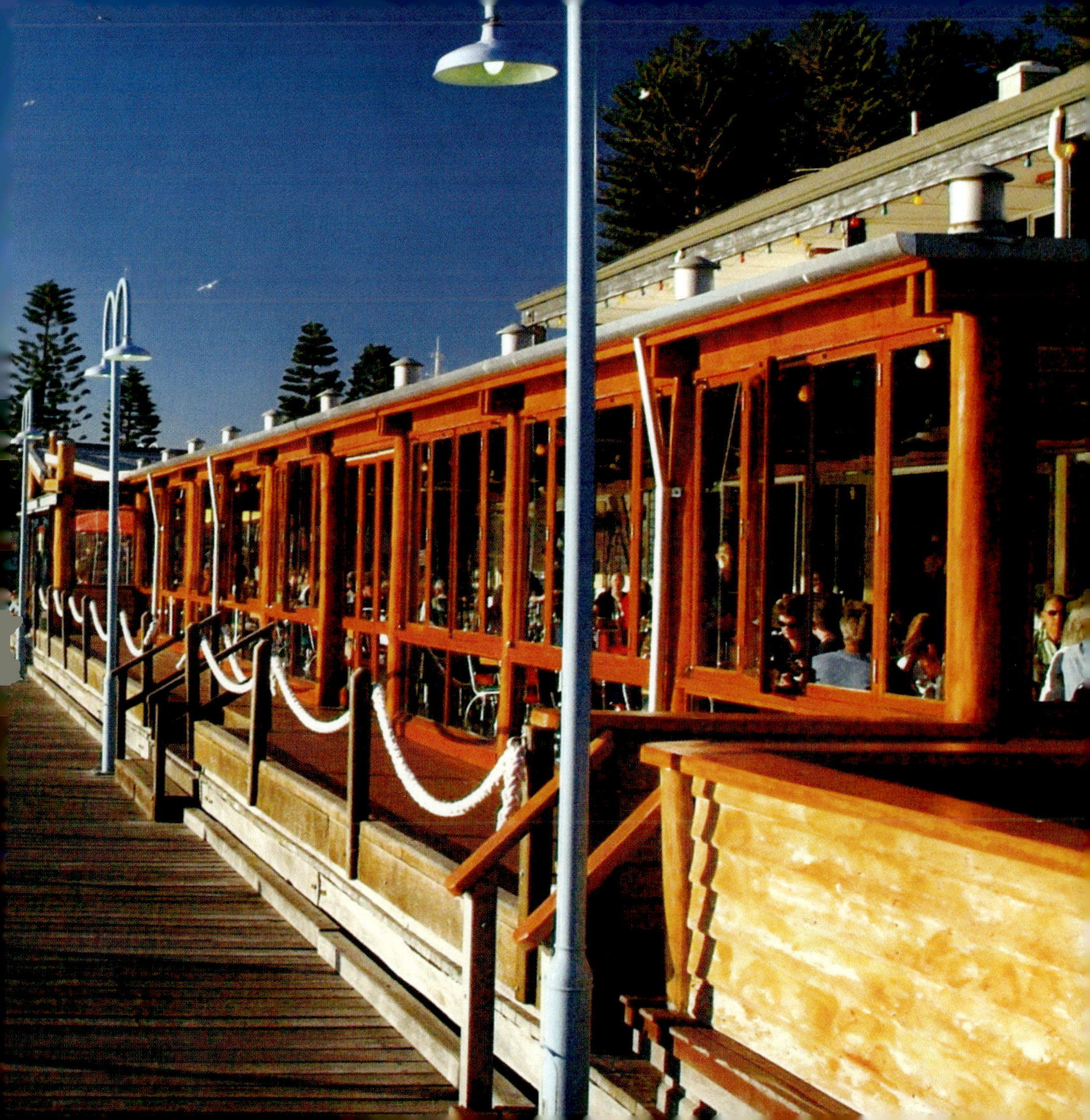

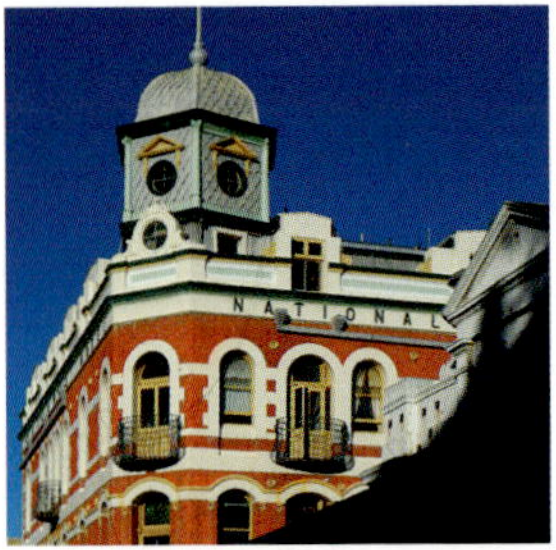
NATIONAL

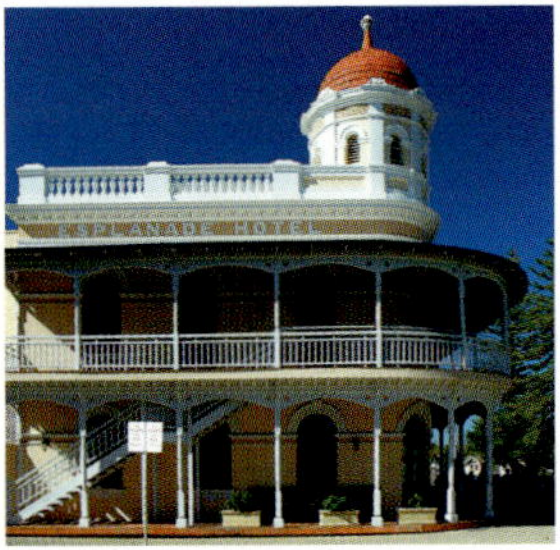
ESPLANADE HOTEL

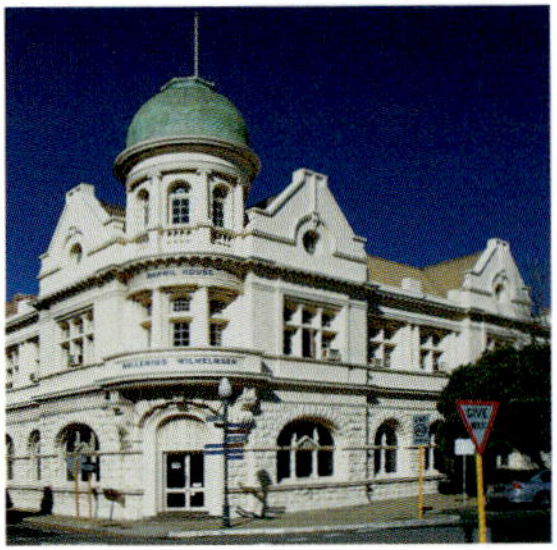

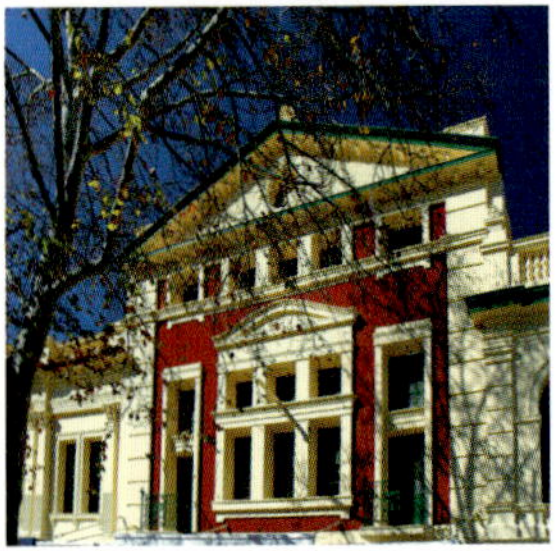

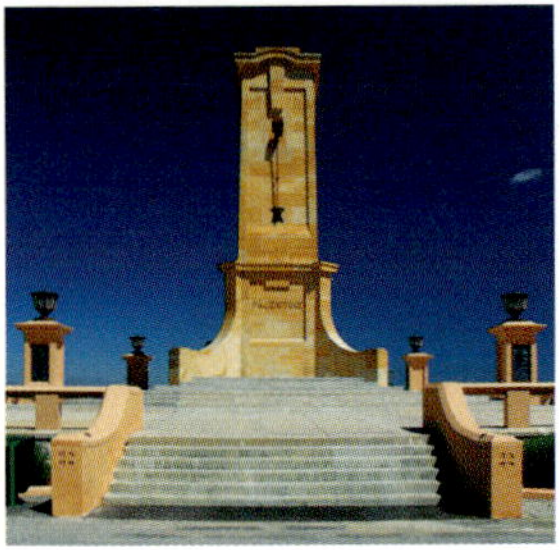

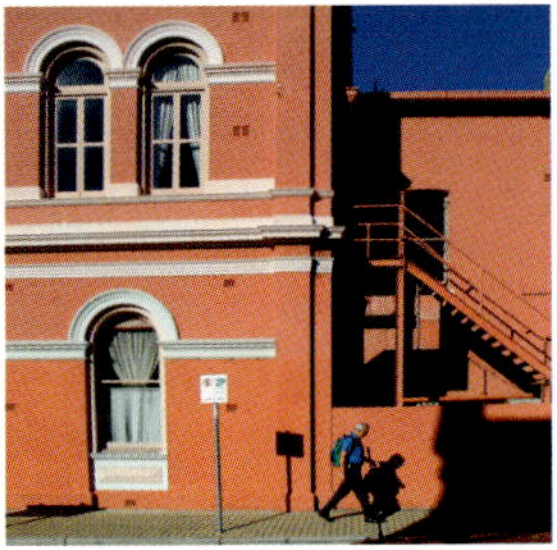

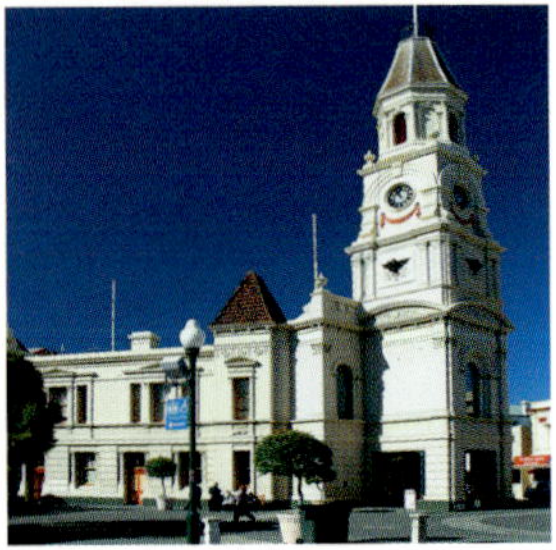

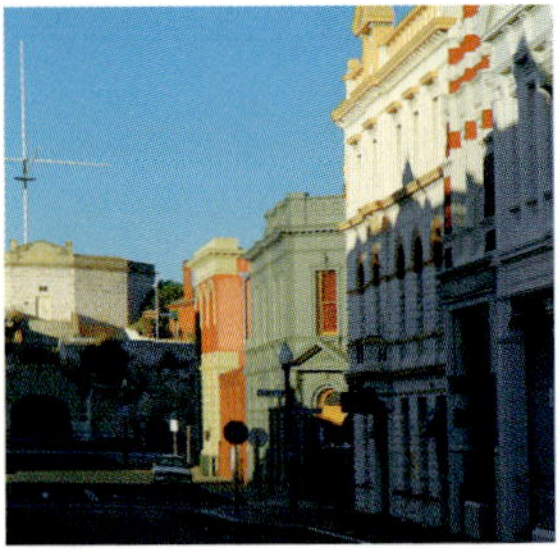

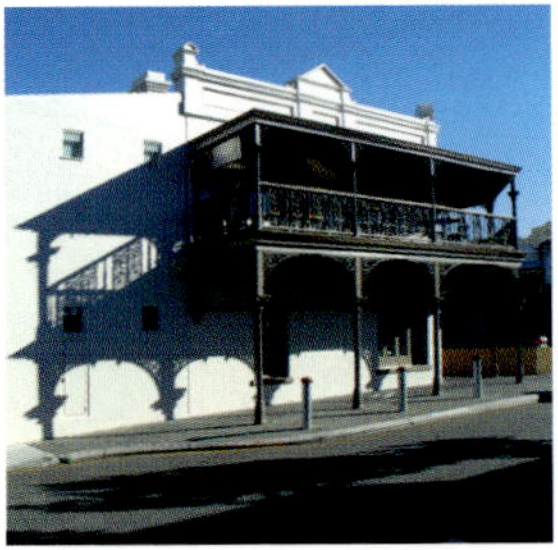

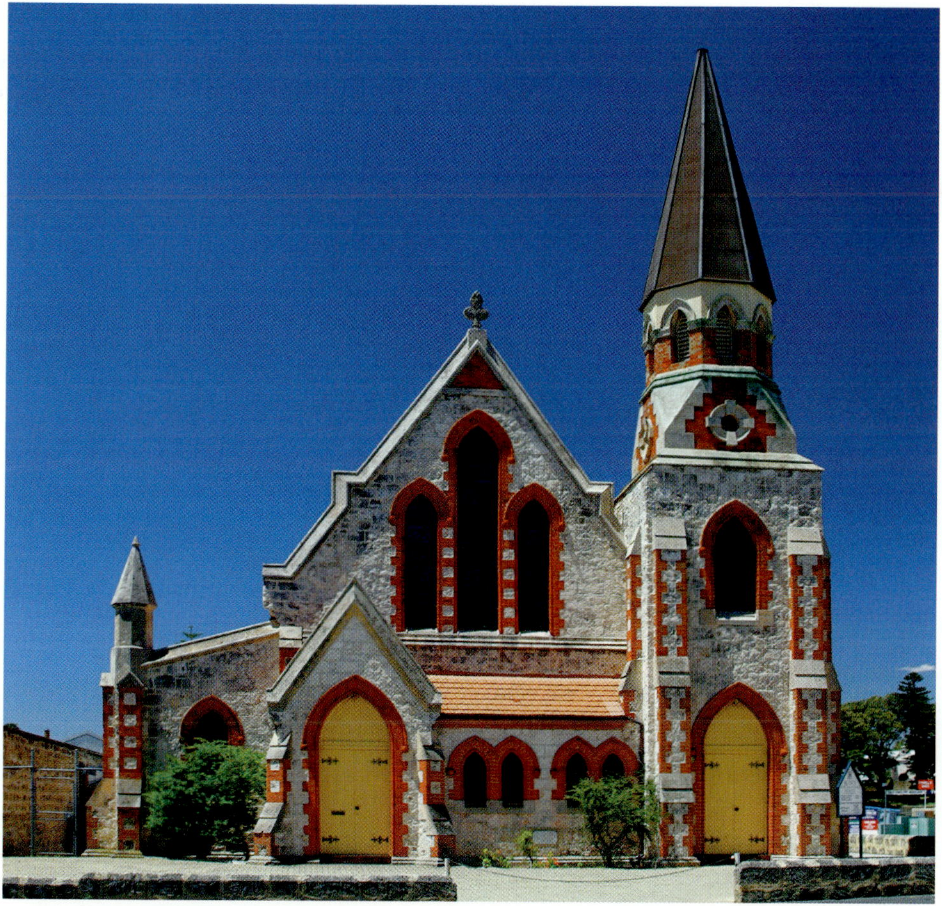

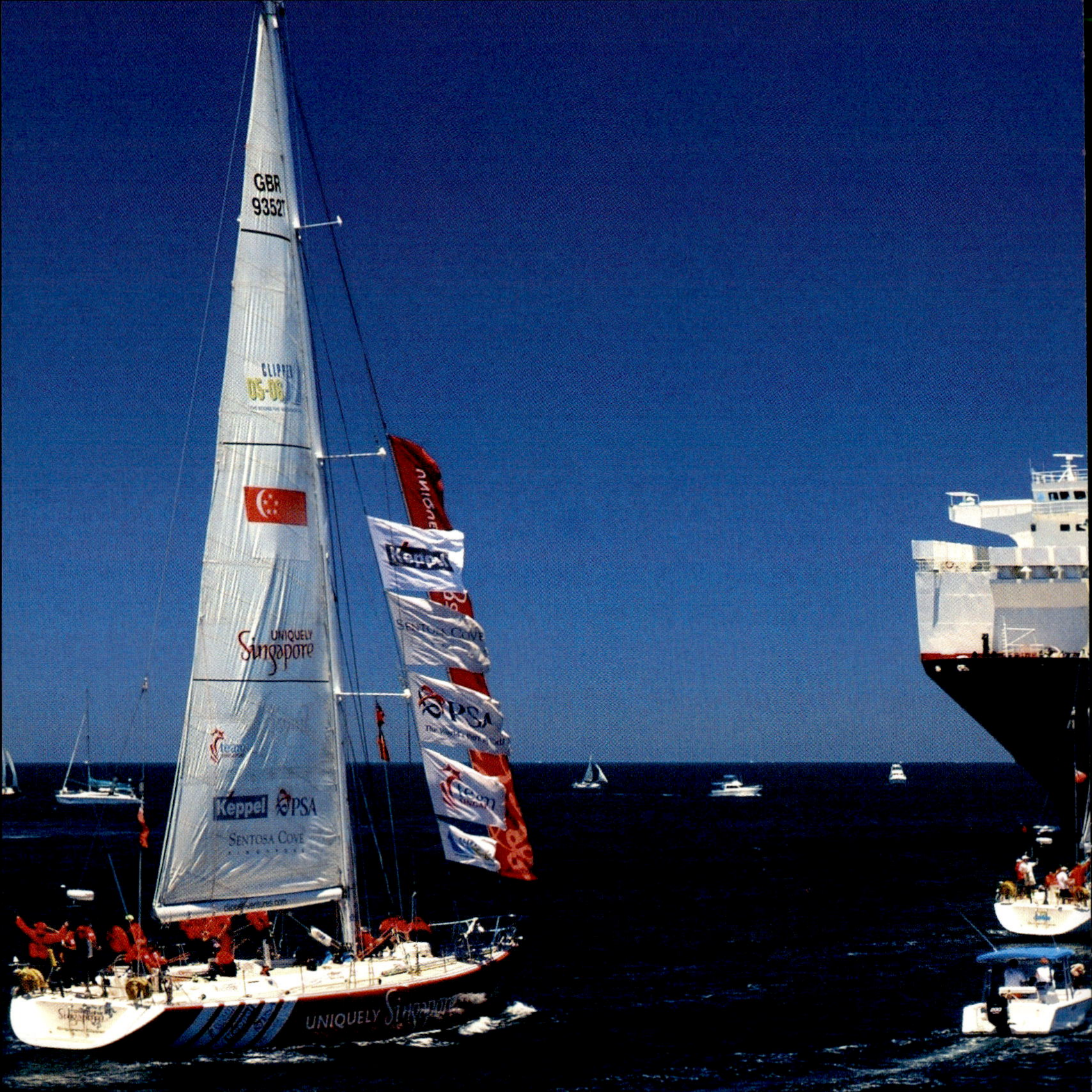
GBR
9352T
CLIPPER
05-06
UNIQUELY
Singapore
Keppel
PSA
SENTOSA COVE
Keppel
PSA
SENTOSA COVE
UNIQUELY Singapore

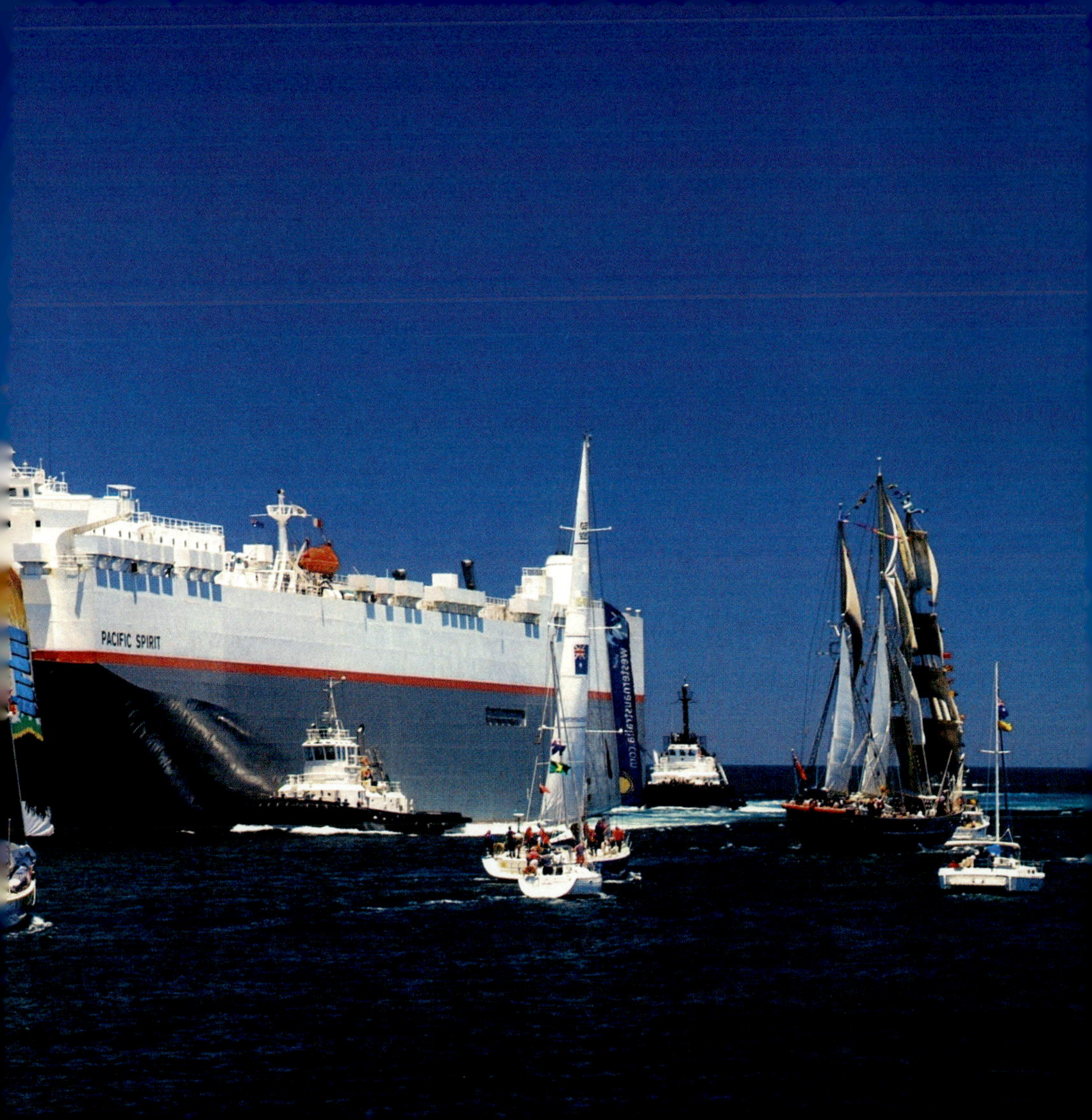
PACIFIC SPIRIT

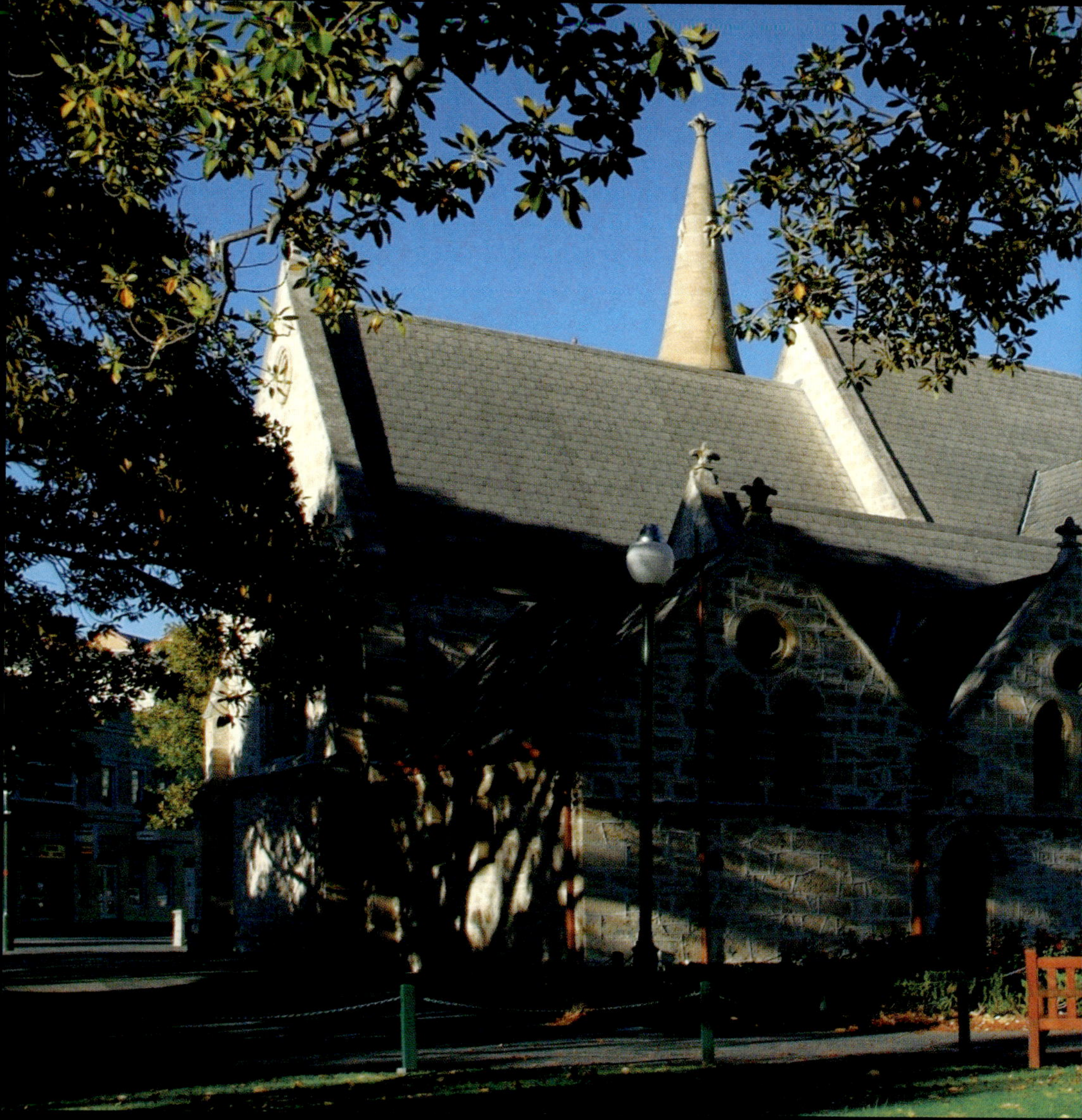

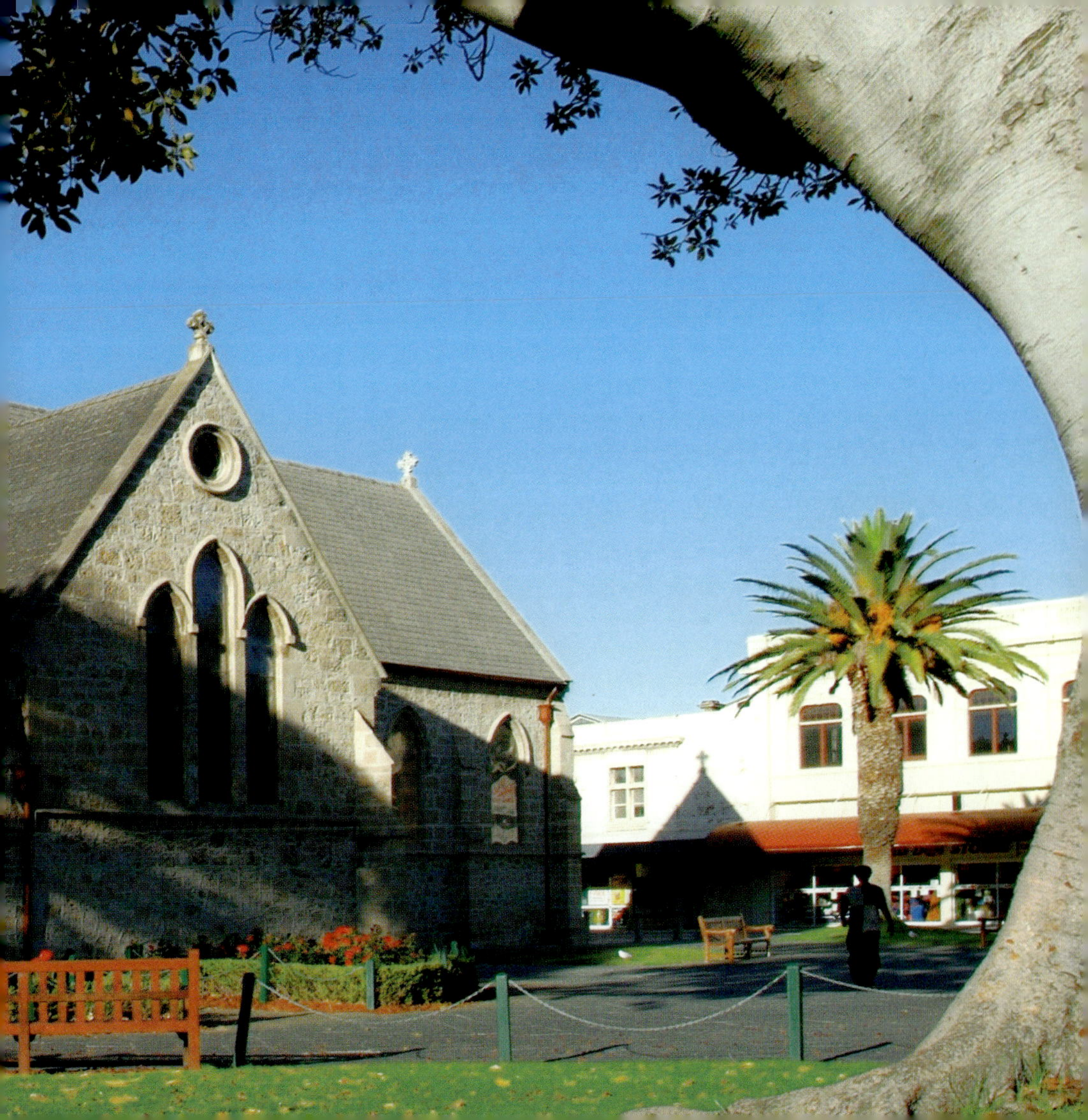

previous page. kings square, fremantle

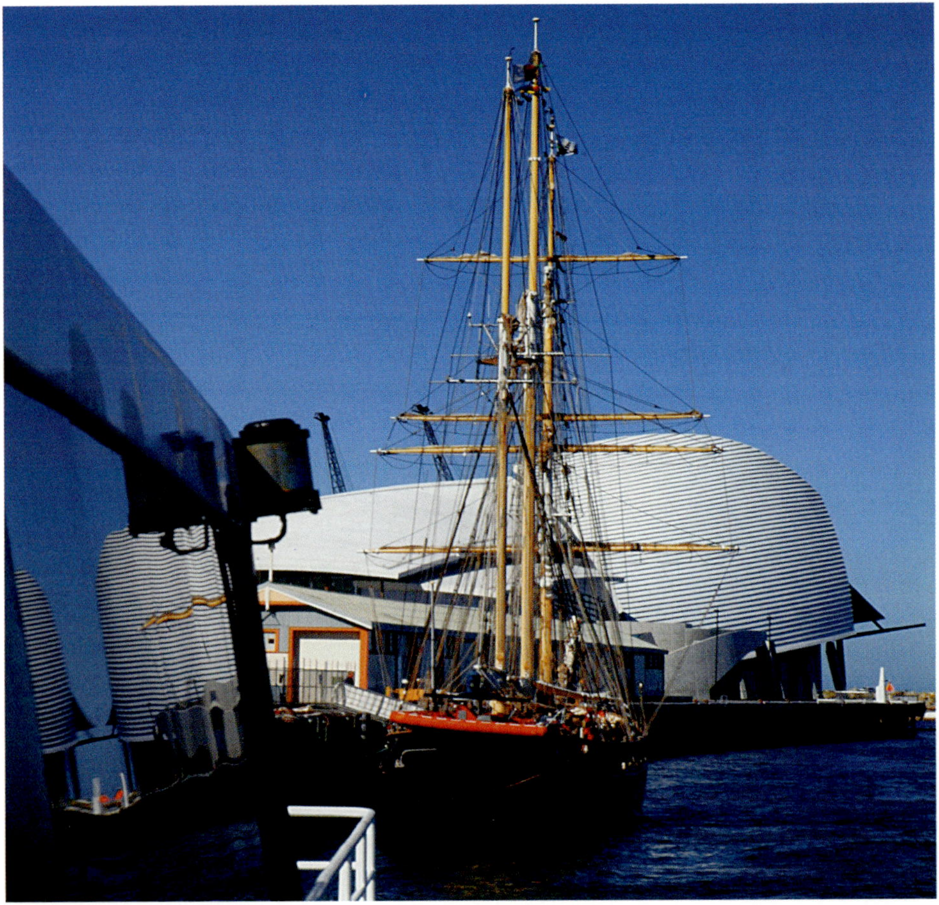

100. victoria quay, fremantle

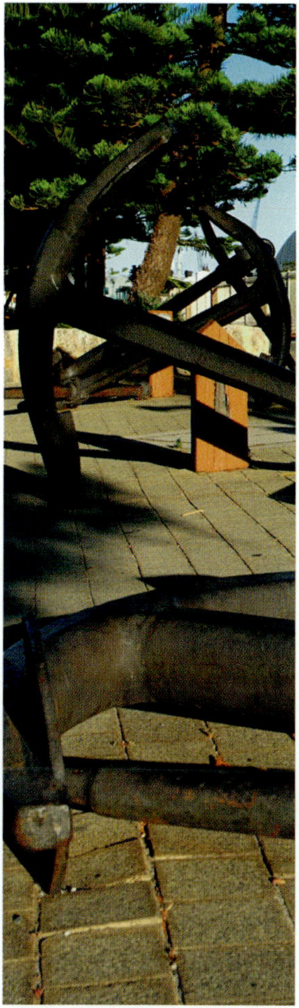

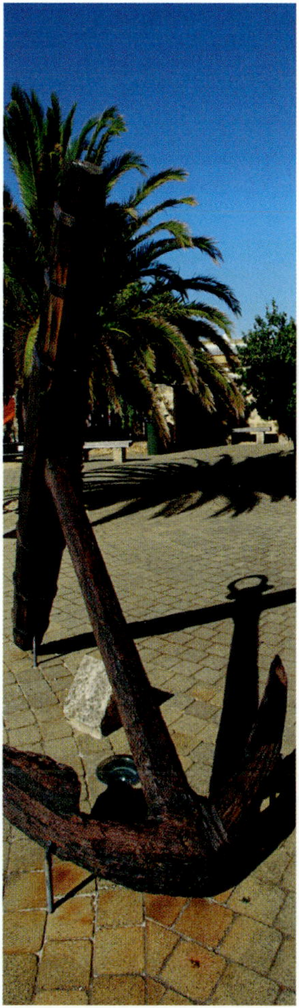

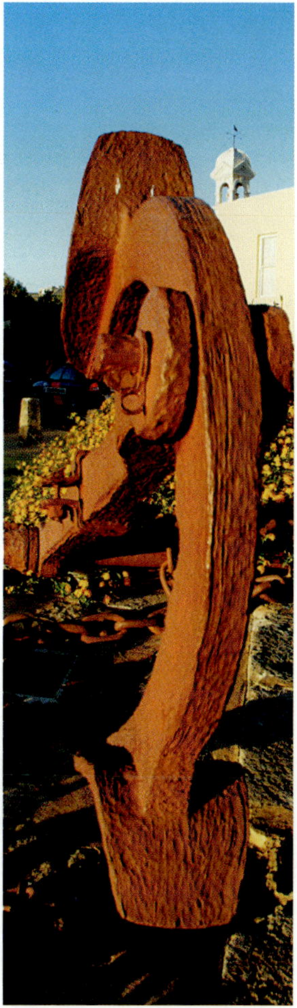

next page. victoria quay, fremantle

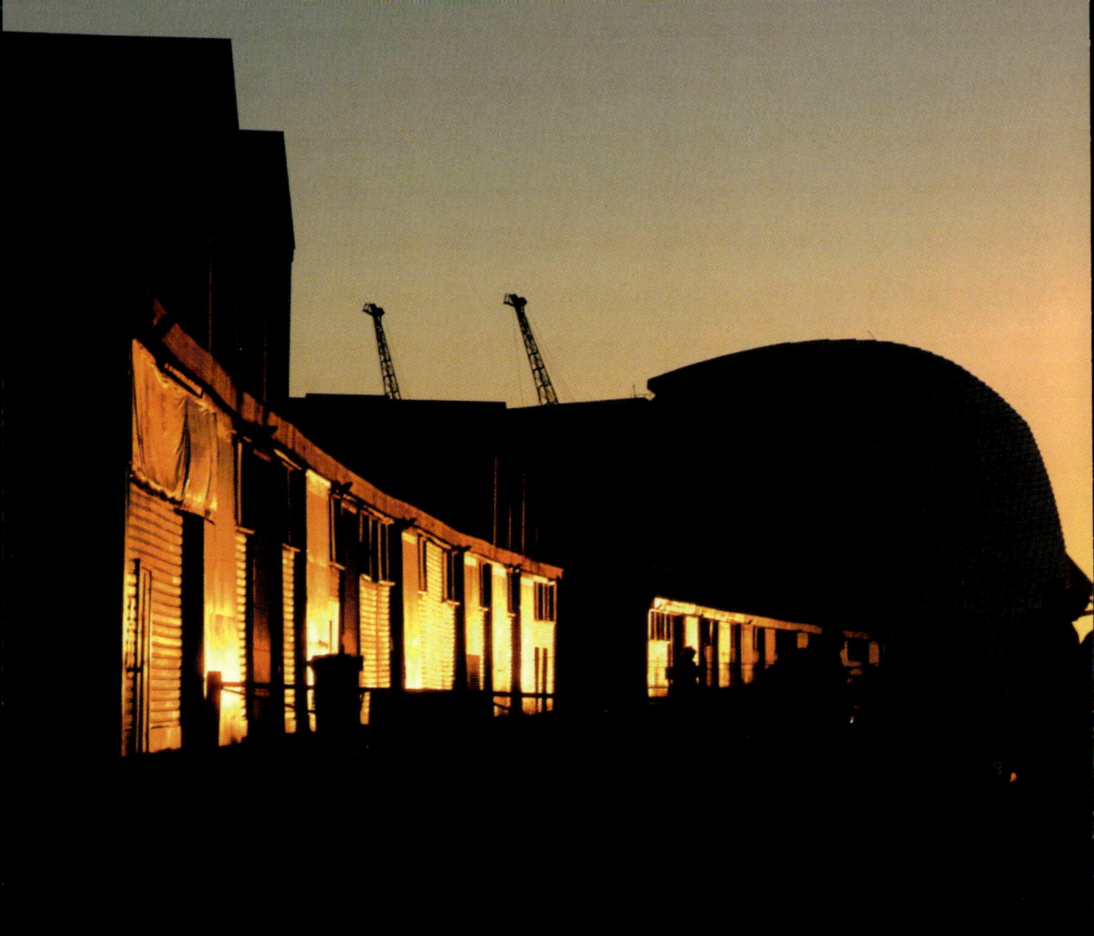

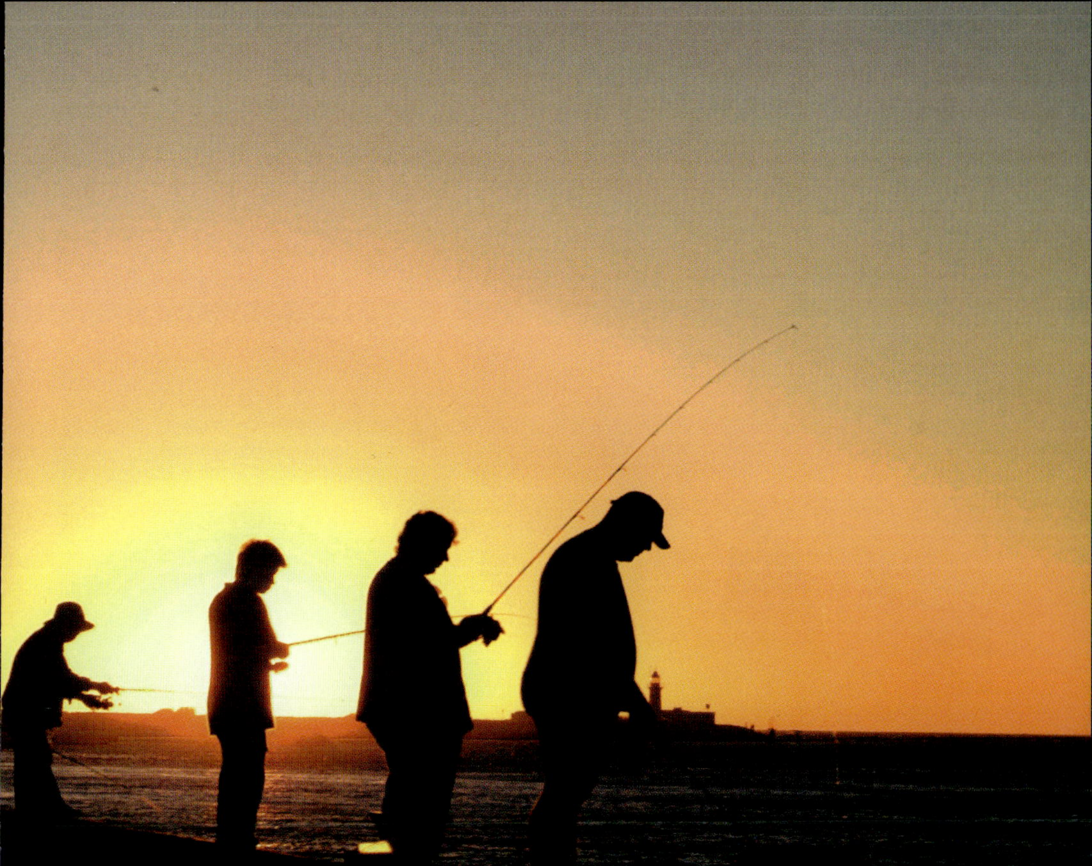

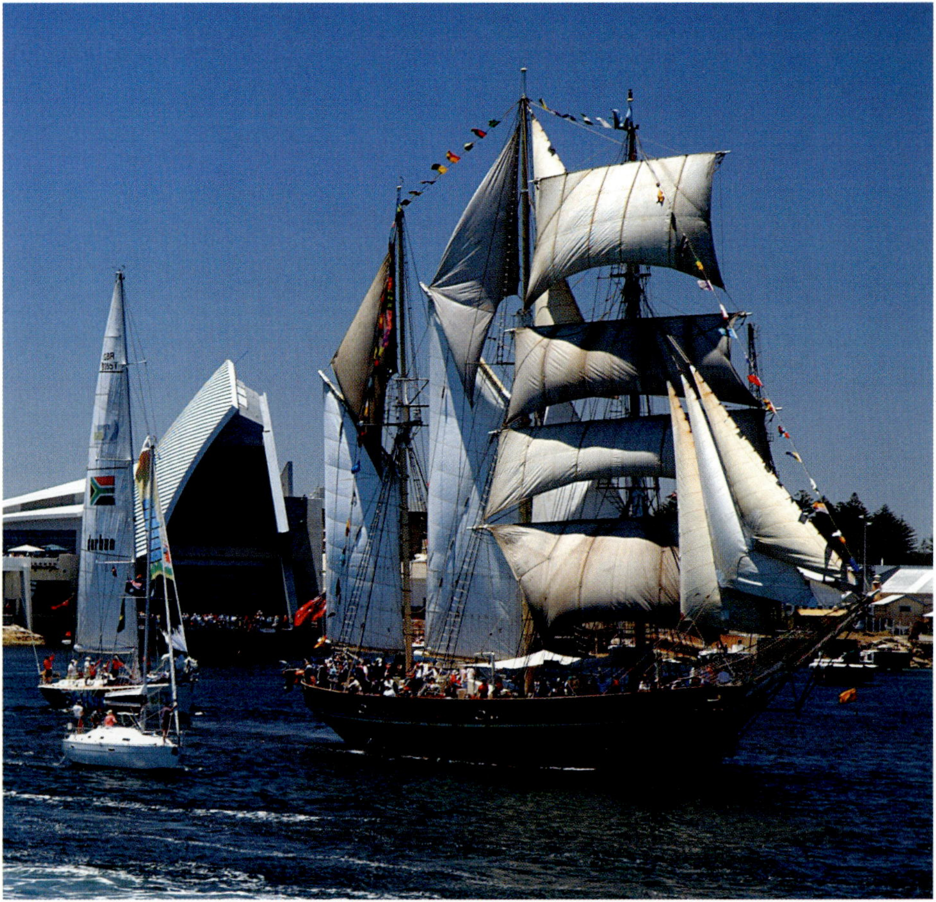
GBR

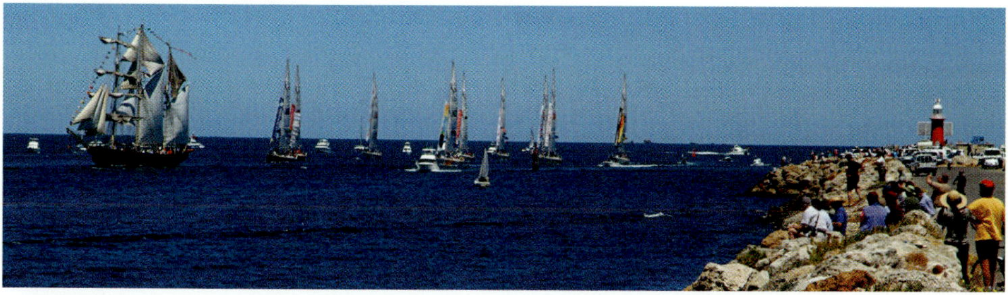

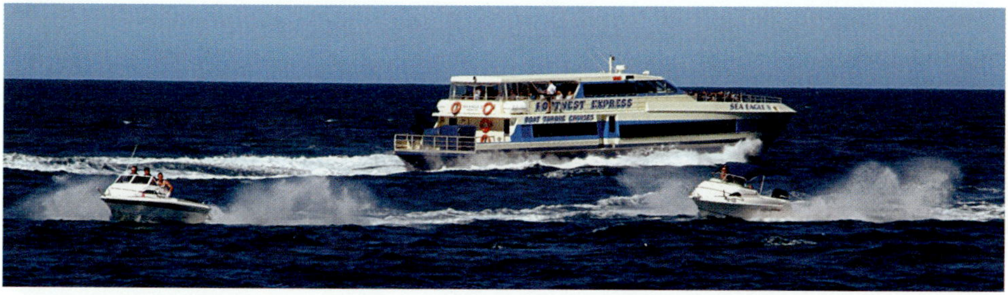
EXPRESS
CRUISES

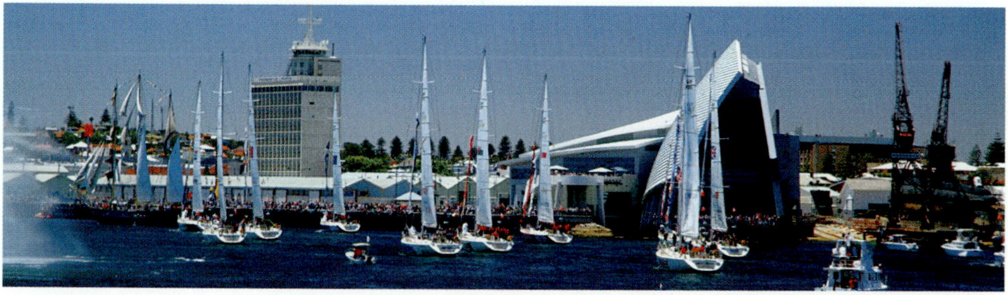

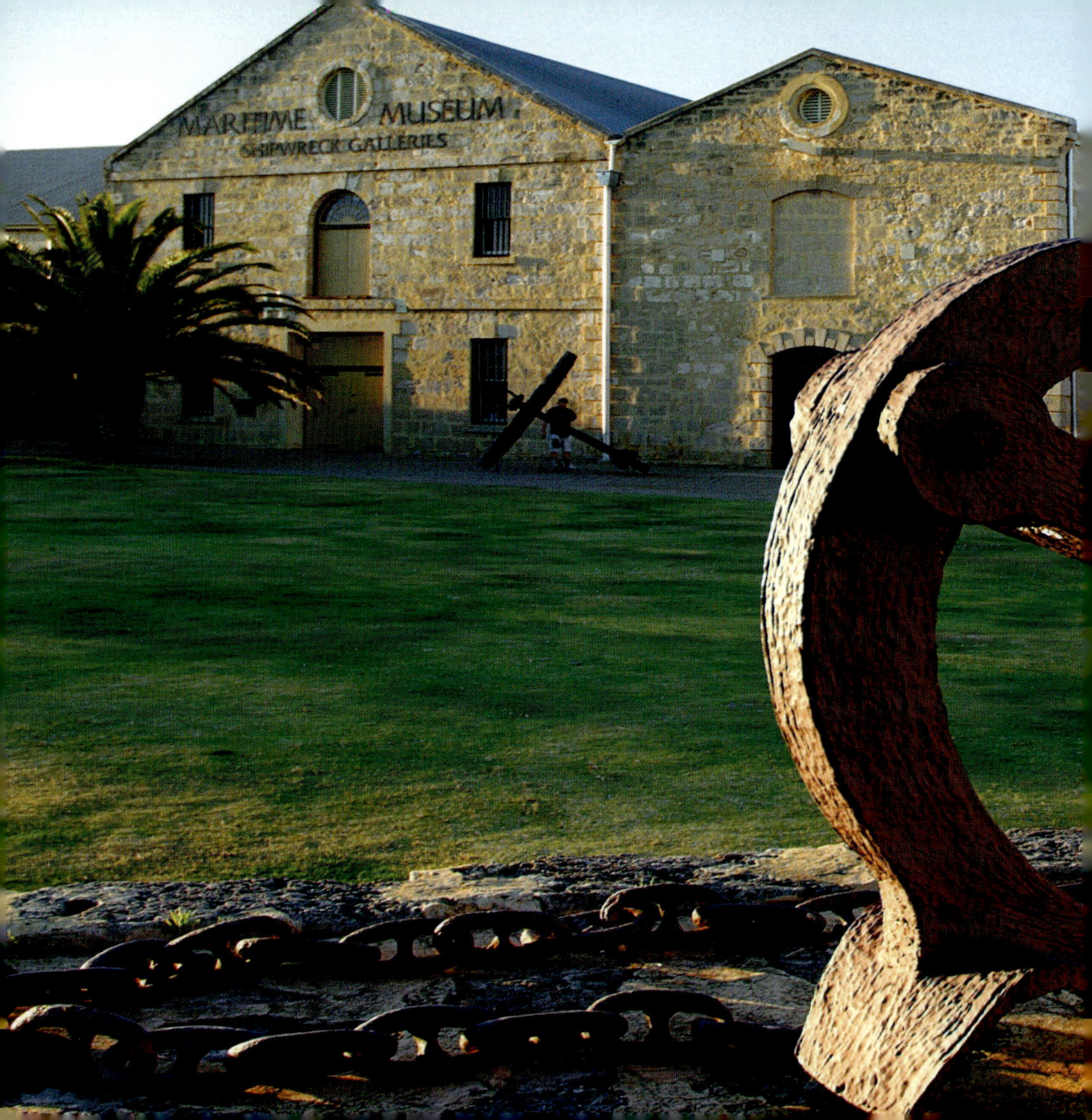
MARITIME MUSEUM
SHIPWRECK GALLERIES

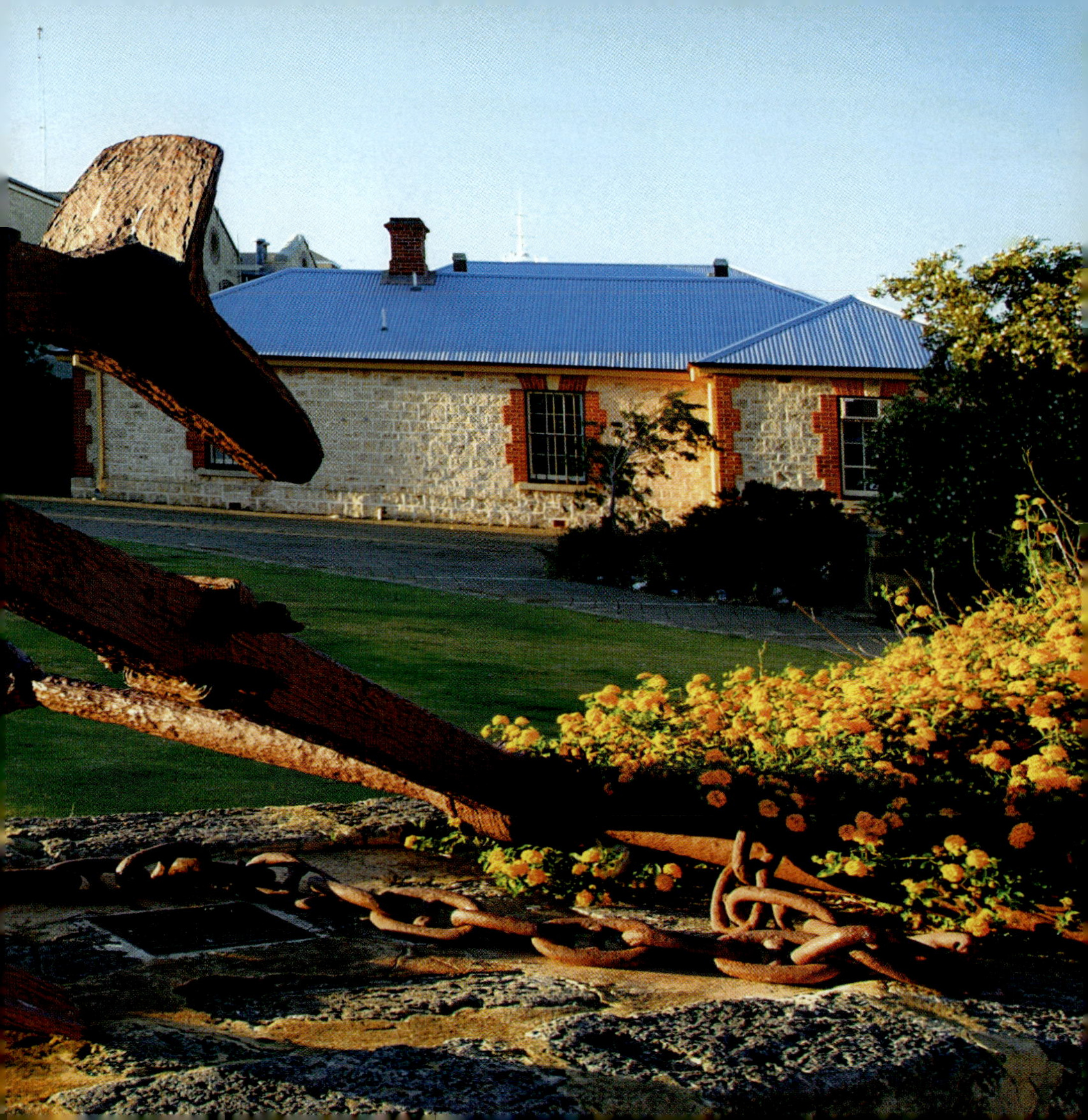

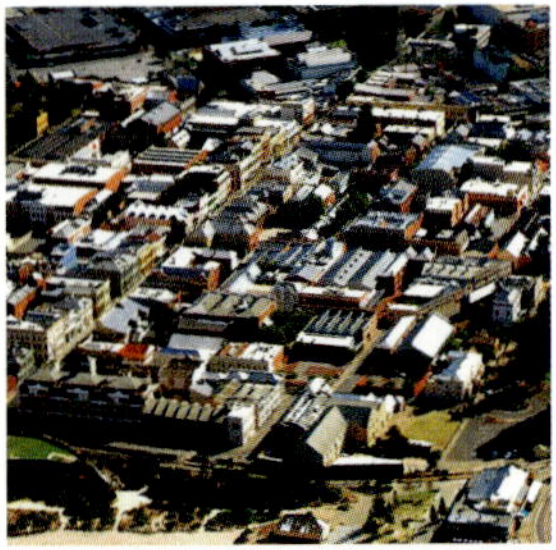
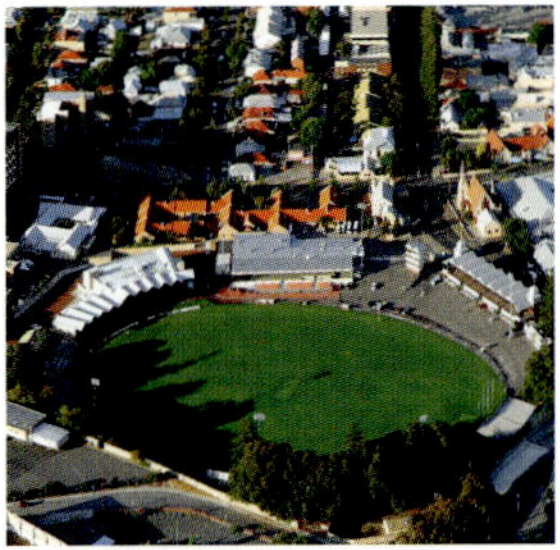
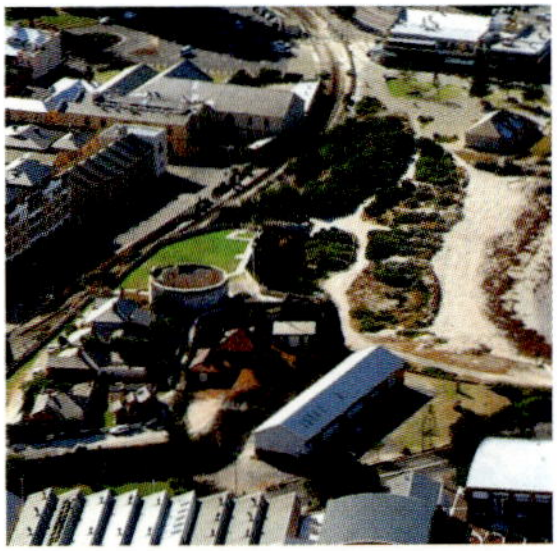
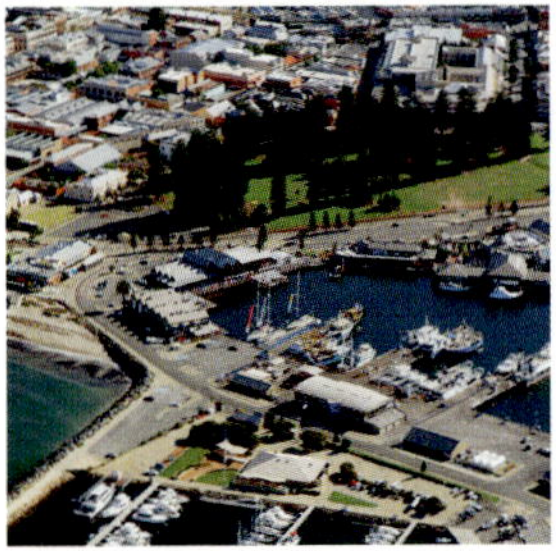
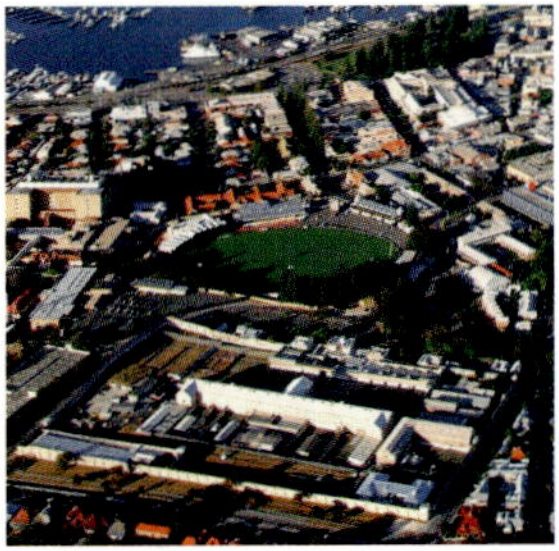
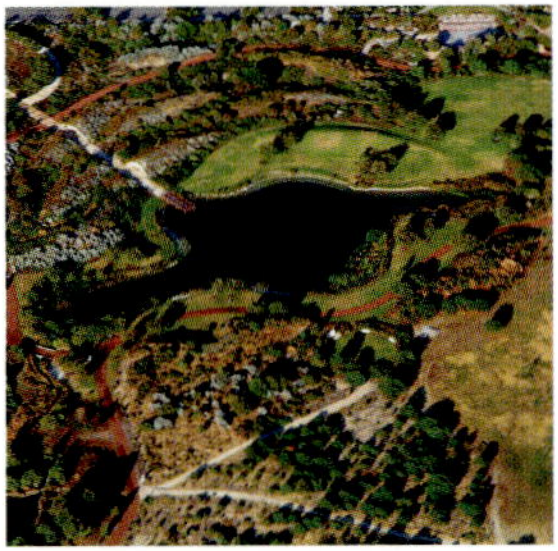
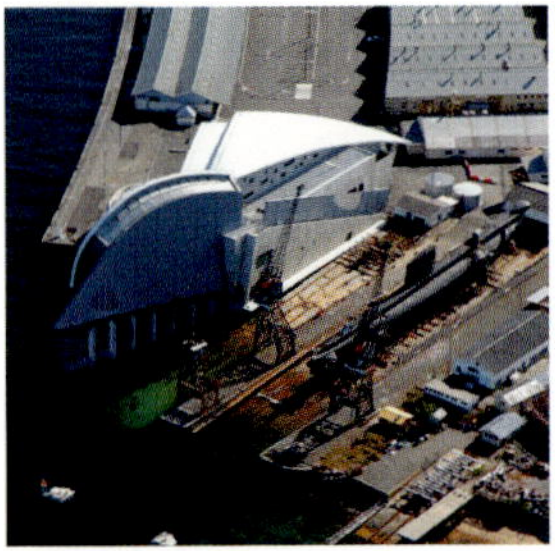
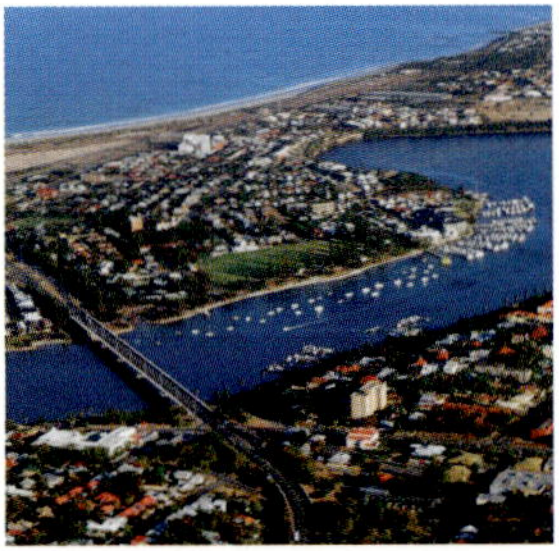
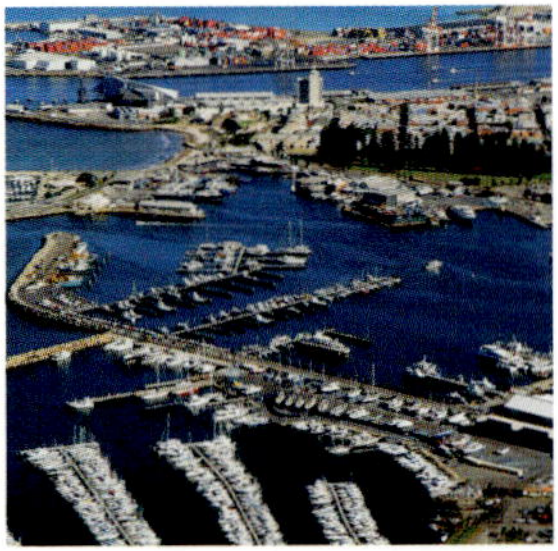

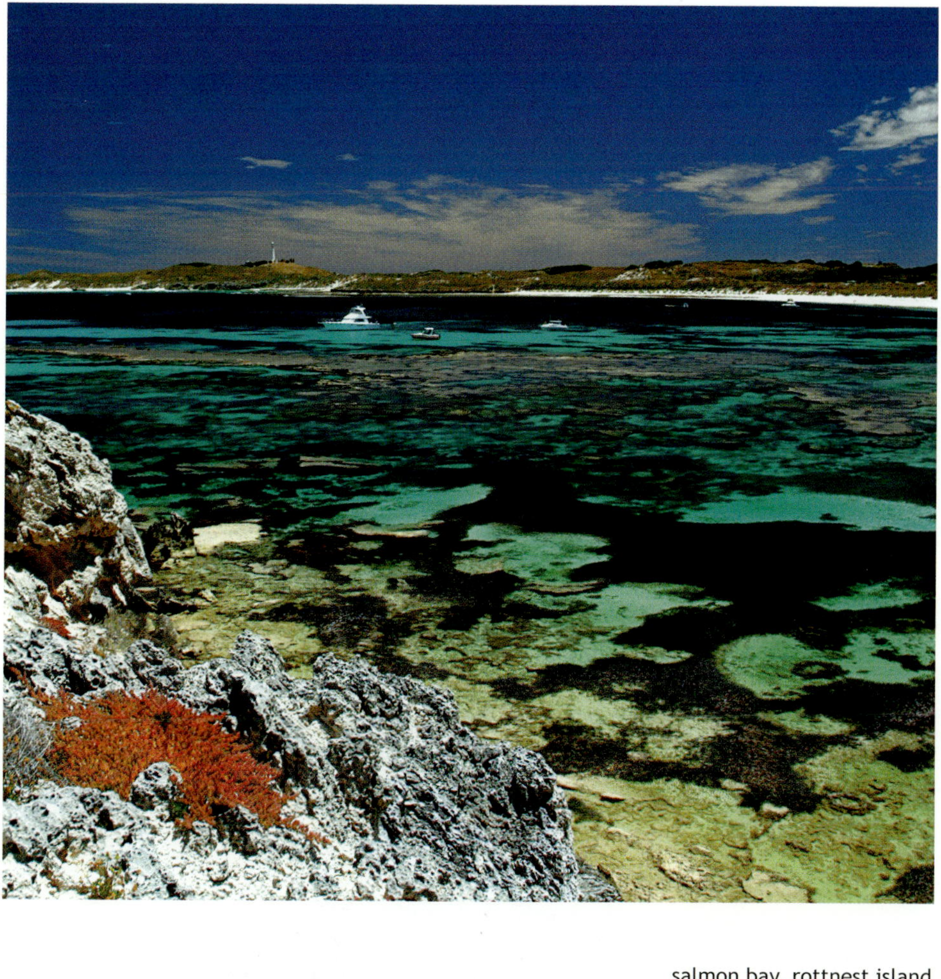

next page. rottnest island

salmon bay, rottnest island

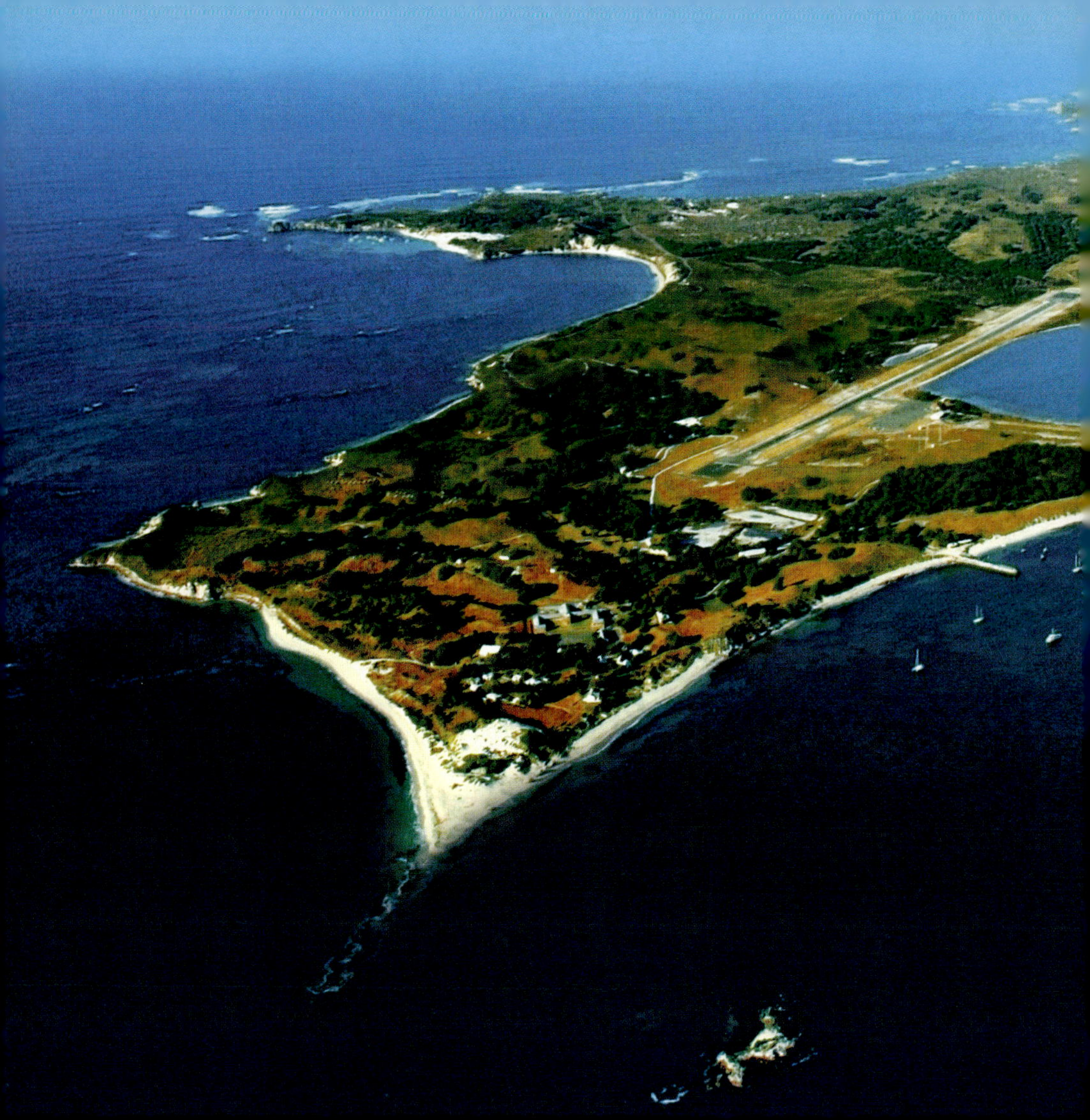

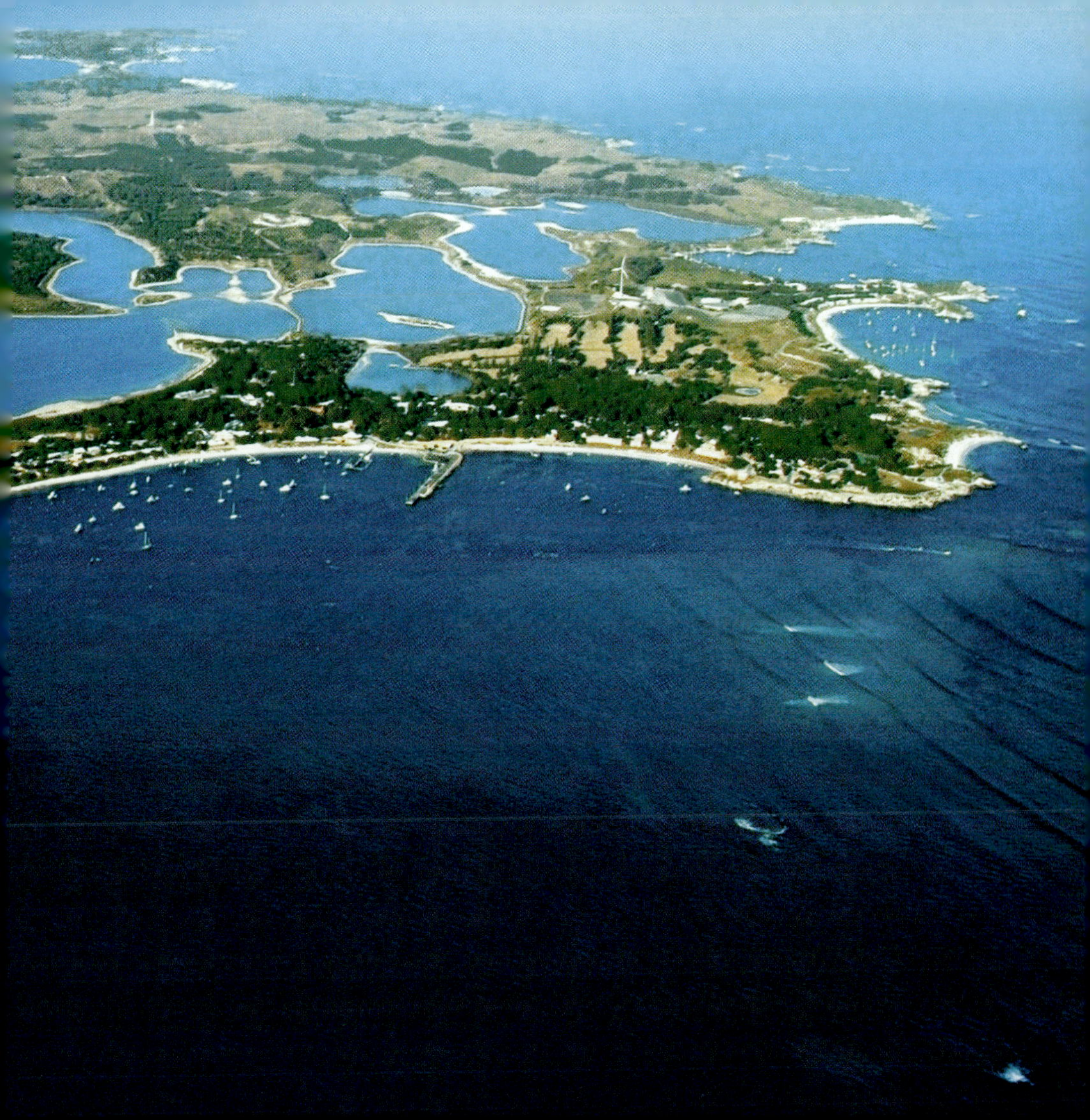

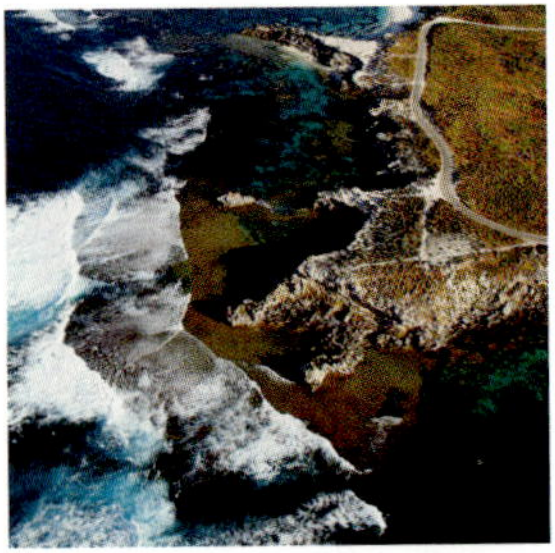
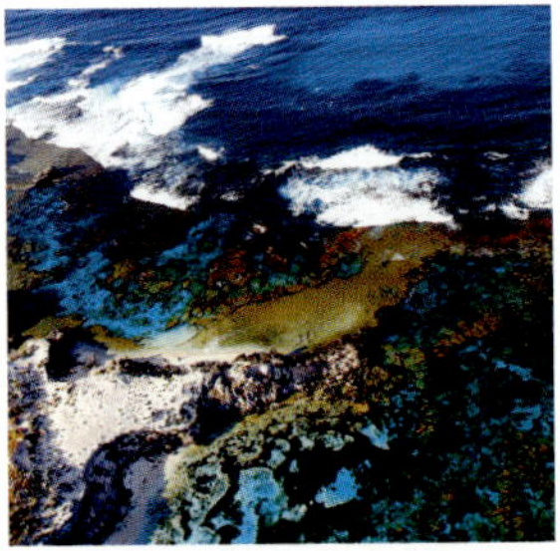
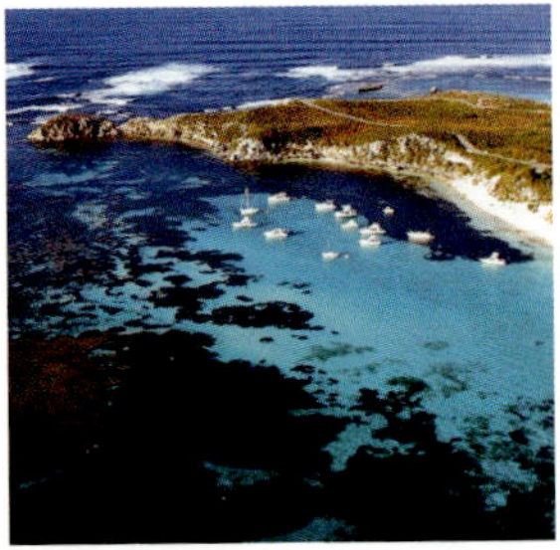
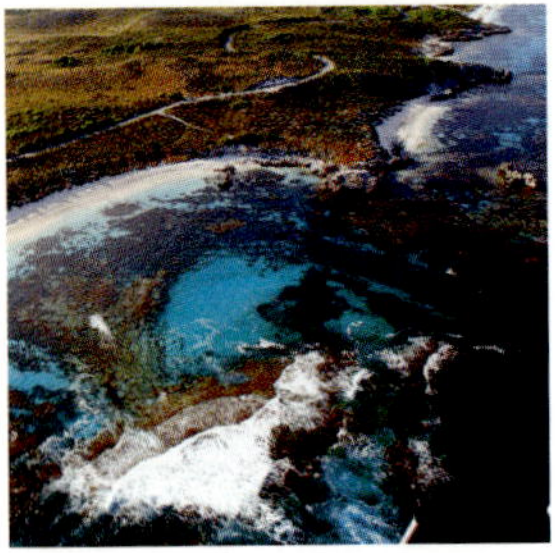
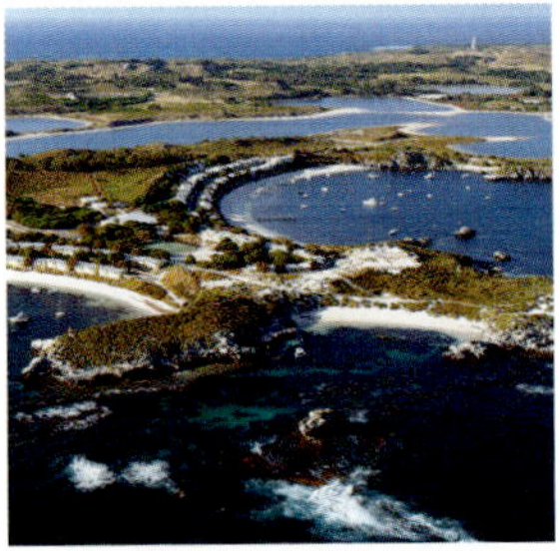
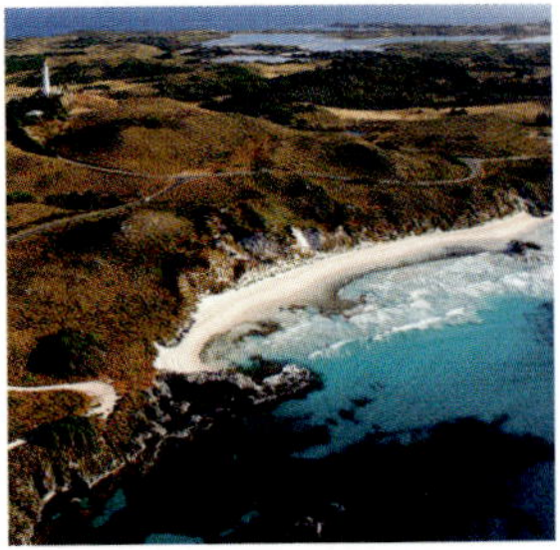
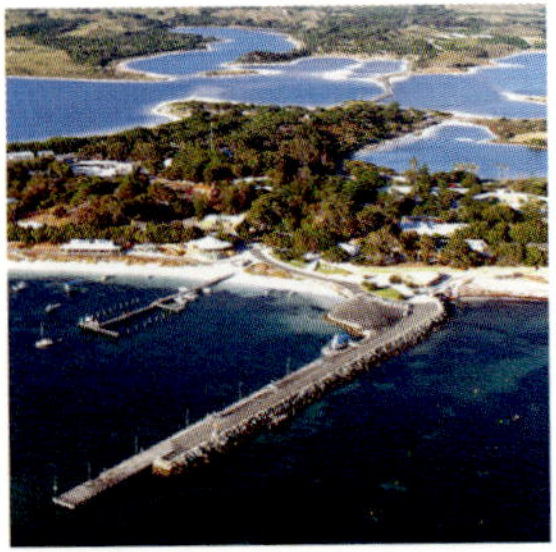
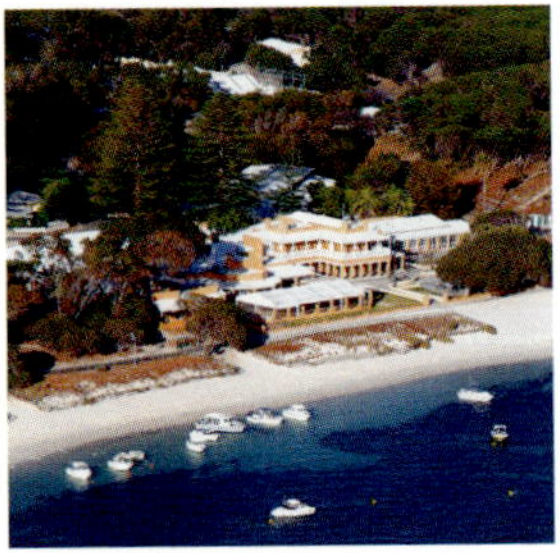
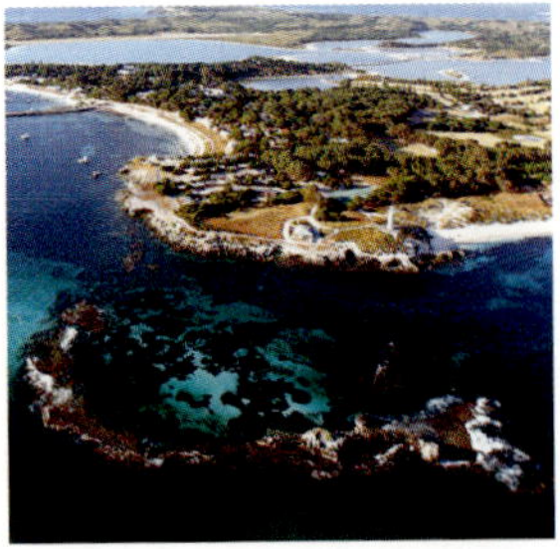

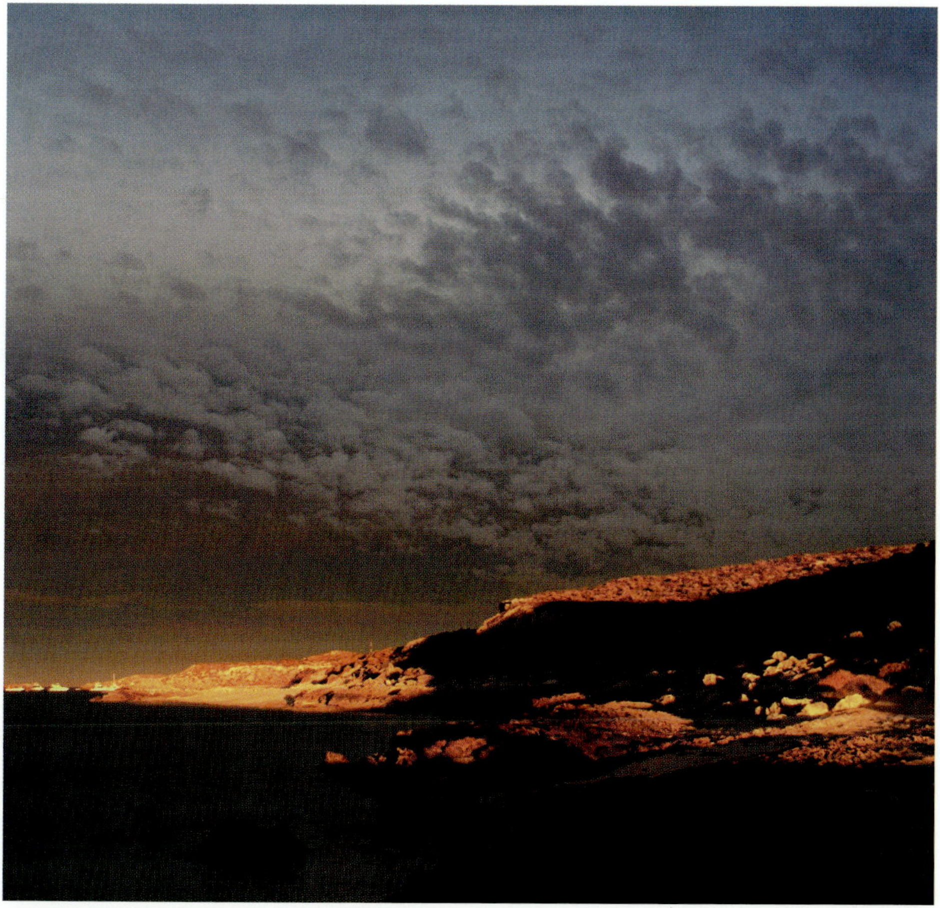

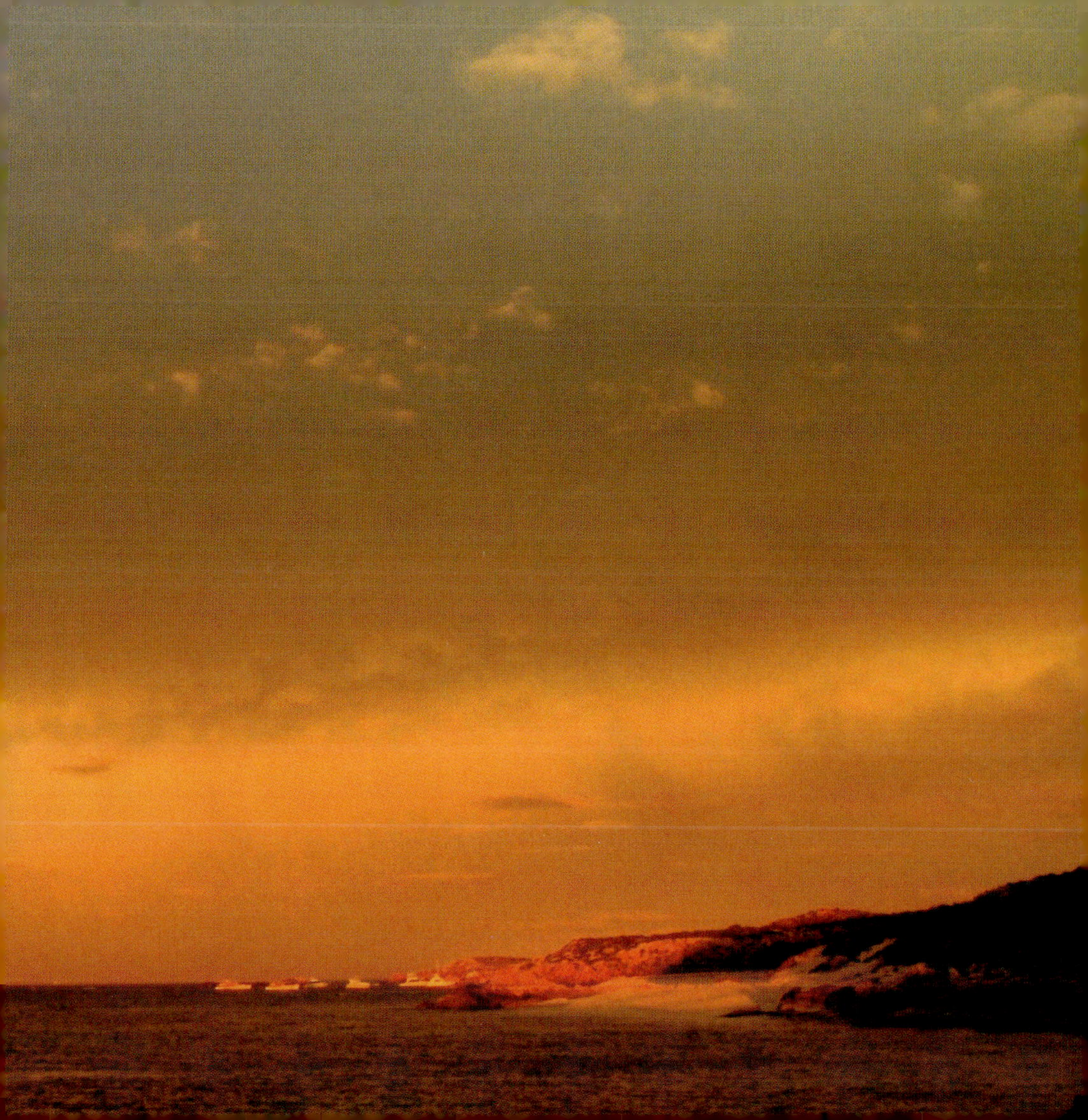

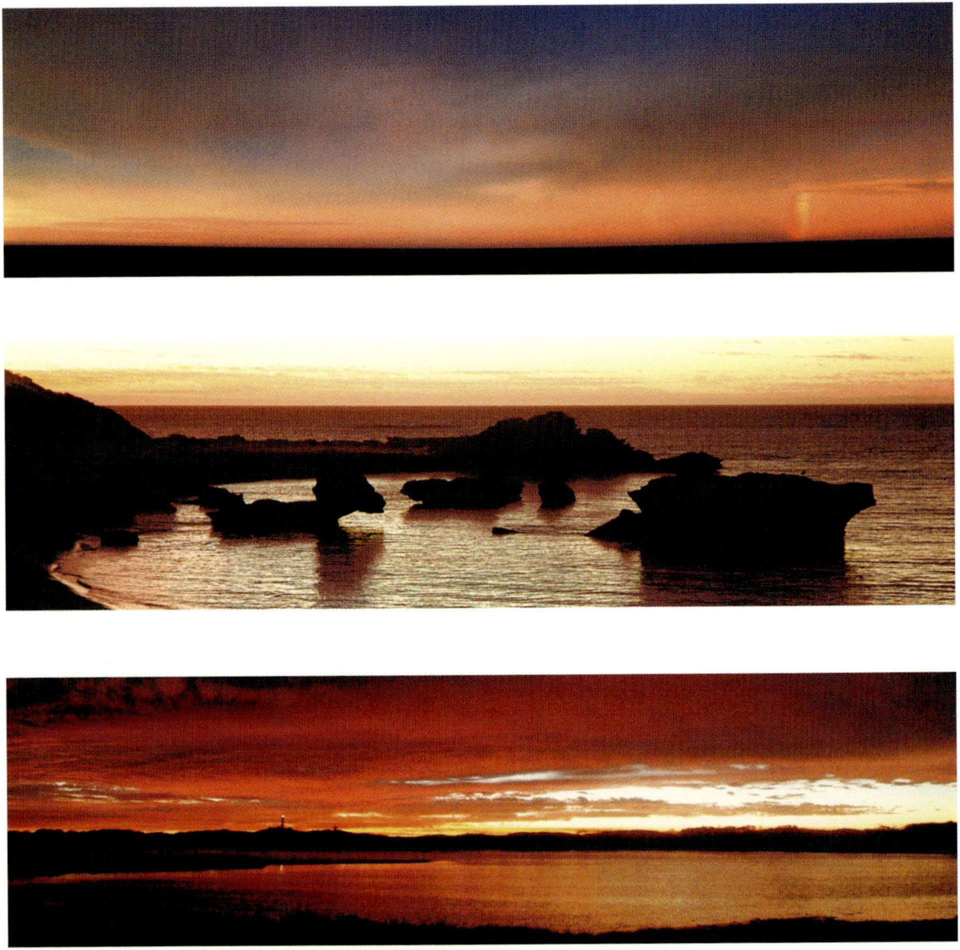

116. a. indian ocean b. city of york bay c. lake baghdad

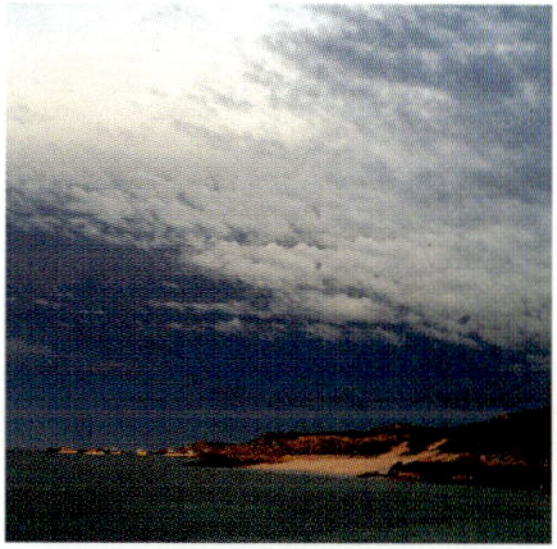
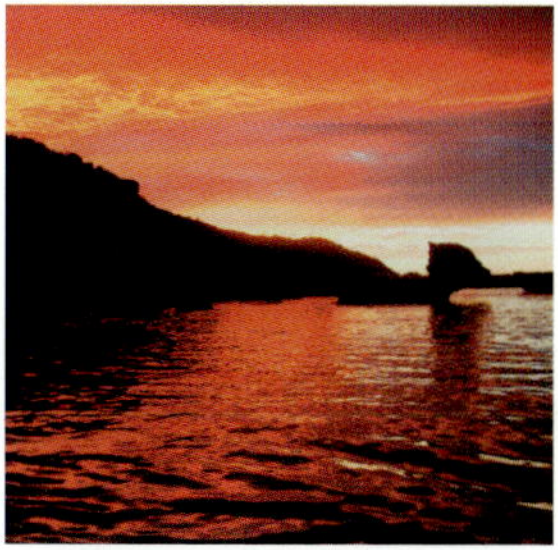
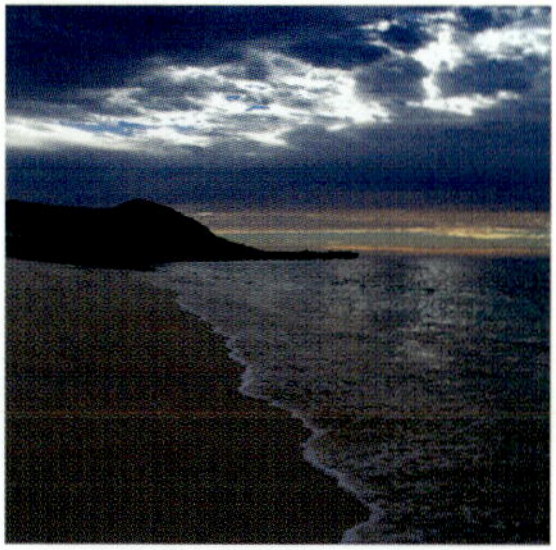
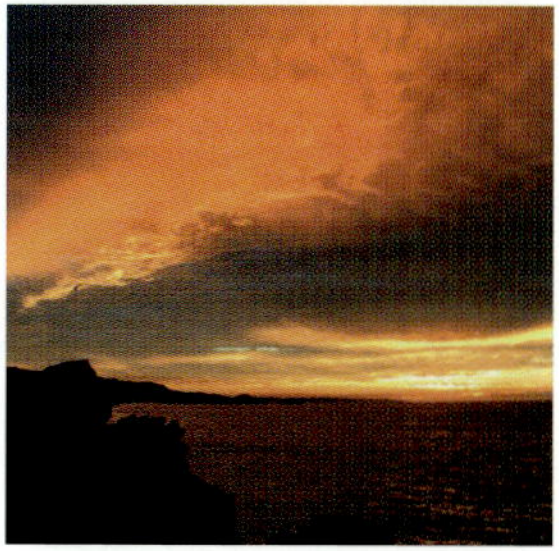
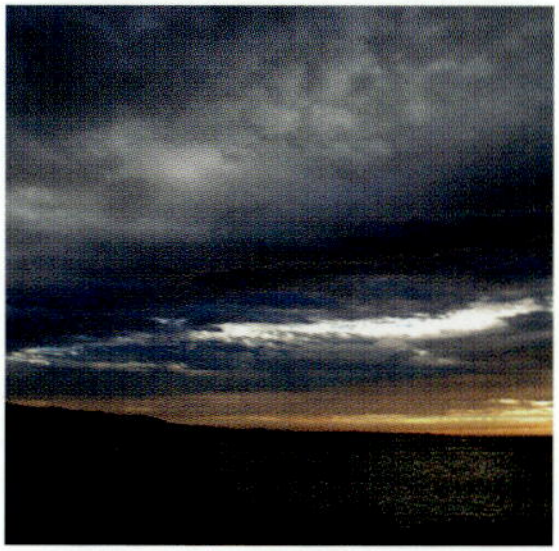
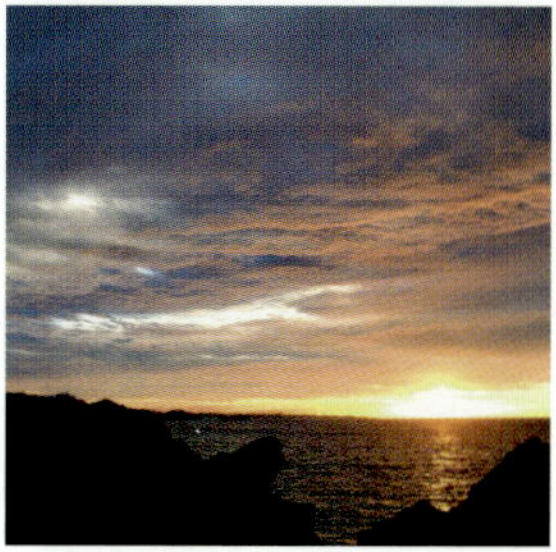
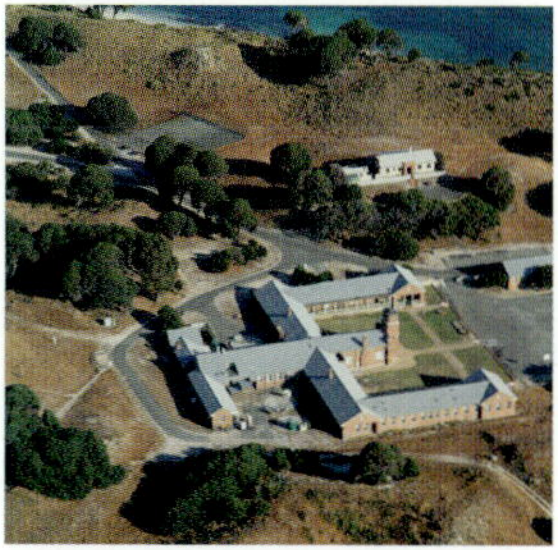
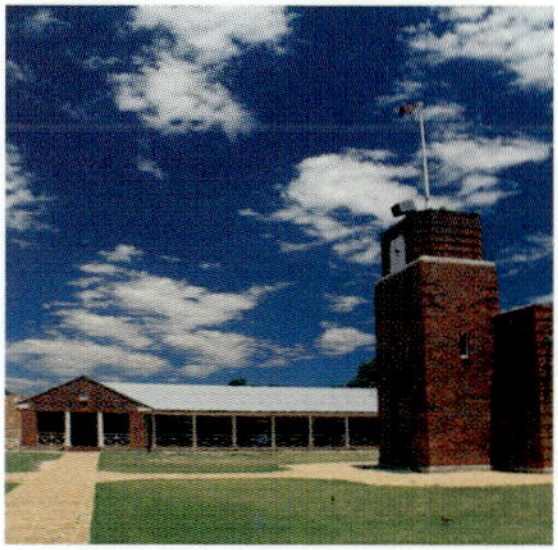
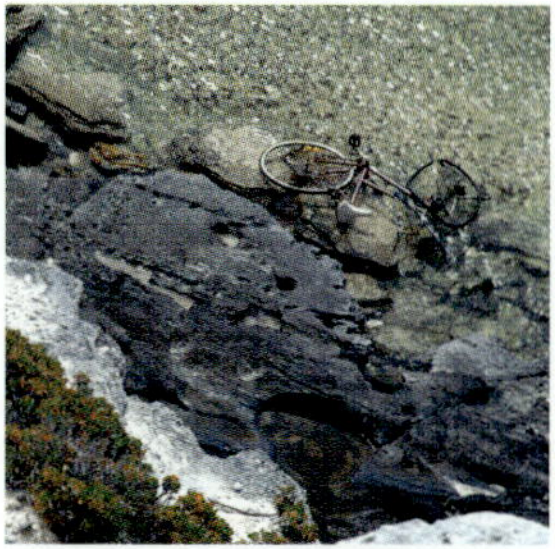

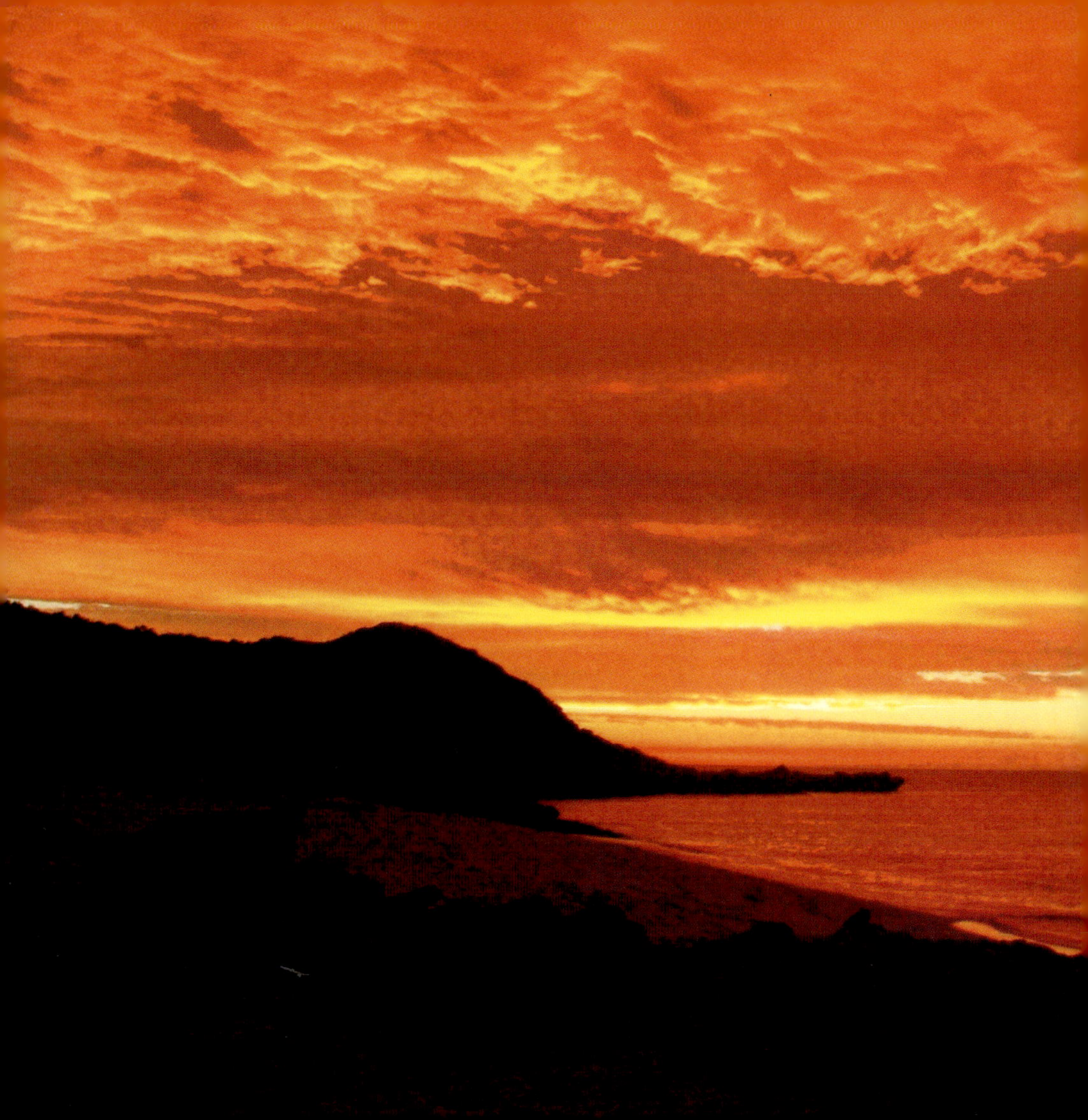

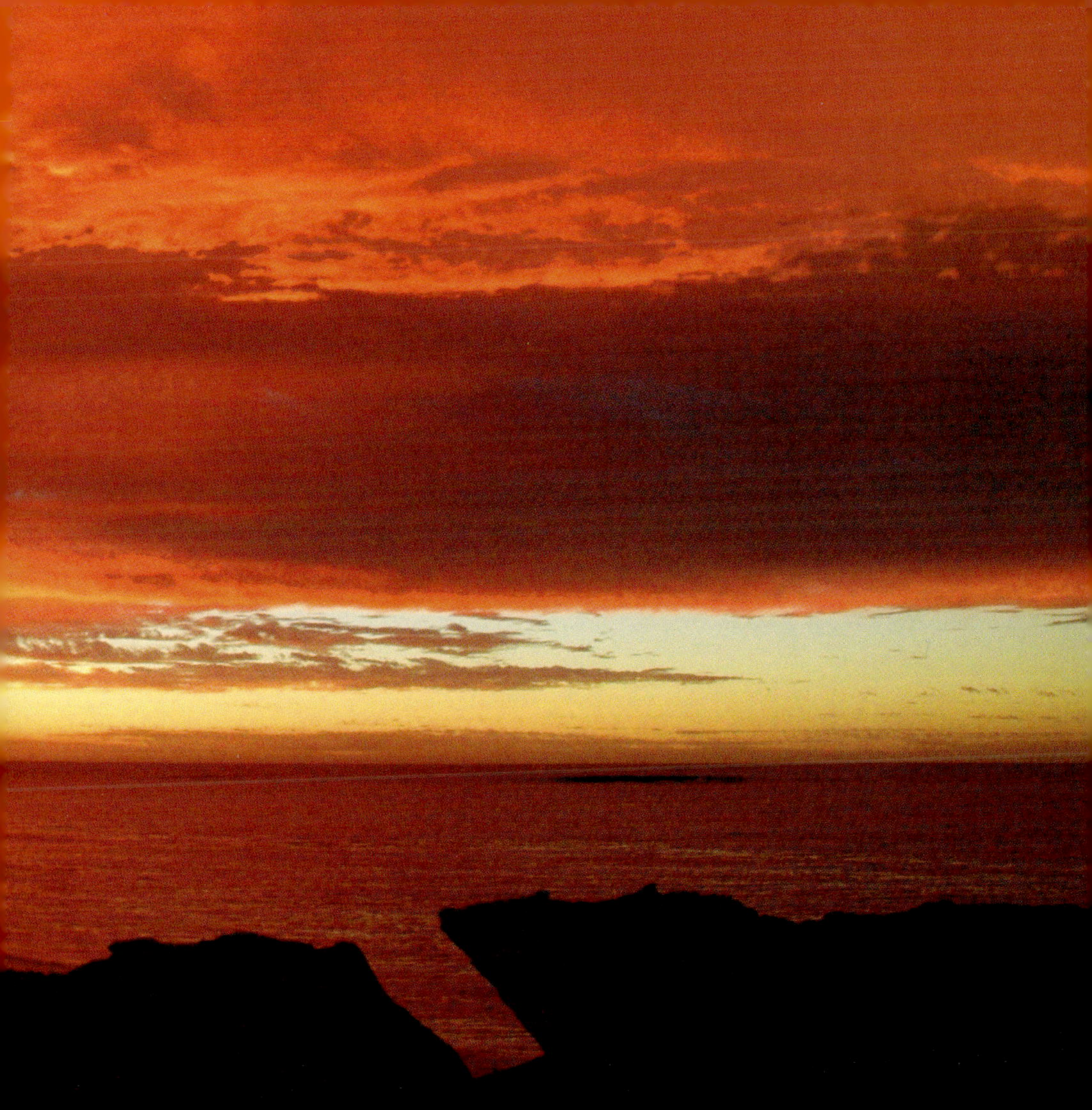

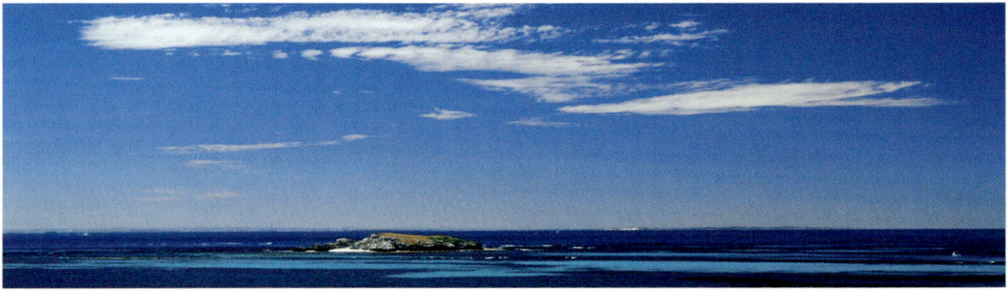

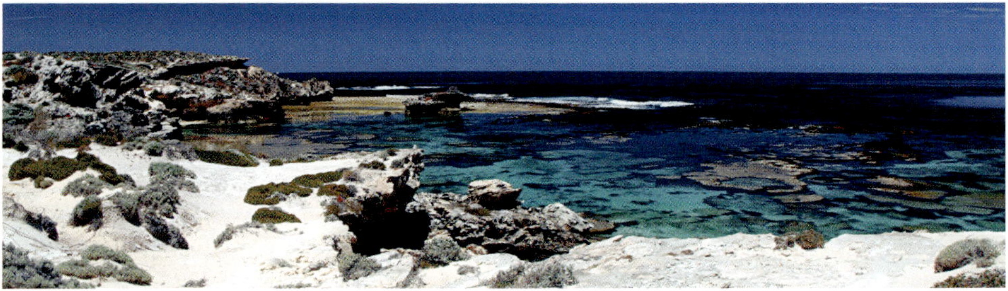

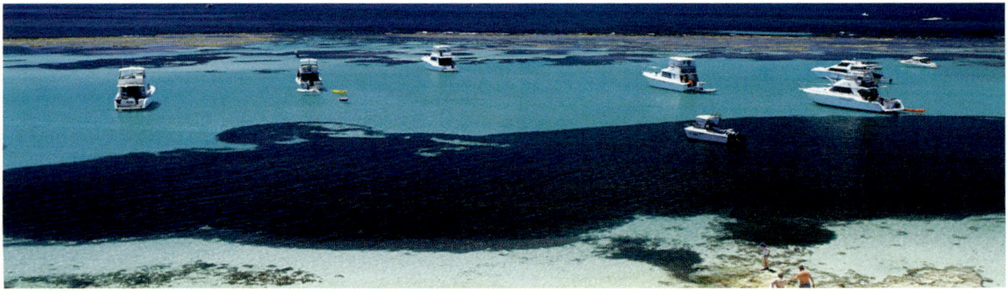

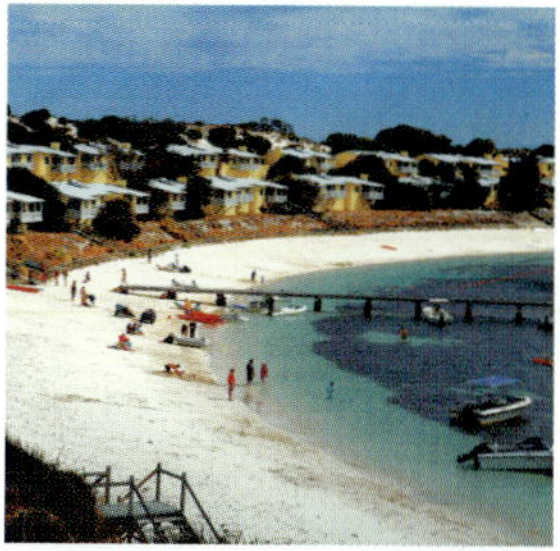

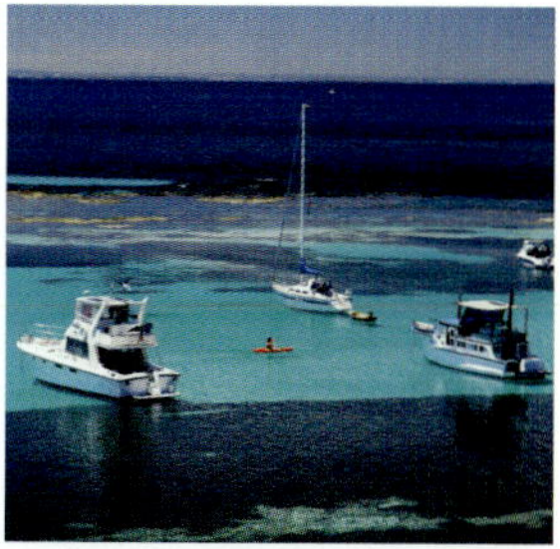

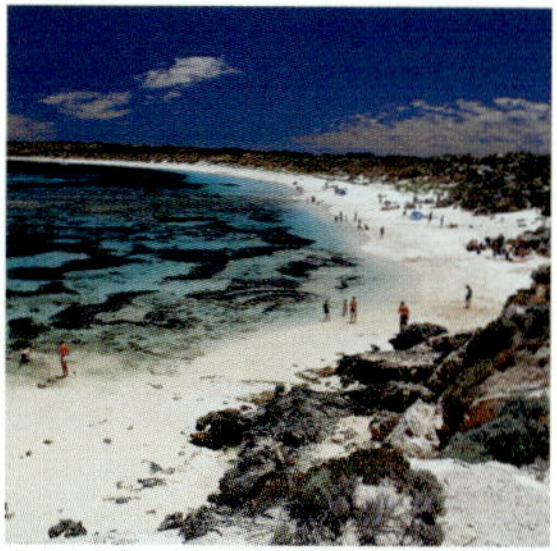

next page. little salmon bay

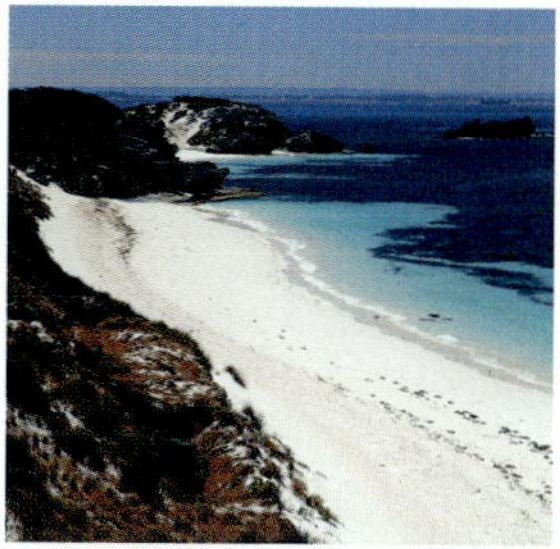

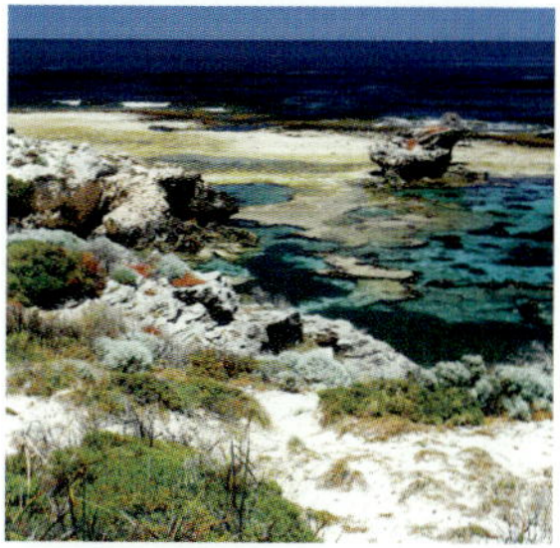

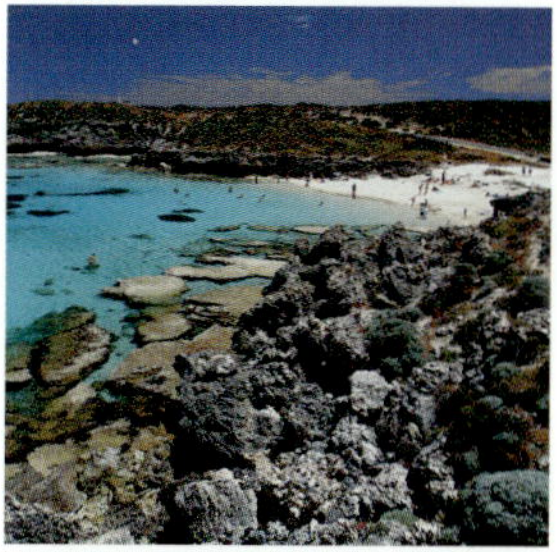

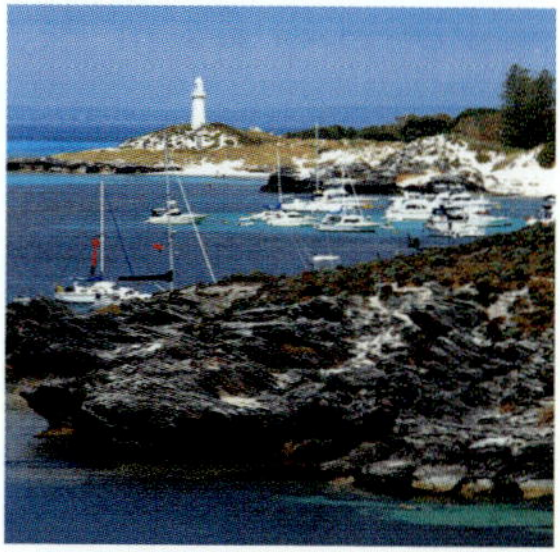

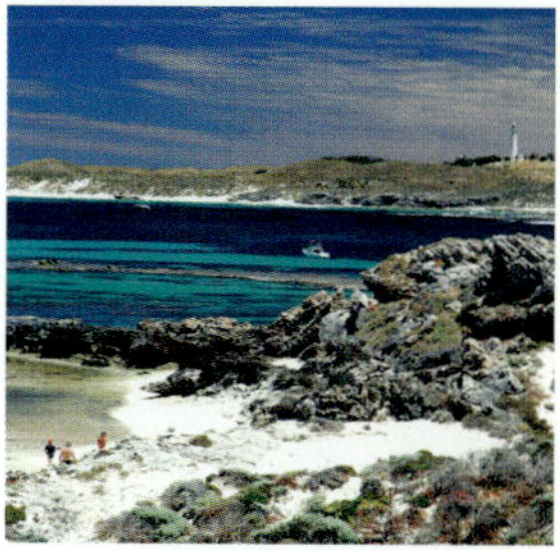

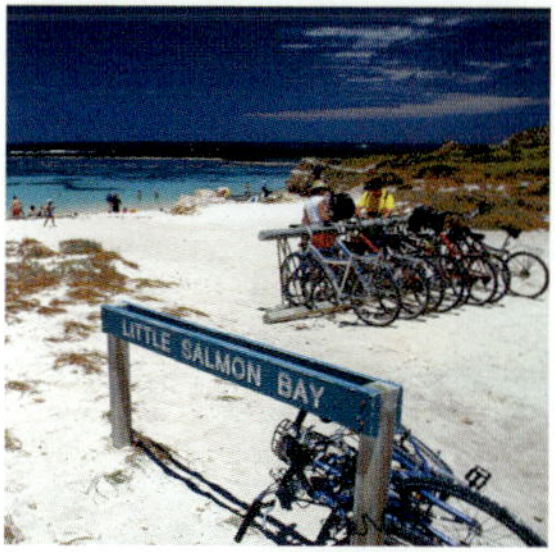

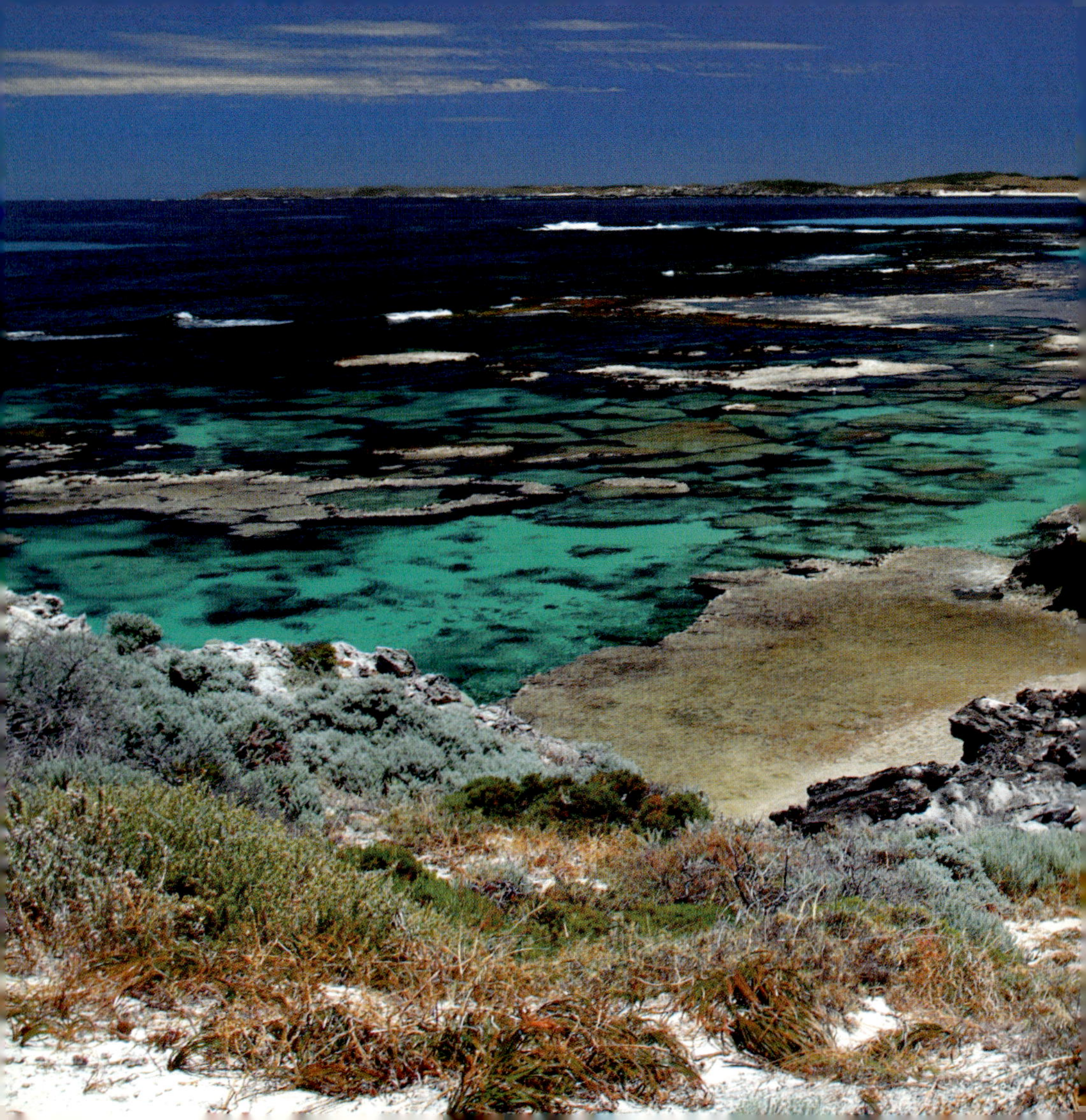

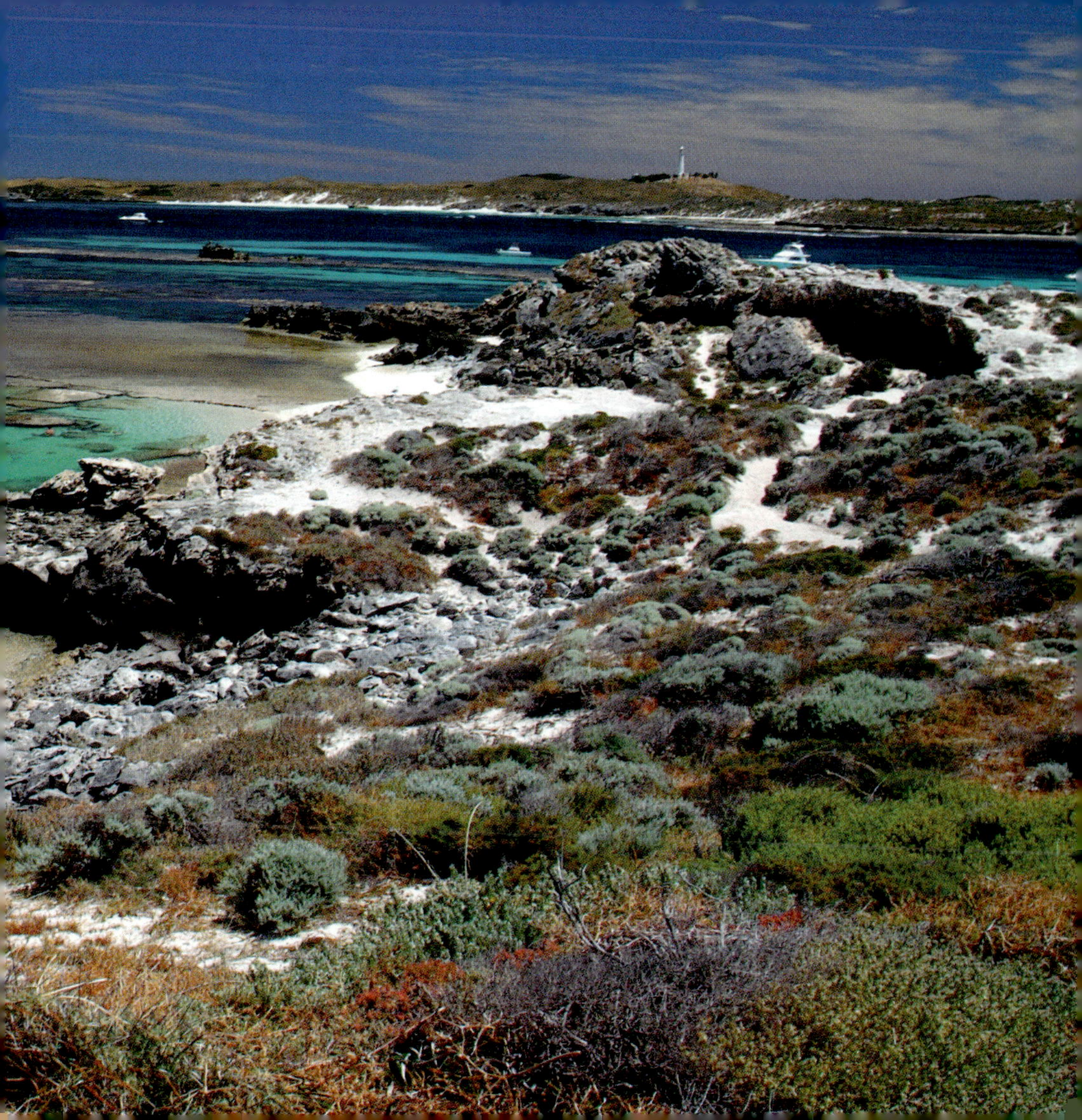

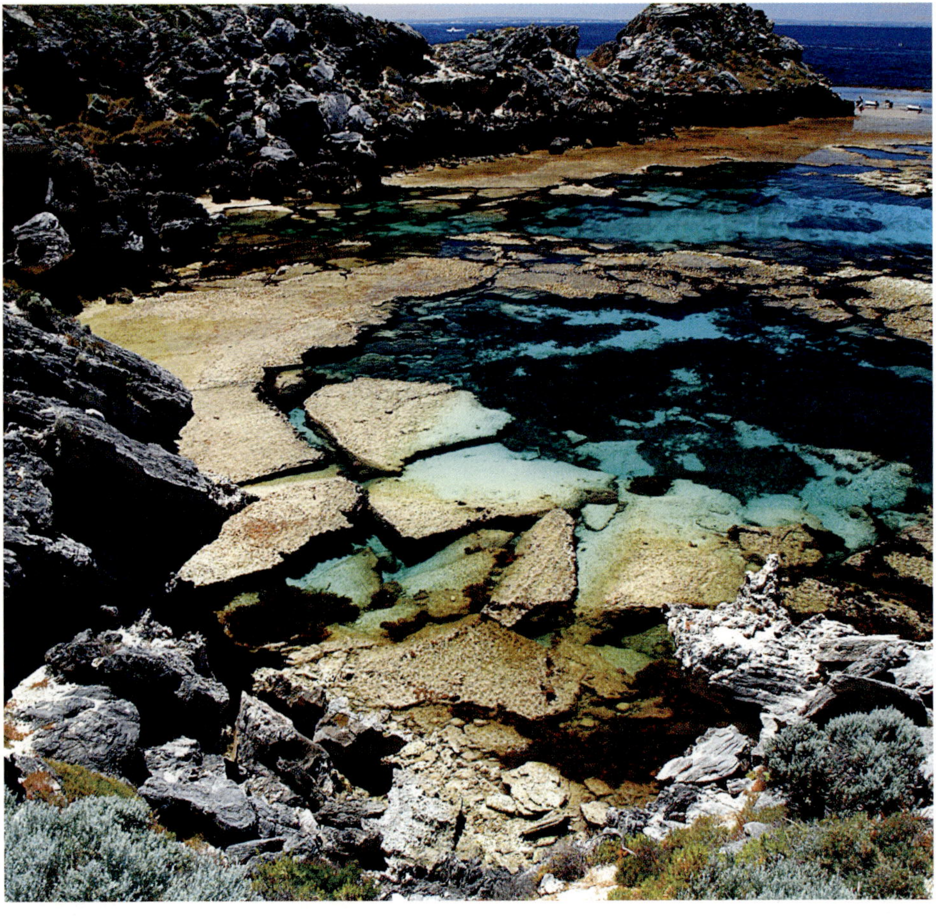

124. parker point

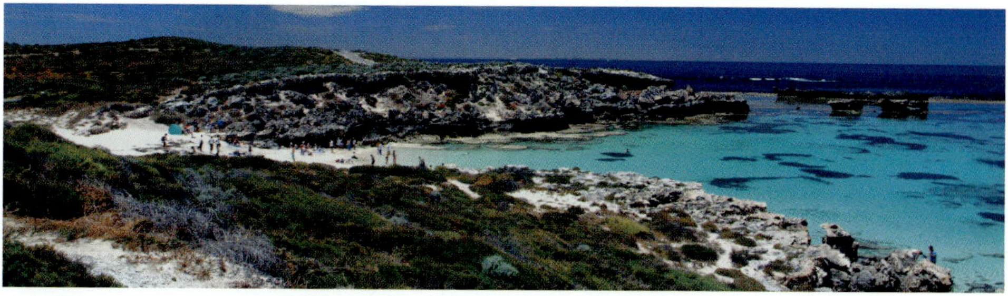

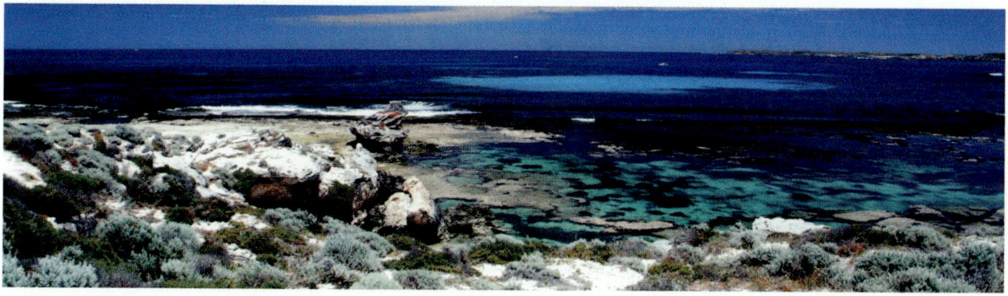

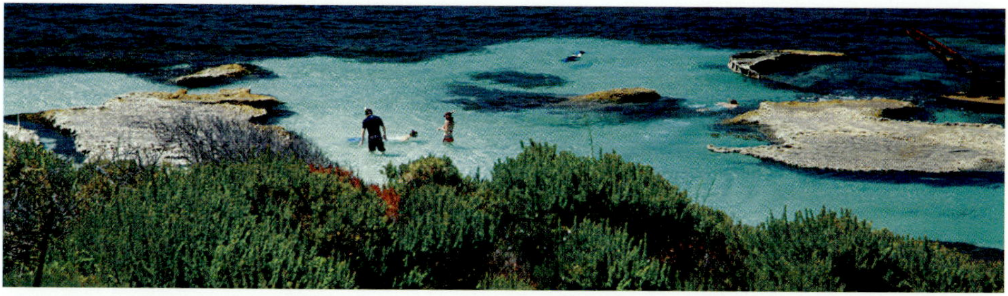

a. little salmon bay b. salmon point c. henrietta rocks

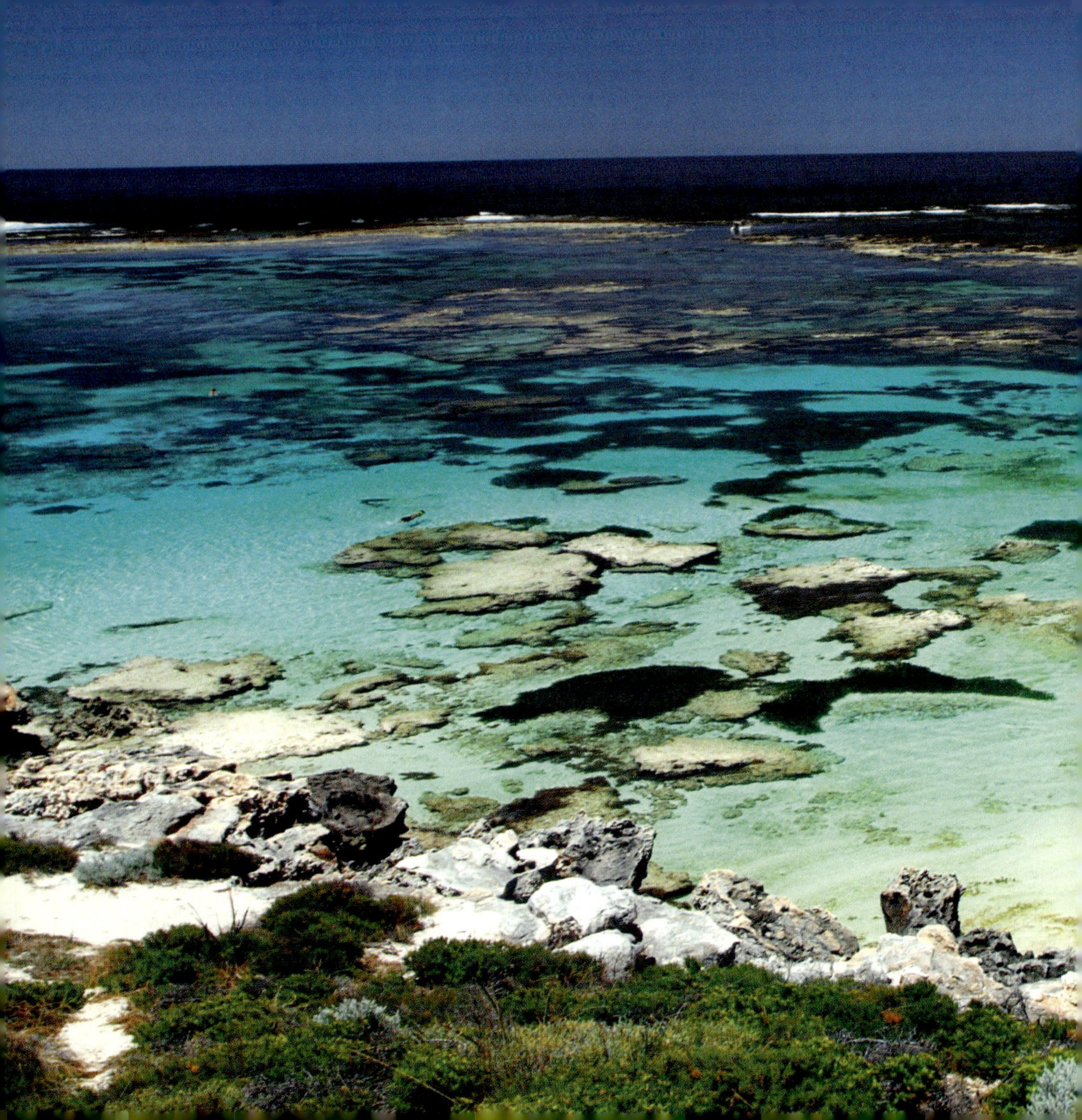

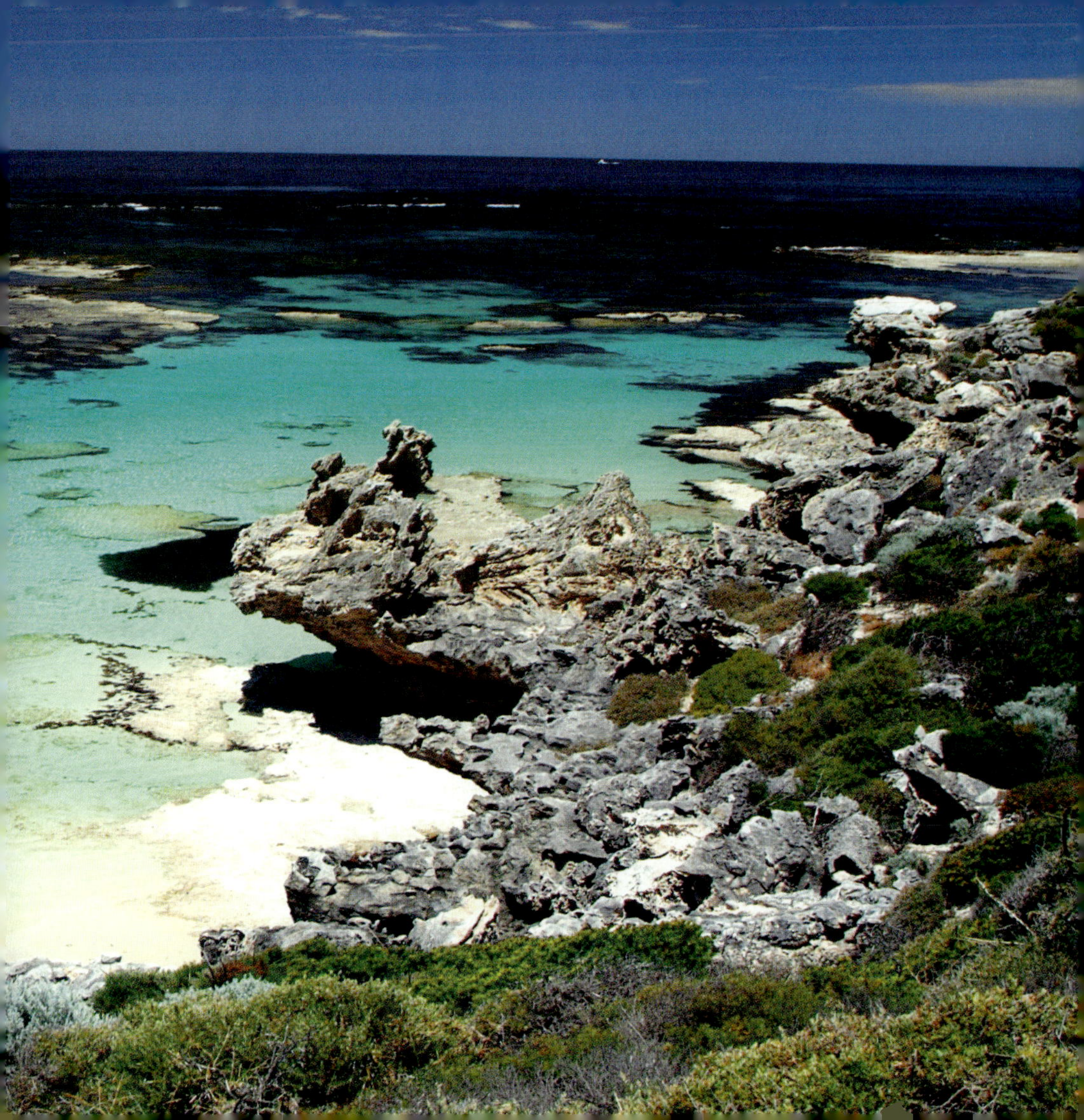

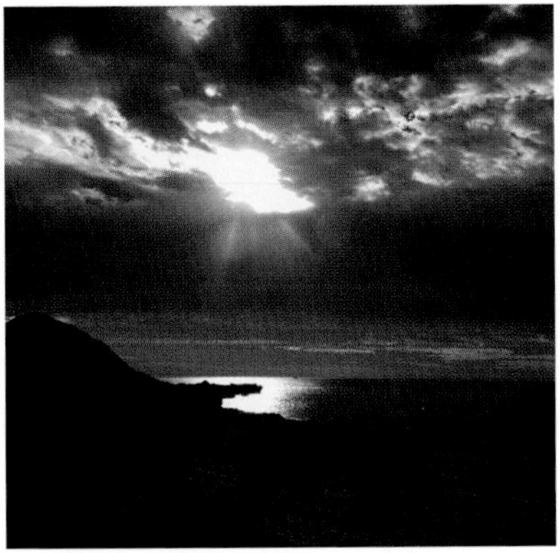

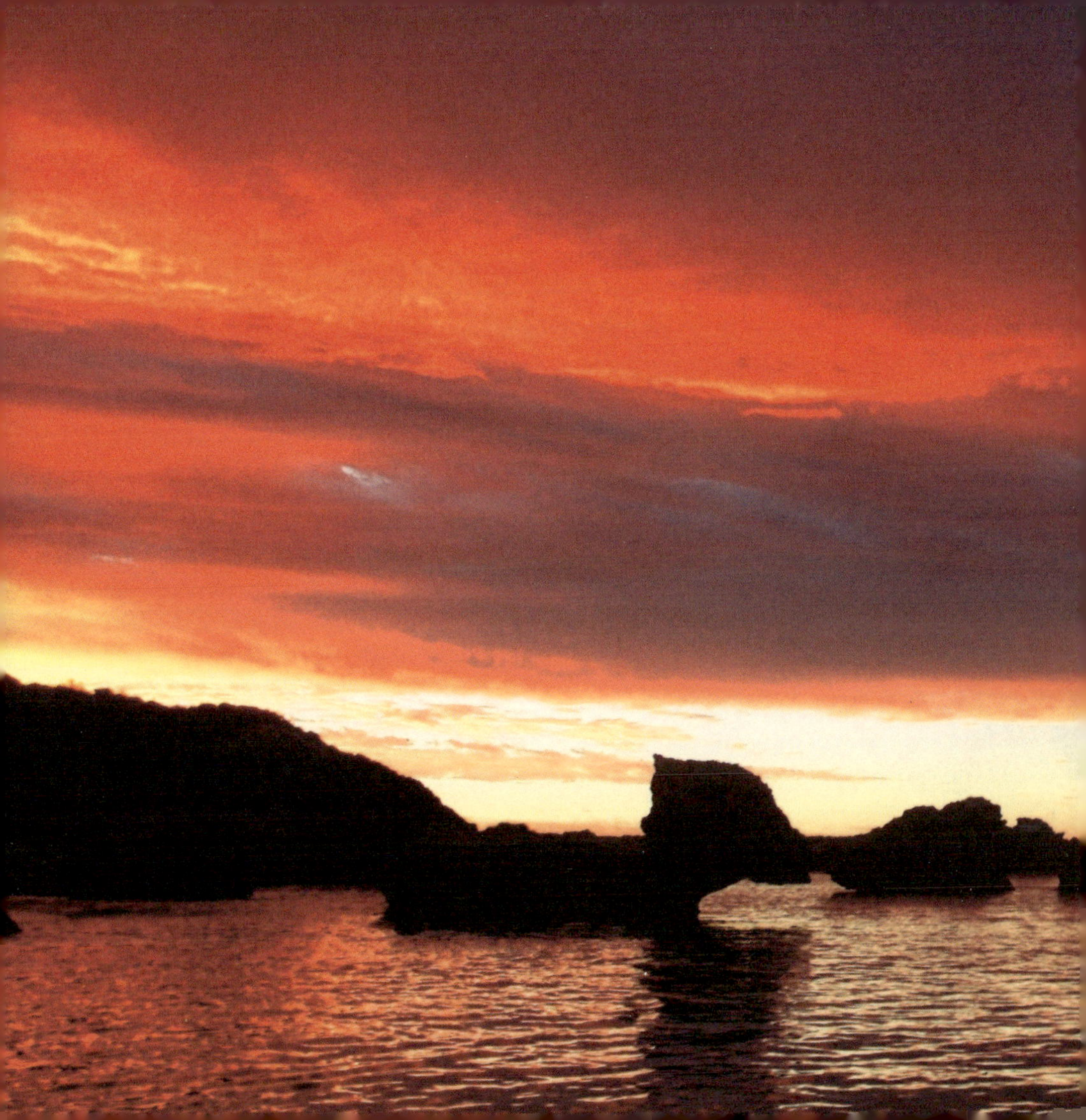